MEDIEVAL
AND
RENAISSANCE
DRAMA
IN ENGLAND

Volume 35

Editorial Board

Editors

MEDIEVAL AND RENAISSANCE DRAMA IN ENGLAND

Volume 35

Editor
S. P. Cerasano

Associate Editor
Mary Bly

Book Review Editor
Heather Anne Hirschfeld

Madison • Teaneck
Fairleigh Dickinson University Press
London: Associated University Presses

Associated University Presses
10 Schalks Crossing Road
Suite 501-330
Plainsboro, NJ 08536

The paper used in this publication meets the requirements of the American National Standard for Permanence of Paper for Printed Library Materials Z39.48-1984.

International Standard Book Number 978-0-8386-4505-5 (vol. 35)
International Standard Serial Number 0731-3403

All editorial correspondence concerning *Medieval and Renaissance Drama in England* should be addressed to Prof. S. P. Cerasano, Department of English, Colgage University, Hamilton, N.Y., 13346. Orders and subscriptions should be directed to Associated University Presses, 10 Schalks Crossing Road, Suite 501-330, Plainsboro, New Jersey 08536.

Medieval and Renaissance Drama in England disclaims responsibility for statements, either of fact or opinion, made by contributors.

Contents

Reviews

Foreword

*M*aRD*i*E *35* brings together seven unique essays, balanced between Shake-spearean and non-Shakespearean drama. A collection of four essays explores various aspects of Ben Jonson. Peter Berek reconsiders Jonson's engagement with the emerging idea of a public while John Pitcher creates a new historical and biographical picture of Jonson's relationship to Samuel Daniel. Given our continuing life with COVID, Fran Teague can't resist thinking about Jonson's writing of *The Alchemist* as a "plague play." Steve Roth re-examines the poets' war, finding a potential tie-in between Jonson's early career and some of the bombastic tragedies of the 1590s, as well as a later "purge" of Jonson in Shakespeare's *Hamlet*. Douglas Arrell places *The Tempest* in con-versation with Heywood's *Ages* and Peter Krause reconsiders aspects of sorcery in the play. David M. Bevington discovers new dimensions of the mercer in *Timon of Athens*. Gregory M. Sargent uncovers the function of city walls and other types of boundaries in *Coriolanus*. A collection of select reviews completes the volume.

—S. P. Cerasano, Editor

Contributors

JESSICA APOLLONI is an Assistant Professor of English at Christopher Newport University. She specializes in comparative law and literature in the early modern period and is currently completing her book manuscript, *Violent Ends: Shakespeare and Comparative Law*. Her scholarship and reviews have appeared in journals such as *Shakespeare Bulletin, Renaissance Quarterly, Studies in Philology, ANQ,* and *Forum Italicum*.

DOUGLAS ARRELL is a Senior Scholar at the University of Winnipeg, where he was Professor and Chair of the Department of Theatre and Film for many years. Since his retirement he has focused his research on the early modern English theatre. His most recent publication is "Heywood's *The Rape of Lucrece* and *Macbeth*" in *MaRDiE 33.*

EMMA KATHERINE ATWOOD is Assistant Professor of English at the University of Montevallo. She has published articles in *Comparative Drama, JSTOR Daily, Early Modern Women: An Interdisciplinary Journal,* and *Borrowers and Lenders*. She earned her PhD from Boston College and ther BA from Kalamazoo College.

MARK BAYER is Associate Professor of English at the University of Texas at San Antonio. He is the author of *Theatre, Community and Civic Engagement in Jacobean London* (2011) and co-editor of *Shakespeare and Civil Unrest in Britain and the United States* (2021). His articles and chapters have appeared in numerous venues including *Comparative Drama, Early Theatre, Shakespeare,* and *Shakespeare Quarterly*.

PETER BEREK, after serving as Professor of English professor and Dean at Williams and Mount Holyoke Colleges, and also being a multiyear visitor at Amherst, is now Professor Emeritus of English at Mount Holyoke and a visiting scholar at Amherst College. He has written about the emerging public sphere in "The Market for Playbooks and the Development of the Reading Public" *PQ* 91, 2 (Spring 2012), 151–184 and "Defoliating Playbooks and the Reading Public, *SEL* 56, 2 (Spring 2016), 395–416.

DAVID M. BERGERON is Professor Emeritus of English at the University of Kansas. As a researcher and scholar, he has written or edited seventeen books, focused primarily on Shakespeare, English civic pageantry, the Stuart royal family, and patronage. His books include, for example, the path-breaking *English Civic Pageantry 1558–1642*; *Shakespeare's Romances and the Royal Family*; *Royal Family, Royal Lovers: King James of England and Scotland*; *Textual Patronage in English Drama, 1570–1640*. In 2017, he published *Shakespeare's London 1613*, and in 2020, *Shakespeare through Letters*. In 2022, he will publish *Duke of Lennox, 1574–1624: A Jacobean Courtier's Life* (Edinburgh University Press). Bergeron has edited the pageants of Anthony Munday, Thomas Heywood, and Thomas Middleton. He edited *Research Opportunities in Renaissance Drama* for 28 years. He has presented papers at universities and conferences in 20 different countries.

PETER KRAUSE is a PhD candidate at Fordham University in New York City studying, among other topics, the contemporary American novel. In particular, he is interested in post-9/11 literature, writing about contemporary war, and the progression in arts and letters from postmodernism to what has been dubbed "the new sincerity." He is also interested in critical theory and counterintuitive readings of those canonical texts, such as Homer and Shakespeare, that reach the most undergraduate students and non-majors. His most recent book reviews can be found in World Literature Today. www.peterwkrause.com.

DAVID LANDRETH is an Associate Professor of English at the University of California, Berkeley. He is the author of *The Face of Mammon: The Matter of Money in English Renaissance Literature*, and of several articles and chapters on money matters in the poetry, prose, and drama of the period. His new work thinks about how Renaissance writers draw value from the changing matters of the past, in terms of four affects that haunt those transactions: glory, envy, shame, and charity.

JOHN PITCHER is Professor of English Literature at Oxford University. His publications include editions of Bacon's *Essays*, *Cymbeline* and *The Winter's Tale*. He has published extensively on the poet Samuel Daniel as the groundwork for his multivolume original-spelling critical edition of Daniel's poems and plays. Currently, he is completing the two Daniel volumes that will contain the shorter poems, life and reputation records, biography and critical and textual commentaries.

SID RAY is Professor of English and Women's and Gender Studies at Pace University (NYC campus). Publications include *Mother Queens and Princely Sons: Rogue Madonnas in the Age of Shakespeare* (2013) and a co-edited collection (with Catherine Loomis), *Shaping Shakespeare for Performance: The Bear Stage* (Fairleigh Dickinson University Press, 2015).

LINDSAY ANN REID is a Lecturer in English at the National University of Ireland, Galway. She is the author of *Ovidian Bibliofictions and the Tudor Book* and *Shakespeare's Ovid and the Spectre of the Medieval*.

STEVE ROTH is an independent scholar of Shakespeare and early modern drama. His work has appeared in *Ben Jonson Journal* and *Early Modern Literary Studies*, and he has presented papers at multiple international conferences. His Shakespeare website is at princehamlet.com.

GREGORY W. SARGENT is a PhD candidate at the University of Massachusetts, Amherst where he is completing his dissertation, "Spatial Violations in the Drama of Shakespeare and his Contemporaries." His project investigates the intersection of dramatic space and representations of violence as they circumscribe cultural geography through fluctuating networks of economic and artistic exchange.

BRIAN SHEERIN is an Associate Professor of English Literature at St. Edward's University (Austin, TX). His work focuses on the intersection of economics, mathematics, and literature in early modern England. He is the author of *Desires of Credit in Early Modern Theory and Drama: Commerce, Poesy, and the Profitable Imagination* (2016).

FRAN TEAGUE is Meigs Professor and Distinguished University Professor at the University of Georgia. Her research is on Renaissance drama performance history and theory and on early modern women writers. Recent books include *Shakespeare and the American Popular Theatre* (2006) and with Margaret Ezell, *Educating English Daughters: Bathsua Makin and Mary More* (2016).

CATHERINE WINIARSKI is Lecturer in the Department of English at the University of California, Irvine. She has published on the religious and political significance of marriage and adultery in early modern drama and most recently on the adaptation of Ovid, Virgil, and Paul in Shakespeare's *Titus Andronicus*. She also researches and teaches environmental writing, ecocriticism, and animal studies.

MOLLY YARN is an independent scholar and the author of *Shakespeare's 'Lady Editors': A New History of the Shakespearean Text* (2021). She serves as a co-editor of the revised edition of the Royal Shakespeare Company's *Complete Works* (ed. Bate and Rasmussen).

In Memoriam
J. Leeds Barroll III, 1928–2022

Susan Cerasano and John Pitcher

We remember, ever so fondly, a gathering at a small and gracious restaurant in Washington, DC, on the evening of November 5th, 2004. There, the two of us—tucked into a cozy table alongside Laetitia Yeandle, Joan Holmer, Raphael Falco, Susan Zimmerman, and Leeds Barroll—were surrounded by velvet curtains and plush carpets. The food was impressive, the wine liberal, and the conversation sprightly. It was a wonderful occasion. Leeds at first thought this would be simply a gathering of friends who had convened to celebrate twenty years of this journal. Instead, we had a surprise waiting. It was a box of page proofs for Volume 17, a collection of essays written in Leeds's honor, which everyone had actually managed to keep secret. When the moment came to present the gift, Leeds at first looked puzzled, and then when he opened the box, bemused; but finally, once he had taken in the moment, he began to look pleased and even jolly. Nevertheless, it was several weeks before he was able to assimilate the full meaning of the volume—it showed just how much we admired him—during which time he wrote and thanked everyone individually with his usual deftness of touch. As well as the scholarly essays in the volume, we were fortunate to have three special contributions, personal tributes from Ann Jennalie Cook, Richard Kuhta, and Raphael Falco. In turn, they wrote about the very great things Leeds had done for the Shakespeare Association of America, the Folger Library, and the Department of English at the University of Maryland (Baltimore County). They each remembered him as an outstanding fellow-scholar and as a generous friend and colleague. Now, so soon after his passing, we recall how much we wanted to honor Leeds—our friend and mentor, and the founding editor of *MaRDiE*. So we ask readers to turn back to Volume 17. The words we wrote almost two decades ago are as true now as they were then.

MEDIEVAL
AND
RENAISSANCE
DRAMA
IN ENGLAND

SYMPOSIUM
Reconsidering Ben Jonson

Ben Jonson and the Public Sphere

Peter Berek

The story of a developing public sphere has a double plot—perhaps even multiple plots. When Jürgen Habermas introduced the idea of the bourgeois public sphere in 1962, he said that it developed in England during the Restoration and flourished in the eighteenth century.[1] More recently, scholars have pushed the origin of a public sphere into the 1590s, or even the mid-sixteenth century.[2] The main plot of the story of an emerging seventeenth- and eighteenth-century public sphere is political: it tells how discussion of statecraft and governance moved from being the province of a small elite clustered around the monarch to being available to a much broader bourgeois community.[3] The Habermassian main plot is a narrative of progress culminating in democratic societies. It's a story worth telling in full, but not here. I want to focus on a subplot, the story of Ben Jonson's engagement with the emerging idea of a public. Both theater and print call publics into being.[4] Jonson is an important figure in the theater and a crucial figure in the development of the playbook in print. But Jonson doesn't do democracy and Jonson doesn't do progress. As in a good early modern play, the Jonson subplot reflects upon and critiques the main story.

Let me quickly sum up the shape of my argument. In the theatrical dialogue between Jonson's *Poetaster* and Thomas Dekker's *Satiromastix*—both plays of 1601—Jonson participates in the development of a theatrical public. In *Sejanus His Fall* (probably performed in 1603, printed in 1605) Jonson puts public making into a political context. Near the end of his career, Jonson's *The Staple of News* (1626) engages with Thomas Middleton's *A Game at Chess*. Here the dialogue is one-sided; Middleton's play doesn't talk back. In *Staple* Jonson comments on the role of print and rejects the very idea of a political public sphere even as he participates in its creation. There are analogous contradictions in the main plot of emerging public making in the sixteenth and seventeenth centuries. Like the three moments I select from Jonson's career, resistance to public making in the word of politics and governance, because of its inevitable engagement in dialogue, cannot help participating in the very project it resists. Criticizing challenges to authority opens a dialogue that calls authority itself into question.

Bruster, Halasz, Mears, Lake, the many authors in the Lake-Pincus, Yachnin-Wilson, Vanhaelen-Ward, and Yachnin-Eberhart collections (all cited below), achieve no consensus on when a public sphere can be perceived in Early Modern England. Publics in their varied definitions can be local or extensive; they may or may not be linked causally to other publics. I make no attempt here to trace the evolution of publics in the first third of the seventeenth century, though I'd be willing to venture there are fewer early and more later. (Habermas may have been wrong about when they begin, but right about when they begin visibly flourishing.) Similarly, I make no claim to be tracing in detail the evidence of an interest in publics throughout Jonson's career. I focus on three events: the remarkable dialogue between plays and writers in *Poetaster* and *Satiromastix*; Jonson's turn soon after to politics in *Sejanus*, and the spectacularly relevant *The Staple of News*. Think of this essay as three (I hope powerfully suggestive) case studies.

Dialogue is vital to the idea of a public. Habermas defined the "bourgeois public sphere" as an arena of conversation and debate. The debate is grounded in critical reason, facilitated by the circulation of print, exists independently of royal or state power, and exerts influence on that power. Conversation in a coffeehouse, conversation in a drawing room is where Habermas finds the public sphere in action. Michael Warner, even more important to my argument than Habermas, adds the idea of reflexivity: "a public is the social space created by the reflexive circulation of discourse" (p. 90).[5] "Only when a previously existing discourse can be supposed, and a responding discourse be postulated, can a text address a public" (p. 90). Warner's focus on reflexivity helps make clear how plays that allude to and echo other plays can call into being a theatrical public. Such performed allusions and echoes bring together reflexively both the previously existing discourse and the responding discourse. This quality of "reflexivity" is crucial to my understanding of *Poetaster*, *Satiromastix*, and *Staple of News*. Discourse among texts matters at least as much as discourse among people or characters.

In *Forms of Association*, Marlene Eberhardt, Amy Scott and Paul Yachnin define a "public" as "forms of association based on the shared interests, tastes and desires of individuals, most of them ordinary 'private' people."[6] Contrasting a public with a "discursive community," they say a public has political content (p. 2). I disagree; a public may or may not be political. Moreover, this definition neglects the importance of reflexivity. *Forms of Association* sees being part of a public as a status, akin to, but less powerful than, being a member of a social class.[7] Amy Rodgers proposes the term "discursive spectator"—spectatorship made visible in discourse about plays rather than in the theater itself. Rodgers's version of spectatorship focuses more on emotional responses and sensory stimuli than cognitive exchanges.[8] Jeffery S. Doty points out that for a political figure to seek popular support is to create a public—to imply that those who are not rulers have a right to discuss those

who rule. (King Henry IV accuses Richard II of having "enfeoffed himself
to popularity," though arguably Prince Hal more effectively pursues the same
strategy.)[9] Doty and Musa Gurnis claim (I think with insufficient evidence)
that Elizabethan and Jacobean taverns were filed with people who drank with
theater folk and talked in playscraps, thereby becoming a theatrical public.[10]
Like Warner, I see being part of a public not as a status but as an activity. It
is participating in reflexive activity rather than being in the same place that
calls a public into being. If I'm right, then it is the reflexive activity of a script
or performance or a printed text that turns its audience into a public. I use
the term "theatrical public" to identify the form of public making elicited by
conversation among playgoers. As more and more plays become available in
print, the distinction between a theatrical public and a reading public dimin-
ishes. Unlike the Habermassian coffeehouse model, which makes rational
discussion the activity and does not demand a text, I believe that a public is
called into being by the shared experience of attending the theater (not necessarily at the same performance) or of reading common texts.

*   *   *

Poetaster and *Satiromastix* are texts that call a public into being by their
sustained reflexive relationship with one another.[11] The two plays are part of
the so-called "Poets' War" or *poetomachia*. Briefly stated, John Marston,
Thomas Dekker, and William Shakespeare feuded with Jonson. Marston
attacked Jonson in *Histriomastix*; Jonson retaliated in *Every Man out of His
Humor*; Marston struck back in *Jack Drum's Entertainment* and *What You
Will*; then Jonson mocked Marston and Dekker in *Poetaster*, and Dekker
replied in *Satiromastix*. Shakespeare participated by portraying Jonson as
Ajax in *Troilus and Cressida*. Older discussions of the Poets' War presume
it arose from personal animosity among Marston, Dekker, and Jonson. James
Bednarz argues instead that the battle is between two different conceptions
of comedy—Jonsonian corrective satire and Shakespeare's, and occasionally
Marston's, "festive comedy." Roslyn Lander Knutson sees the "war" as
something like a marketing ploy—though theater companies competed, they
were also collaborators in a common enterprise.[12] The war seems to me more
collaborative than competitive. Though the conventional scholarly opinion
says Dekker wrote his play to retaliate against Jonson's, the two plays are so
close in time and language that one can imagine the playwrights, ostensibly
rivals, working with knowledge of one another's evolving scripts.[13] The very
existence of such a "war" shows that playwrights and acting companies presumed an audience that took pleasure in seeing plays in dialogue with one
another. *Poetaster* and *Satiromastix* enact a dialogue that includes one another's
audiences—audiences that thereby become a public.

Alan Sinfield points out that by representing himself as Horace and by
bringing other writers on stage as characters, Jonson in *Poetaster* foregrounds

the emerging idea of the "author"; he also suggests that the *poetomachia* helps create the idea of a theatrical public.[14] Though the setting of the play is Roman, there are many allusions to Elizabethan writing, especially echoes of plays of its contemporary theater. Jonson seems to want to make his Romans very Roman indeed, all the while incorporating characters and references that flamboyantly belong to the world of 1600. The play combines earnest defense of the social value of satire, endorsed by a solemn Augustus Caesar, and bathroom humor at its comic climax. The Augustan setting is at odds with the boisterous, very un-Roman Captain Tucca. While Gabrielle Bernhard Jackson may well be right in saying that the Roman setting lends "universality" to a topical play, I don't want to efface the sheer peculiarity of *Poetaster*.[15]

The language of precursor plays and poems circulates in *Poetaster*. As its title suggests, the play is about bad poetry and bad poets. It arraigns Jonson's theatrical colleagues and sometime friends, Crispinus-Marston and Demetrius-Dekker for writing badly. But the play's prime examples of good writers are Augustan Romans—figures from the play's setting, not Elizabethans. Horace-Jonson is an example of the good poet; Virgil may be even better. *Poetaster* sometimes seems to take itself very seriously, especially on the subject of the social role of satire and the satirist.[16] Horace speaks often and at length on the subject; in revising the play Jonson added 3.5, a scene that translates the historical Horace's defense of poetic satire in his own *Satires*.

The massive allusiveness of *Poetaster* gives some indication of how much Jonson thought the audience for the boys playing at Blackfriars might know about contemporary plays and their performers. We now trace this knowledge through learned footnotes in scholarly editions. But Jonson in the theater had to depend on what was in his audience's minds, not on what they could read or look up. Some of their knowledge came from schooling: the audience needs to know a little about major Roman poets to get the significance in the play of characters named Horace, Ovid, and Virgil. Perhaps some auditors knew Horace's *Satires* and *Ars Poetica* well enough to recognize moments when Jonson translates and adapts those texts, but such knowledge is not essential. The meaning of the passages and their purpose in the play is plain whether or not you know their source. Allusions to Elizabethan plays, I believe, work quite differently. When Histrio enters in Act 3 scene 4, the play invites its audience into a world of playhouse gossip that calls on a range of awareness far more complex than simply knowing the color—presumably red—of John Marston's hair. Without such knowledge, the jokes aren't funny.

Histrio's entrance sets Tucca off with a series of jokes about such matters as the way players like Edward Alleyn and Richard Burbage have grown rich, though they may have begun their careers as fiddler and bass players at "Goose Fair" (3.4.114). Tucca mocks Marston-Crispinus both for his genteel origins and his "stalking strain" (3.4.133). Proposing Crispinus to Histrio as a play-maker the actor might hire, Tucca assures Histrio that with the help of

Marston-Crispinus he will no longer need to trudge rough rural roads and act on makeshift barrel-and-board stages. To get the joke, the audience needs to be aware of Alleyn's strutting, Marlowe's grandiloquence and Marston's idiosyncratic versifying. He or she also needs some sense of the business—the economics—of theater. For the passages to work on stage, their audience in the moment of hearing the lines needs to know what the theater historian recovers with his or her research.

Tucca himself is an informed theatergoer and active conversationalist about the stage. He tells Histrio "I would fain come with my cockatrices one day and see a play, if I knew when there were a good bawdy one; but they say you ha' nothing but humours, revels, and satires that gird and fart at the time, you slave" (3.4.153–56). Times have changed; the plays nowadays are no match for the ones I used to see. Histrio assures Tucca he's just been looking in the wrong place. Those "humours, revels and satires" "are on the other side of Tiber. We have as much ribaldry in our plays as can be, as you would wish, Captain. All the sinners in the suburbs come and applaud our action daily" (3.4.157–59). If you want the good old-fashioned stuff, Histrio says, don't look to theaters like Blackfriars on the north bank—the very theater where Tucca himself is a character in Jonson's comical satire, the very theater in which we are now the audience. The men on the south bank, performing daily and not weekly, will serve your turn.

This scene is wildly metadramatic. Not only does Tucca remind the audience of his real-life model by his accent and (one guesses) his costume, but speaking in character he anticipates being imitated on another stage by another actor. Of the south bank of the river, Tucca says, "I hear you'll bring me o' the stage there: you'll play me, they say; I shall be presented by a sort of copper-laced scoundrels of you. Life of Pluto, an you stage me, stinkard, your mansions shall sweat for't, your tabernacles, varlets, your Globes and your triumphs!" (3.4.160–63). The Blackfriars audience needs to imagine seeing Tucca across the river at the Globe. The boy Tucca at Blackfriars, mimicking a known model from the streets of London, anticipates being re-mimicked by a Chamberlain's Man in Dekker's *Satiromastix*. Not merely corrective imitation of life, *Poetaster* asserts a dialogic relationship within theater. The play's flamboyant anachronisms and disjunctions of tone give emphasis to the fact that style in performance and taste in theater are matters for controversy.

Like Tucca, the audience of *Poetaster* needs to be continually conscious not just of the experience it is having but of other experiences it has had in the past and might want to have in the future. And the Blackfriars audience presumably has been to the Globe. Though there were no doubt differences between the composition of the audience in the indoor theaters and the amphitheaters, many playgoers, and many book buyers, had attended both. The audience is aware of differences in taste. Tucca's trade, enacted before our eyes in this scene, is "skeldering" or fleecing the people he meets; the actors too "skelder" their paying customers at the expense of true poets such as Horace. When Tucca offers to sell Histrio his own diminutive companions, the Pyrgi, as potential performers, he shows off their skill with speeches from old plays. The audience—at least some of the audience—recognizes parodies of out-of-fashion styles: "O doleful days! O direful deadly dump!/O wicked world! and worldly wickedness!" (3.4.168.169). The audience recognizes speeches from Kyd's *Spanish Tragedy*, quoted at length, and flamboyant cries of *Vindicta!* and *Timoria!* of the sort to be found in creaky plays of revenge. One of the Pyrgi echoes Shakespeare's Pistol—himself a notable borrower from old plays—and offers to play the Moor in Peele's *The Battle of Alcazar*. As the scene continues, Demetrius-Dekker enters; Histrio introduces him as "a dresser of plays about the town here," hired to abuse Horace by putting him in a play that will make the actors a "huge deal of money" (3.4.260–65). As a comic climax to this scene, one Pyrgus stands on the shoulders of the apothecary Minos to create a mock-actor as tall as the towering Edward Alleyn; the other Pyrgus delivers a famous Alleyn speech from *Alcazar*. These old plays performed by the Pyrgi, according to Gabrielle Bernhard Jackson, were revived at about the time of *Poetaster*. Jonson invites his audience to see that his up-to-date comical satire makes these golden oldies into exercises in historicizing or nostalgia. Some of the audience's pleasure in this scene comes from seeing the boys of Blackfriars mock adult actors, some from seeing their own experiences in Blackfriars as a part of an emerging debate about the nature of theatrical value.

Let me now turn to *Satiromastix*, another voice in this public-making debate.[17] Though set in Norman England, not Augustan Rome, Dekker's *Satiromastix* brings on stage many of the characters in *Poetaster*: Rufus Crispinus, Demetrius Fannius, Tucca, Asinius Bubo, and of course Horace. *Poetaster* ends with a medical humiliation of Crispinus-Marston as the character vomits up scraps of vocabulary from Marston's writings; *Satiromastix* counters by "untrussing" Horace. Dekker's play is far less solemn about the value of satire than Jonson's; instead of a long speech translated from the real Horace's *Satires*, Dekker's Horace earnestly rhymes a celebration of baldness. Jonson and Dekker seem to be trying to appeal to some of the same people. Some of the fun for the Globe audience of *Satiromastix* probably arises from seeing adult actors perform roles they have seen performed by boys at Blackfriars. Though we can't know for certain what kinds of costumes the actors wore or what they did on stage, it seems likely that characters who appear in both plays imitated one another both in dress, gesture, and stage business. Why pass up an opportunity for good gags? Sharing so many characters and jokes, the two ostensibly rivalrous plays exchange tribute as well as mockery. Or, perhaps better, the mockery the plays direct at one another is akin to the mockery both direct at the old plays they sometimes echo. Both are a mix of put-down and affection.

The plays are also alike in their references to theater history and allusions to other plays. Act 4 scene 1 of *Satiromastix* brings Captain Tucca and his boy onstage to a banquet hosted by the Welshman Sir Rees ap Vaughan—the play usually calls him "Sir Vaughan"—and a group including both Horace and the rich widow Mistress Miniver. Once again, Tucca speaks in play-scraps. Aggressive Tucca announces his name as "Hamlet revenge," and asks Horace if he has been at "Parris Gardens." Horace replies, "I ha plaide Zulziman there." Perhaps Horace alludes to having played the title part in *Soliman and Perseda*; perhaps not. For certain, Tucca then mocks Jonson-Horace for his unsuccessful acting career.

> Thou call'st *Demetrius* Jorneyman Poet, but thou putst up a Supplication to be a poore Jorneyman Player, and hadst beene still so, but that thou couldst not set a good face upon't: thou hast forgot how thou amblest (in leather pilch) by a play-wagon, in the high way, and took'st mad Jeronimoes part, to get service among the Mimickes: and when the Stagerites banisht thee into the Ile of Dogs, thou turn'dst Ban-Dog (villanous Guy) and ever since bitest, therefore I aske if th'ast been at Parris-garden, because thou hast such a good mouth, thou baitst well; read, *lege*, save thy selfe and read.
>
> (4.1.127–36)

Instead of Horace's defense of satire, Tucca offers a narrative about how Jonson's failure on the road in acting an old-fashioned play like *The Spanish Tragedy* led him to use his dog-like barking and biting mouth in the banned play, *The Isle of Dogs*. Violent Jonson, no even-tempered Horace, had to prove he could read to escape hanging for killing a man in a quarrel. A "journeyman poet" like Dekker is better than a mouthy dog.

Satiromastix dramatizes theatrical naïveté as well as sophistication. Tucca thrusts papers at Horace, and Horace recognizes texts, written by Horace himself, mocking Tucca and read out in 3.1. "Why Captaine these are epigrams compos'd on you." Perhaps alluding to Jonson's description of his laborious composition by candlelight in the "Apologetical Dialogue" after *Poetaster*, Tucca retorts, "Goe not out Farding Candle," and says he'll pledge this epigram in wine. That brings the dialogue back to Sir Vaughn and Mistress Miniver, both of whom seem to have been standing by uncomprehendingly as Horace and Tucca trade insults grounded in theatrical sophistication. Sir Vaughan has difficulty with "epigram" and says to Mistress Miniver, "God blesse us, will he be drunk with nittigrams now." Picking up on the idea of drink, Tucca asks the "sprite ath Buttry" to arise and then echoes Jonson's *Cynthia's Revels*, "arise deere Echo, rise" (4.1.138–43). He turns his mocking attention from Horace to Miniver, whom he calls "my old whore a Babilon." When she says she doesn't know where in London Babylon stands, Tucca replies with more playscraps, "Feede and be fat my faire Calipolis" (4.1.150), conflating two lines from *Alcazar*. All the characters on stage then turn on

Tucca for his traducing of Horace. Exiting, Tucca challenges Asinius Bubo to a duel. Terrified Bubo ends the scene with a phrase echoing an exchange between Prince Hal and Falstaff before Shrewsbury, "I owe God a death, and if he will make me pay it against my will, Ile say tis hard dealing" (4.1.211–12).

What are the pleasures of this scene for the audience hearing *Satiromastix* at the Globe? Some are traditional pleasures of comedy, such as laughing at Sir Rees ap Vaughan's Welsh accent or at Tucca's bombast. Some are like those of the Blackfriars audience for *Poetaster*: the pleasures of theatrical knowingness, the sheer delight in recognition, the fun of seeing how the playwright uses Tucca to insult his rival. But Tucca is just as much mocking Mistress Miniver's incomprehension as he is mocking Horace-Jonson's pretensions. The scene, like the play as a whole, divides the imagined audience into an in-group that understands the mockery and can communicate with one another in a language of allusion and gossip and other auditors who stand by looking dumb. It's the same game as *Knight of the Burning Pestle*. Horace-Jonson is at least as much in on the joke as Tucca, Demetrius, and Crispinus. In the language of Jonson's preface to *Catiline*, these sophisticated denizens of a theatrical world are characters extraordinary being watched by auditors extraordinary; they are capable of judging with distinction.[18] The allusiveness and knowingness of the characters onstage gives pleasure to members of a theatrical audience whom the play is transforming into a public.

Concentrating on print, Michael Warner speaks of "a concatenation of texts through time" (Warner, p. 90). Of course, the sequential or parallel performances of *Poetaster* and *Satiromastix* are not textual events, even though our evidence for those performances is textual. But the continual allusions in both plays to other plays and to one another are surely "concatenations." Not only do the allusions invite the theatergoer to think about older plays; the allusions imply that the author and actors can count on an audience that has some sophisticated understanding of theater history. I am not insisting that I know precisely what that understanding was or that all members of the audience thought the same way. Indeed, my point is precisely that the plays provoke discussion and debate among their auditors. When Jonson speaks in his preface to *Catiline* about wanting readers who can "judge with distinction," or when he speaks of "readers extraordinary," he implies he wants readers who will see things his way. But at the same time, he acknowledges the prevalence of the ordinary readers he scorns. The way in which the Widow Miniver misses jokes in *Satiromastix* dramatizes the possibility of multiple responses by an auditor, just as the disagreements among Crispinus, Demetrius, and Horace in both plays dramatize the conflicts among different styles of playmaking. While no one is likely to have misunderstood the humiliations of Crispinus-Marston at the end of *Poetaster* or of Horace-Jonson at the end of *Satiromastix*, that doesn't mean that all auditors took the side of Dekker in his play, or Jonson in his. Controversy is the marketing premise of *Poetaster* and *Satiromastix*;

an acting company interested in maximizing its revenue will happily sell admission to customers on either side of that controversy.

It may not seem like news to my readers to hear that people who attended Elizabethan and Jacobean plays argued with one another about those plays. What we get from plays of the *poetomachia* is confirmation of our speculation, not an entirely new idea. Because these plays take theater as their subject, they give us a vivid dramatization of disagreements about taste that in all likelihood were on display among theatergoers attending less explicitly metadramatic performances. We see a form of public making, of participation in a reflexive process. Though both *Poetaster* and *Satiromastix* are intensely literary, both also foreground questions of royal authority. *Poetaster* uses Augustus Caesar to ratify the poetic authority of Horace. In an un-Habermassian way, the play first fosters debate about poetry and theater but then subordinates that debate to royal authority. Dekker's *Satiromastix* works differently. Dekker's play represents royal authority in the person of the Norman king William Rufus and displays him as a notable if ineffective lecher. Other characters trick King William and by doing so save the wedding-night virginity of the soon-to-be-married Caelestine. Did Dekker patch his mockery of Jonson-Horace into a preexisting script about William Rufus?[19] Or is his portrayal of the lecherous and inept William a conscious mockery of Jonson's near-sycophantic devotion to Caesar? If the latter, the play may participate in a public debate about the relationship between monarchic and literary authority. Yet the presence of the preposterous Captain Tucca onstage casts a screen of frivolity over the action. Falstaff-like Tucca is a kind of Lord of Misrule who creates an atmosphere of carnival license.

If we call what we are seeing in these plays political, we are using the word in an attenuated way, as when we say, "the political is personal, the personal is political." By these standards, everything is political. That seems to me to efface an often-useful distinction. Rebelling against fashion is not the same as rebelling against a government. But with public debate about matters of state by ordinary subjects forbidden under Elizabeth and James, debate about matters of poetry or theater could serve as a rehearsal—a way of shaping habits and skills of discourse that would eventually prove useful in the changed political climate of the Restoration. Theater is a sphere for thought. Plays don't so much take positions on public matters as they create the occasion for audiences to play with the idea of taking positions. Instead of "a willing suspension of disbelief," I suggest audiences play with a willing suspension of real-world consequences. Serious play in the playhouse matures into play with serious matters in the public sphere. Showing this proposition to be true goes far beyond the scope of this essay. Yet Jonson's own move to political tragedy from the comical satire of *Poetaster* may suggest such a desire on his part.

*   *   *

We don't see much playful suspension of consequences when Jonson turns to tragedy in *Sejanus His Fall*. Here Jonson seems to be able to imagine a political public, but not to imagine the efficacy of such a public.[20] His subject matter is explicitly political—imperial Roman politics. He represents discussion among the Germanicans, the faction out of power, about the rise and fall of Sejanus, favorite of the emperor Tiberius. These discussions take place at the margins of the stage, heard by the audience but not by the powerful figures upon whom the Germanicans comment.[21] Of course, *Sejanus* is a play in which the margins have a central role. The 1605 quarto includes extensive marginal annotations in which Jonson cites and sometimes quotes the classical sources for his play; with those annotations Jonson makes his playbook look like an edition of a classic. For the learned "reader extraordinary," the marginalia invite a conversation about whether Jonson's representation of the ancient world matches the sources he cites. A potential learned conversation in the margins of print is very different from a conversation about seventeenth-century politics. Jonson may be trying to insulate himself from the scandal that might arise from any implication of a topical meaning.[22] But margins on stage (though not a Habermassian coffeehouse or bourgeois parlor) are a place for conversations about politics. However, the play shows that these marginal conversations have no political effect.[23]

In the first four acts of *Sejanus*, important events occur while Germanicans observe from the side of the platform or comment unheard (except by the audience) while their rivals conspire. Jonson introduces us to the characters in the world of Sejanus and Tiberius largely through the marginal commentary of the Germanicans. After beginning with a conversation in which Germanicans Sabinus and Silius say they lack the criminal talents needed for court politics (see esp. ll. 4–18), the play brings Sejanus's allies Satrius, Natta, and Latiaris onstage (l. 20) while Sabinus and Silius, remaining onstage though presumably out of earshot, make derogatory comments on the new arrivals. When Germanicans Cremutius Cordus and Arruntius enter, representatives of both factions talk with their allies, heard by the theater audience but not heard by their rivals. Cordus and Arruntius continue their commentary as Drusus and Haterius pass over the stage. Admittedly, my description of what happens onstage depends heavily on the editorial stage directions in the Cambridge edition—Jonson's own texts are almost bare of directions. But the text only makes sense if we presume (with Cambridge editor Tom Cain) that the audience both sees and hears groups of characters on the stage that see, but do not hear, one another.[24]

Sejanus himself first appears while the four Germanicans are onstage. Looking at the Germanicans, Sejanus says to his cronies, "I note 'em well," and continues, unfazed, his ongoing conversation about accepting a bribe from Eudemus in return for a place as consul. The Germanicans remain onstage while Sejanus persuades Eudemus, her physician, to help him woo Livia, sister of the late Germanicus and wife of Drusus; they remain onstage when Tiberius enters. As Tiberius rejects a kneeling suitor and says he has no need for flattery, Germanican Arruntius points out the flattery in Sejanus's line, "How like a god speaks Caesar" (1.1.378). Jonson effectively dramatizes the brazen self-assurance of Sejanus by showing how little he cares whether or not his schemes become known, and at the same time Jonson lets the Germanicans reflect on the desperate state of Tiberian Rome. Critique of action is virtually simultaneous with action, but the critique is largely marginal, ineffective at obstructing the favorite's plans to accumulate power. What the critics can do is talk with one another. Observing, commenting, reflecting, they are like a public.

The comments of the Germanicans about the machinations of Sejanus and Tiberius seem true and just.[25] But neither the comments nor the actions of the Germanicans affect what happens in Rome. Though not agents, they can be victims, as we see in act 3 when Silius is accused, tried, and forced into suicide. His downfall illustrates how Tiberian Rome is a place of surveillance and conspiracy, but the most powerful aspect of his death is his bold, forthright denunciation of tyranny. What he says is not so different from what Sabinus and Arruntius have been saying to one another from the margins of the action; the price of speaking in public, rather than conversing on the margin, is death.

Tiberius' letter to the Senate in *Sejanus* (5.542 ff.) implies without explicitly stating that Tiberius would not mind seeing the Senate use its authority against Sejanus. As a modern politician might say, Tiberius maintains his deniability. Responsibility for the dismemberment of Sejanus and slaughter of his children lies with the Senate and the people. Germanicans Arruntius and Lepidus stand on the margins of this Senate scene, observing and commenting wryly to one another. They have no better information than anyone else onstage; they too can only make interpretations of the oblique letter from Caesar. Better judgment, not better knowledge, differentiates them from the others.

The Germanicans, for most of the action of *Sejanus*, make clear that the actions and opinions of Sejanus, Tiberius, and their followers are appropriate matters for their debate and discussion. But the play does not initially embrace their opinions: they comment in the manner of a chorus, but without the special authority of a chorus. Observers but not agents, they are a bit like conversationalists in a Habermassian coffeehouse. This changes as the play draws to a close. Arruntius and Lepidus stop speaking to one another in asides and begin to engage with other characters who are not necessarily their allies. When Sejanus' friend Terentius begins to narrate the offstage horror of the favorite's death, the Germanicans engage with him both as questioners asking for amplification and as commentators reinforcing his judgments. At the end of the play, there is little difference between the judgments of Terentius and the two Germanicans. All three jointly reflect on the gullibility of the mob and the fickleness of Fortune.

By the end of *Sejanus*, moralizing commentary reflecting values shared by characters, authors and audience supplants judicious but impotent political conversations among the Germanicans. Moving to the center from the edges or margins of the stage, the Germanicans lose their edginess and marginality. The disgrace and dismemberment of Sejanus shows how wrong it is to try to pry power away from its legitimate source, however corrupt the immediate exemplar of that legitimacy. Commonplaces expressed in a common voice supplant overheard debates among conflicting judgments.

Poetaster, like *Satiromastix*, was frequently in conversation with other plays. Not marginal, those conversations are in the midst of the play's action. But the play's representation of political life, when not jokey, is flamboyantly in service to Jonson's own self-proclaimed Horatian persona. The "public" *Poetaster* adumbrates, though deferential to Augustus, debates only theatrical and literary taste. Conversation in *Sejanus* is different. Observing and discussing actions, Jonson's Germanicans have some resemblance to the politically engaged public of which Habermas or Yachnin and his colleagues speak. The Germanicans offer one another, and the audience, rational judgments of political appeals to irrationality or to the selfish pursuit of private desires. Standing aside, standing on the margin of the stage, characters such as Arruntius offer in the theater a version of performed reflection analogous to the textual reflexivity Warner describes. But the reflexivity of the Germanicans onstage is not textual, but theatrical, though the reader of *Sejanus His Fall* in print can be part of a reading public. Jonson can imagine public discourse; he is committed to reason's power to expose knaves and fools; he may or may not have republican sympathies.[26] Jonson, obviously, is not Habermas, and surely has no interest in anything Habermas would recognize as democracy. Yet in 1603, in his first tragedy and first overtly political play, he adumbrates what will eventually become a public sphere.

*   *   *

Discussing *Poetaster*, *Satiromastix*, and *Sejanus*, I've been attending to what I've called the Jonsonian subplot of an evolving public sphere. The main plot continues to advance in the seventeenth century. By the 1620s the emergent phenomenon of "the news"—a phenomenon of print—shows that matters once deemed the province only of those around the monarch are now available for reading and debate among all who can afford to buy a coranto or newsbook or visit a tavern where one is read aloud.[27] It is in this new context that Jonson's 1626 *The Staple of News* creates another set of conversations and more theatrical concatenations that bear upon the public sphere. *Staple* in its Intermeans enacts conversations about theater and its history, conversations of a kind familiar to us from *Poetaster*. But the Staple of News that gives Jonson's play its title—the Staple from which news is sold and circulated for money—represents the possibility of widespread public conversation and debate about seventeenth-century issues of national and dynastic importance. Some of the publics called into being by the news have much in common with our modern, more political understanding of the public sphere. England has changed, and "the news" is a symptom of those changes. The principal subject is the Thirty Years War, not the wars of the theater. Jonson shows in *Staple* that he can imagine a Habermassian future. But the prospect fills him with contempt.

A decade after monumentalizing his plays in *The Works of Ben Jonson*, and after a decade of theatrical silence, Jonson's return to the stage in *Staple* raises not just questions about publics, but also the question of whether the play's real life is on the stage or in print. The "news" Jonson mocks is textual, whether circulated in manuscript or print: though commercial, like theater, it is read, not performed.[28] The news is more like playbooks than plays. *Staple* queries the relationship between news and theater. Are they parallel media that can be used well or badly? Or is theater—Jonson's kind of theater—a form of poetry with a privileged relationship to moral improvement that newsbooks can never match? Jonson seems to be bringing to the fore, though not resolving, questions about the differences between a theatrical audience and a reading public. As Jane Rickard argues, Jonson wants his play to educate his audience about the difference between news and theater.[29] But does being in print create affinities between a play and the news?

Extensive allusions to other plays appear in the Intermeans, choric scenes in which gossipy women seated on the stage (named Mirth, Censure, Expectation, and Tattle) criticize the play they've been watching. (These Intermean characters remind us, and probably would have reminded Jonson's seventeenth-century readers, of the onstage "Grex" in Jonson's *Every Man Out of His Humor*).[30] In the first Intermean, following act 1, the women complain that the play they are watching has neither a Fool nor a Devil—they contrast it unfavorably with Jonson's own 1616 *The Devil is an Ass* and the 1603 *Merry Devil of Edmondton*.[31] This play doesn't amuse the Intermean viewers as much as old-fashioned plays with slapstick Vice characters. The gossips in the second Intermean continue to complain that *Staple* is not like an old play with a devil and a vice, but that doesn't keep them from guessing that Pennyboy Senior, miserly uncle of protagonist Pennyboy Junior, is a vice or speculating that the rich, marriageable Pecunia doesn't "do any more but express the property of money" (2 Int 22–23). Even while complaining, the gossips recognize the affinities of *Staple* with the old allegorical drama. They also deny, quite unconvincingly, that the character Pecunia is meant to allude to the Spanish princesses, much in the news as potential matches for the English heir, who, like her, have three names. From outside the play—or in reality, from the margins of the stage—the gossips act like a theatrical public.

The Intermean characters discuss the relationship between Jonson's play and another King's Men play, Middleton's 1624 *A Game at Chess*. Unlike the other theatrical references I've been discussing, those to *A Game at Chess* bring recent politics into Jonson's play. *A Game at Chess* is the most explicitly topical early modern play—an allegory that uses chess pieces to dramatize the politicking about the prospect of a Spanish marriage for Prince Charles. *Staple*'s references to *A Game of Chess* and its imagining of a commercial enterprise for the production and dissemination of news simultaneously represents and helps create a politically engaged public.

In an argument that, like my own, embraces the ideas of Michael Warner, Stephen Wittek shows how *A Game at Chess* helps call a public into being both by drawing on contemporary news pamphlets and by generating multiple versions of itself in manuscript and print.[32] I won't rehearse here Wittek's argument about Middleton, but will concentrate on Jonson's own strategies as he intermingles a very up-to-date representation of the burgeoning news culture of the 1620s, an old-fashioned story about a prodigal young heir, and a story about "Pecunia" that oscillates between treating the character of that name as a real rich woman and as an allegorical figure for money.

A Game at Chess shows up in a scene in which the newly hired staff of the Staple are selling news to Jonson's protagonist, Pennyboy Junior. Thomas (formerly Pennyboy Junior's barber) and Lickfinger (a cook) offer news in the form of theatrical gossip. Thomas describes a legacy left to the King's Players by the Archbishop of Spalato, the Fat Bishop in Middleton's play (a part performed by the recently deceased William Rowley) and then makes his allusion to the play more specific by saying that its central character, the fistula-afflicted Spanish ambassador Gondomar, has developed a second fistula "for putting the poor English play of him / To such a sordid use, as is said he did, / Of cleansing his posteriors" (3.2.208–10). (A marginal note in the 1640 Folio reads "Gondomar's use of the Game at Chess, or play so-called.") The reference to Middleton, while based in theater, reminds us of *Game at Chess* in print. The other news in the scene has nothing to do with plays. Thomas itemizes seventeen "events" ranging from the King of Spain's being elected Pope to the Rosicrucians drawing farts out of dead bodies.[33] *Staple*'s relationship to *Game at Chess* doesn't have the playful interpenetration of *Poetaster* and *Satiromastix*; Middleton's play is news for which Jonson can offer scatological contempt.[34]

A political public sphere seems to make Jonson exceedingly uncomfortable. In print, after the second Intermean, he inserts a paragraph addressed "To the Reader" (pp. 79–80) that berates both the reader and his own characters for misunderstanding the play. Speaking of the news-office, the "Staple," that gives the play its name, Jonson writes,

> In this following act, the Office is opened and shown to the Prodigal and his princess, Pecunia, wherein the allegory and purpose of the author hath hitherto been wholly mistaken, and so sinister an interpretation been made as if the souls of most

of the spectators had lived in the eyes and ears of these ridiculous gossips that tattle between the acts. But he prays you thus to mend it: to consider the news here vented to be none of his news or any reasonable man's, but news made like the time's news—a weekly cheat to draw money—and could not be fitter reprehended than in raising this ridiculous office of the Staple, wherein the age may see her own folly or hunger and thirst after published pamphlets of news, set out every Saturday, but made all at home, and no syllable of truth in them, than which there cannot be a greater disease in nature or a fouler scorn put upon the times. And so apprehending it, you shall do the author and your own judgement a courtesy, and perceive the trick of alluring money to the Office and there cozening the people. If you have the truth, rest quiet, and consider that *Ficta, voluptatis causa, sint proxima veris.* ["Let what thou feign'st for pleasure's sake be near the truth"][35]

This "office of the Staple," Jonson's own brilliant invention and the heart of his play, is both "ridiculous" and a truthful representation of the "folly or hunger and thirst after published pamphlets of news, set out every Saturday." Inveighing against fakery, Jonson assures that his own fakery—the text we are reading—creates a curative truth. Theater, even in print, is better than news. Yet while praising his fakery, he strips characterization from his protagonist, Pennyboy Junior, and turns him into the stock type, "the Prodigal."

Most significantly, Jonson turns on his own public as it is represented in the Intermeans. Perhaps Jonson wants to distress "readers in ordinary" by saying they are like the gossipy women in the Intermeans, all the better to celebrate the "reader extraordinary" who interprets as the author does. That's a characteristic Jonsonian move. But the fact that Jonson speaks out in his own voice after two acts of his play suggests he's aware that the vitality of his script is potentially at some variance with what he believes to be his own opinion. Jonson's cozeners, exposing the folly of those they cozen (including the members of the audience), win our admiration—that's part of their ill-gotten gains. You don't expend so much authorial energy lecturing your audience about its response unless you are aware that the audience is debating its own analyses of the materials with which you present them. Lecturing suggests you perceive your audience is turning into a public.

In the third Intermean, the four gossips agree with Jonson. The news vended at the Staple is worth no more than the stories they learn from chatter at the conduit or the bakehouse. All are "stale" (Third Intermean, 21); the vendors ineffectively try to compensate for the loaf's staleness with "butter"—another one of *Staple*'s many puns on the name of the celebrated news merchant, Nathaniel Butter. Scorning "butter" and the world of newsbooks, the gossips—or at least Censure—try instead to become a theatrical public, but that strategy can't work. Censure chastises schoolmasters who turn their scholars into "playboys" (36) who learn "play-books" instead of Terence (Censure misses the joke) and calls on the aid of Zeal-of-the-Land Busy to drive out theater. To Censure, theater seems essential to drive out theatricality, just as

Jonson's play, to drive out news, becomes news itself. You can't shut down (or shut up) a public without creating yet another public.

Jonson himself has a hard time getting past the Staple of News—the idea, not the play. His last two acts are a kind of variety show. The workers at the Staple become "jeerers" who devote themselves, not to fake stories, but to empty insults. Then we have a sequence about Pecunia's heraldic coat of arms, and then a sequence about canting. Arguably, all these have some thematic significance—they show words being used solely to attack or to impress without any meaningful referent or object of knowledge. News, too, exists for its own self-referential sake, ungrounded in fact or reality. With a stretch, the audience can find some unity. The fifth act of the play barely touches the subject of "news." There's a very funny scene in which Pennyboy Senior imprisons his dogs, a less funny scene in which the jeerers jeer at him. But the resolution of the action comes when Pennyboy Canter, the father of Pennyboy Junior, presides over the restoration of Pecunia to his son and the repentance of Pennyboy Senior for his previous miserly attachment to Pecunia-money. Canter reminds all that we should value money for its use, not just treat it as an object of accumulation. None of the Pennyboys seems to notice the irony that the use they celebrate is the enrichment of a foolish prodigal heir. The audience seems to be expected to take pleasure in this ending precisely because it is the stock resolution of old-fashioned comedy. It isn't clear what we are expected to make of the complaints in the preceding Intermean—quite correct—that the play in which the four gossips are characters has lost sight of its own subject, the news.

The Staple of News gives distress even to its most recent editor, Joseph Loewenstein. Loewenstein argues in his introduction that *Staple* embraces contradictory attitudes toward money. Early in the play, the Pennyboy household is the object of mockery for its pursuit of Pecunia, the princess whose name fully speaks her identity. By the play's end the audience seems to be expected to celebrate the wedding of the prodigal Pennyboy Junior with the rich princess: the pursuit of riches may be corrupt, but the achievement of riches is a cause for celebration.[36] The parts of *Staple* still don't clearly fit together. In *Poetaster*, the Roman setting is slightly incongruous for satire of Marston and Dekker. In *Satiromastix* it is a challenge to see how the William Rufus story fits together with the mockery of Jonson-Horace. The problems in *Staple* are different, and more intense, because they involve both vagaries in plotting and inconsistencies in values. Jonson cannot satirize the news without making his own play a participant in the novel discourse he scorns. As the play says, "the very printing of them makes them news" (1.5.52). If the news critiques political life, criticism of the news itself becomes a political event.

Crucial to the inconsistencies in *Staple* is Jonson's long-standing self-division about how to value theater. The theatrical events celebrated by the gossips of the Intermeans are events of Jonson's own past. Lynn S. Meskill describes what she calls Jonson's "auto-allusions": his references in *Staple* both to his own plays and to aspects of his own biography.[37] The contradictions in *Staple*, she argues, arise from Jonson's personal history and psychology. Some of these allusions I've already mentioned. Meskill is especially telling when she discusses the "black box" that Picklock, Pennyboy Canter's attorney, denies is an appropriate container for the deed that will assure Pennyboy Junior's inheritance (*Staple* 5.1.88). She connects that black box to "the container in which the all-important marriage license (and thus the inheritance of a dowry of £6,000) is passed from hand to hand in *Bartholomew Fair*."[38] Both boxes—the feigned and the unfeigned—allude to the box in Kyd's *Spanish Tragedy* that Pedringano thinks contains his pardon but in fact is empty. The three boxes represent three stages of Ben Jonson's career: the unsuccessful touring actor in *The Spanish Tragedy* mocked by Dekker, the successful playwright who monumentalized his *Works* in 1616 (a year after *Bartholomew Fair*, though that play is not printed until 1631), and the old man struggling to revive a career in theater after a decade of silence. Meskill reads *The Staple of News* as an allegory of Jonson's career. Like Pennyboy Junior, Jonson wants to secure his own inheritance. (The concern for inheritance harks back to *Every Man in His Humor*.) Jonson's "fortune" includes both the old-fashioned Elizabethan theater of Kyd, whose *Spanish Tragedy* Jonson mocks even as Hieronimo's cloak provides a disguise for Face in *The Alchemist*. Pennyboy Canter offers the exuberant play with canting languages in plays such as *The Alchemist* and *Bartholomew Fair*; miserly Pennyboy Senior reflects such Jonsonian achievements as Sordido in *Every Man Out* and *Volpone*. After a decade of theatrical silence, Jonson divides the paternity his own past offers so he can make a new play that uses the past without being bound by that past. Jonson wants to "make it new." However, as I have tried to show, doing so may "make it news."

Jonson's evocation of his own past creates yet another conversation, this one not among plays or playgoers but within Jonson himself. Should he rejoice in his satirist's gift for staging disruption or subsume that gift to the demands of authority? The Jonson who took delight in the clamor of stagey jargons, who relishes confidence tricks on both his characters and his theatrical audience, should take delight as well in the generative abundance of the Staple's news-making machine.[39] Yet when he turns playscript into playbook, Jonson interjects a passage in his own voice—or better yet, one of his own voices—and summarily rejects "this ridiculous office of the Staple." Readers who admire the Staple are fools. That Jonson interrupts his own playbook with this assertion of disapproval and desire for control suggests the intensity of his own ambivalence. Having made a play that takes sides in a public controversy, he implicitly puts himself on the same footing as other participants in that controversy. Jonson himself has become "news." Or, perhaps one can say, the Jonson who amused, delighted, and tried to teach a theatrical public is now in conversation with the monumentalizing Jonson who tried to fix his relation to authority in folio print. Scorning the public, Jonson is himself becoming a public.

To say Jonson is "becoming a public" is far from saying that the Jonson subplot I've been narrating has merged with the Habermassian main plot. The development of "the news" and of newsbooks is part of the main plot of the development of a public sphere in the seventeenth century. A topical, overtly political play such as *A Game at Chess* is also part of that main plot, as Wittek has shown. The Jonson subplot I have been describing sometimes advances and sometimes critiques the main plot's narrative. The subplot critique is especially vivid on the subject of print, even though Jonson himself arguably did more than any other early modern playwright to advance the importance of plays in print. He begins to call a reading public into being as early as his first play in print, *Every Man Out of his Humor* (1601). The 1616 Jonson folio monumentalizes his plays as "works" to be read, just as one would read Ovid, Horace, or Virgil. But for Jonson in the 1620s, print has more meanings than it did in 1616. The news in print, in its regularity of appearance and cheapness, competes with theater as well as with playbooks; the news by its ready availability implies that anyone who can pay the price has the right to his or her own opinions about affairs of state. That's a good way of describing a Habermassian public sphere. But is this a sphere of which Ben Jonson wishes to be a part? Does he wish to be in print conversation with upstart barbers and cooks? The answer, it seems to me, is relentlessly "yes" and "no." Print may once have seemed to Jonson to offer an authority to teach of the sort Augustus conferred on Virgil and Horace. But what if Jonson-Horace shares that authority with Nathaniel Butter? Print, the medium in which he once transformed stage voices into monumental works, is now itself Saturday ephemera. Like the printed text of *A Game at Chess*, print is what you use to wipe your posteriors.

I said at the start of this essay that the Jonson subplot reflects upon and critiques the main plot of the development of a public sphere in Early Modern England. While of course Jonson did not intend his writings as a critique of the emerging public sphere, we can see in the plays I've been discussing some of the same qualities that make it hard to specify when one can usefully talk of a public sphere in England. That writers and other subjects disagreed and argued is surely the case; how far these disagreements called their readers into something Habermas or Warner would recognize as a public is much harder to ascertain. But as I have shown, Jonson's example helps us to realize that even assertions denying the legitimacy of making arguments about *arcana imperii* cannot help but legitimate the idea of controversy, including the very controversies they want to efface. Attempts to repress debate about public matters themselves become part of the debate. Authority, whether poetic or political, cannot engage in dialogue with its critics without calling itself into question. To use some old-fashioned terms, "containment" and "subversion" may be the same. Writers and speakers don't proclaim themselves as part of a public sphere, even though the discourse they deploy helps call such a sphere into being. Caring about authority, both his own and the monarch's, Jonson in *Poetaster* tries to be both self-promotional and funny and brings in Augustus to clinch his argument. Dekker in *Satiromastix* is content with being funny. But the dialogue their plays create with one another calls their audience into being as a public. *Sejanus*, as I have shown, imagines a political public even as it marginalizes that public. Only by merging their voices with the imperial authority that would not hear their voices—only by bringing dialogue to an end—do the Germanicans end their marginality. In *Staple of News* questions of authority are everywhere: familial among the Pennyboys, political at the Staple and its newsbooks; literary and interpretive in the Intermeans. And Jonson's efforts to silence debate with his own authority are as paradoxically ineffective as those of the controversialists whose writings call into being a public sphere.

The Staple of News may show a theatrical public becoming a reading public; it surely shows Jonson engaging with an emerging world of public discourse about matters of state. Perhaps hyperbolically, I have claimed *Staple* shows Jonson himself becoming a conversational public. But *Staple* seems impatient with conversations among plays and equally impatient with conversations among texts in print. Mixing an old-fashioned prodigal son plot, an everlasting concern for money, and a newfangled focus on the news, *The Staple of News* talks to itself and expresses its loathing of its subject. Even as he helps call the public sphere into being, Jonson condemns the very sphere he helps to create.[40]

Notes

1. Jürgen Habermas's account of the public sphere appeared in German in 1962. The English translation is *The Structural Transformation of the Public Sphere: An Inquiry into a Category of Bourgeois Society*, tr. Thomas Burger with the assistance of Frederick Lawrence (Cambridge MA: The MIT Press, 1989).
2. Douglas Bruster, "The Structural Transformation of Print in Late Elizabethan England," in Arthur F. Marotti and Michael D. Bristol, eds., *Print, Manuscript, Performance: The Changing Relations of the Media in Early Modern England* (Columbus: Ohio State University Press, 2000), 49–89; Alexandra Halasz, *The Marketplace of Print: Pamphlets and the Public Sphere in Early Modern England* (Cambridge: Cambridge University Press, 1997). For the mid-sixteenth century, see Natalie Mears, *Queenship and Political Discourse in the Elizabethan Realms* (Cambridge: Cambridge University Press, 2005), and Peter Lake, *How Shakespeare Put Politics on the Stage: Power and Succession in the History Plays* (New Haven: Yale University Press, 2016).
3. For most of Ben Jonson's lifetime, conversations about public policy were the province of the monarch and his or her counselors. *Arcana imperii* were off limits to ordinary people; expressing opinions about matters of domestic or foreign policy could lead to severe penalties. Only elites had a legitimate voice in such conversations. Most

of what we think of as "news" was closely held; for example, it was an offense to make known to others the debates in Parliament. For extensive discussion of the usefulness of Habermas's ideas in studying the Early Modern period, see Peter Lake and Steven Pincus, eds., *The Politics of the Public Sphere in Early Modern England*, (Manchester: Manchester University Press, 2007) and Bronwen Wilson and Paul Yachnin, eds., *Making Publics in Early Modern Europe: People, Things, Forms of Knowledge*, (New York: Routledge, 2010). Harold Mah writes, "Analysis of the public sphere should begin, I would suggest, with a recognition that its location is strictly in the political imaginary. The public sphere is a fiction, which, because it can appear real, exerts real political force. The enabling condition of a successfully staged public sphere is the ability of certain groups to make their social or group particularity invisible so that they can then appear as abstract individuals and hence universal." "Phantasies of the Public Sphere: Rethinking the Habermas of Historians," *Journal of Modern History* 72, no. 1 (March 2000): 168.

4. Steven Mullaney makes the case for the role of performance as well as print in his critique of Habermas: "What's Hamlet to Habermas? Spatial Literacy, Theatrical Publication and the Publics of the Early Modern Public Stage," in Angela Vanhaelen and Joseph P. Ward, eds., *Making Space Public in Early Modern Europe: Performance, Geography, Privacy*, (New York: Routledge, 2013), 17–40.

5. Michael Warner, *Publics and Counterpublics* (New York: Zone Books, 2005), pp. 65–124. Warner first explained these ideas in "Publics and Counterpublics," *Public Culture* 14, no. 1 (2002): 49–90. He reprints the essay in the book of the same title.

6. Marlene Eberhart, Amy Scott, and Paul Yachnin, "Introduction," in *Forms of Association: Making Publics in Early Modern Europe*, ed. Paul Yachnin and Marlene Eberhart (Amherst: University of Massachusetts Press, 2015), p. 1.

7. These distinctions are most fully articulated by Javier Castro-Ibaseta in "Sonnets from Carthage, Ballads from Prison: Entertainment and Public-Making in Early Modern Spain," *Forms of Association*, pp. 140–41.

8. Amy Rodgers, *A Monster with a Thousand Hands: The Discursive Spectator in Early Modern England* (Philadelphia: University of Pennsylvania Press, 2018).

9. *1Hen4* 3.2.69, *The Norton Shakespeare,* 3rd ed. Jeffrey S. Doty, *Shakespeare, Popularity and the Public Sphere* (Cambridge: Cambridge University Press, 2017), esp. pp. 1–29.

10. Jeffrey S. Doty and Musa Gurnis, "Theatre Scene and Theatre Public in Early Modern London," *SHAKESPEARE 2018* 14, 1,12–25.

11. Two recent books discuss intertextuality in the early modern theater but make no connection with an emerging public sphere: Janet Clare, *Shakespeare's Stage Traffic: Imitation, Borrowing and Competition in Renaissance Theater* (Cambridge: Cambridge University Press, 2014); Laurence Publicover, *Dramatic Geography: Romance, Intertheatricality, and Cultural Encounter in Early Modern Mediterranean Drama* (Oxford: Oxford University Press, 2017).

12. James Bednarz, *Shakespeare and the Poets' War* (New York: Columbia University Press, 2001); Roslyn Lander Knutson, *Playing Companies and Commerce in Shakespeare's Time* (Cambridge: Cambridge University Press, 2001). Lucy Munro has discovered that Jonson and Marston, rivals in the *poetomachia*, were business partners in 1604–6 with shares in the ownership of the Blackfriars theater. See Munro, "'As it was Played in the Blackfriars': Jonson, Marston and the Business of Playing," *ELR* 50, no. 2 (Spring 2020), 256–95. In "John Marston and the Revolution at Paul's Playhouse (1599–1601)," *MP* 118, 1 (August 2020), 1–24, James Bednarz argues that Jonson, wanting to impose artistic control and didactic purpose on contemporary drama, opposed the "hybridity" that Marston displayed in his plays. I find it useful to

compare the *poetomachia* to the baseball rivalry between the Boston Red Sox and the New York Yankees. Though opposing players try hard to defeat their rivals, they can still be friends after the game or play happily together when traded.

13. Matthew Steggle says that *Poetaster* preceded *Satiromastix* but does not explain how Jonson manages to incorporate allusions to Dekker's play into his own. *Poetaster*, he claims, asserts "literary" status for drama while Dekker insists on the primacy of theater, though Steggle's argument is weakened by its dependence on paratextual materials that could not have been known to an audience in the theater. See *Wars of the Theaters: The Poetics of Personation in the Age of Jonson* (Victoria, B.C.: English Literary Studies, University of Victoria, 1998), esp. 48–61. As the title suggests, the book's central concern is less with dialogue among plays than with the representation of real contemporary figures on stage.

14. Alan Sinfield, "Poetaster, the Author, and the Perils of Cultural Production," in *Material London, ca. 1600*, ed. Lena Cowen Orlin (Philadelphia: University of Pennsylvania Press, 2000), p. 82.

15. *The Cambridge Edition of the Works of Ben Jonson*, ed. David Bevington, Martin Butler, and Ian Donaldson (Cambridge: Cambridge University Press, 2012) 7 vols. *Poetaster* appears in vol. 2, 2–181; I here refer to Gabriele Bernhard Jackson's Introduction, p. 3. Future citations will appear in my text.

16. Lynn S. Meskill argues that *Poetaster* enacts the author's fantasy of being protected from misreading by others—of avoiding the kind of envious critique that Jonson's play directs at Marston and Dekker and that Dekker's *Satiromastix* directs at Jonson. See *Ben Jonson and Envy* (Cambridge: Cambridge University Press, 2009), 94–109. More recently, Eric Vivier reads *Poetaster* as a self-promoting defense of satirical attacks on individuals as well as vices. I think Vivier's essay insufficiently acknowledges the play's comic self-awareness. See Eric D. Vivier, "Judging Jonson: Ben Jonson's Satirical Self-Defense in *Poetaster*," *The Ben Jonson Journal* 24, no. 1 (2017), 1–21. Malcolm Smuts makes a similar argument for the play's self-contradictions: R. Malcolm Smuts, "Jonson's *Poetaster* and the Politics of Defamation," *ELR* 49.2 (2019), 224–47.

17. References to *Satiromastix* are drawn from *The Dramatic Works of Thomas Dekker*, ed. Fredson Bowers, 4 vols., vol. 1 (Cambridge: Cambridge University Press, 1953), 299–395. Introduction and annotations appear in Cyrus Hoy, *Introductions, Notes and Commentaries to texts in "The Dramatic Works of Thomas Dekker, ed. Fredson Bowers,"* 4 vols., vol. 1 (Cambridge: Cambridge University Press, 1980), 179–310. Act-scene-line references appear in my text.

18. See "To the Reader in Ordinary" and "To the Reader Extraordinary" in *Catiline His Conspiracy, Cambridge Edition* 4. 26.

19. The hypothesis that Dekker modified a tragic or tragicomic script already under way is described in Hoy, *Introductions, Notes and Commentaries*, 1, 180.

20. Seeing *Sejanus* as being written from the perspective of Jonson's Roman Catholicism, Victor Lenthe argues the play's opposition to the very idea of "public opinion." See Lenthe, "Ben Jonson's Antagonistic Style, Public Opinion, and *Sejanus*," *SEL* 57, no. 2 (Spring 2017), 349–68.

21. Anne Barton writes, "Like the Elizabethan comical satires, *Sejanus* is a play which reaches its readers or theatre audience largely through the medium of commentators, men who stand a little to one side anatomizing other characters and passing judgment on their behavior." *Ben Jonson, Dramatist* (Cambridge: Cambridge University Press, 1984), p. 100.

22. *Sejanus His Fall*, ed. Tom Cain, in *The Cambridge Edition of the Works of Ben Jonson*, ed. David Bevington, Martin Butler and Ian Donaldson, (Cambridge:

Cambridge University Press, 2012), 2. 197–392. A full discussion of Jonson's marginalia can be found in the electronic edition (http://universitypublishingonline.org.
ezproxy.amherst.edu/cambridge/benjonson/k/essays/Sejanus_textual_essay/1/). My
citations of Jonson refer to this edition. William W. E. Slights has an excellent discussion of "marginality" in *Sejanus* in *Ben Jonson and the Art of Secrecy* (Toronto:
University of Toronto Press, 1994), 48–49.

   23. Adam Zucker persuasively argues that Jonson's marginalia and other forms of
what modern critics see as pedantry "reach out in complex ways to a Jacobean audience
that was only just beginning to understand itself as a potentially objectifiable community—that was, in other words, only just beginning to understand itself as an 'audience.'" "Pedantic Ben Jonson," *Ben Jonson and Posterity*, ed. Jane Rickard and Martin
Butler (Cambridge: Cambridge University Press, 2020), pp. 44–62.

   24. Ian Burrows discusses stage directions in *Sejanus* in "'[Overhearing]': Printing
Parentheses and Reading Power in Ben Jonson's Sejanus," *Early Theatre* 20, no. 2
(2017): 99–120. Burrows claims that the printed text of *Sejanus* refuses to disambiguate
both the complexities of Jonson's syntax and the difficulties created by the absence
of most stage directions, including clear indications of the timing of entrances and
exits. Resisting the by-now-conventional view that Jonson is trying to control the
meaning of his text with his massive marginal annotations, Burrows asserts that Jonson
wants his reader to struggle with figuring out the meaning of words and action just as
do the characters in the play. Burrows says, "While trying to understand the Rome
that Jonson depicts, where so many characters are always potentially traitors or always
potentially spies, the local, logistical problems we encounter in reading resemble the
suspicions and anxieties encountered by the characters themselves (To whom is a
character speaking? For whom is a character speaking?)" (106).

   25. Cynthia Bowers thinks the Germanicans are objects of satire; I disagree. "'I
Will Write Satires Still, in Spite of Fear': History, Satire, and Free Speech in *Poetaster*
and *Sejanus*," *Ben Jonson Journal: Literary Contexts in the Age of Elizabeth, James
and Charles*, 14, 2 (Nov 2007): 153–72.

   26. For a discussion of Jonson's relationship with republican thought, see Julie
Sanders, *Ben Jonson's Theatrical Republics* (Houndmills: Palgrave, 1998).

   27. The best account I know of the emergence of "news" is F. J. Levy, "Staging
the News," in *Print, Manuscript and Performance: The Changing Relations of the
Media in Early Modern England*, ed. Arthur F. Marotti and Michael D. Bristol (Columbus: Ohio State University Press, 2000), 252–78. For an extended account of newsbooks
during the Thirty Years War, see Jayne E. E. Boys, *London's News Press and the Thirty
Years War* (Woodbridge: The Boydell Press, 2011). Boys discusses *Staple* as evidence
for the diffusion and reception of newsbooks.

   28. Alan B. Farmer argues that the play is best understood as a response to the
politics of the year in which it was first printed rather than to the year of its performance.
See "Play-Reading, News-Reading and Ben Jonson's *The Staple of News*" in Marta
Straznicky, ed., *The Book of the Play: Playwrights, Stationers and Readers in Early
Modern England*, (Amherst: University of Massachusetts Press, 2006), 127–58.

   29. Jane Rickard, "A Divided Jonson?: Art and Truth in *The Staple of News*," *ELR*
42, no. 2 (Spring 2012): 294–316. Rickard argues that Jonson tries to present "different
judgments of different kinds of news," sees some affinities between news and theater,
and hopes to educate its audience "to discriminate within and between both media"
(314). She denies Jonson is self-divided.

   30. The "Grex" of Mitis, Cordatus and Asper begin *Every Man Out of His Humor*
with a 360-line Induction in which they comment on the history of comedy and the
actualities of theater. When Asper, as the action begins, takes on the part of Macilente,

Mitis and Cordatus remain onstage—presumably at the margins of the platform—as choric commentators, and continue in that role throughout the performance. While the play in print doesn't have marginal notes, the printed text includes elaborate resources to put *EMO* in dialogue with potential interpreters and the author in dialogue with his reading audience. Jonson tells his reader the printed text includes more lines than the Chamberlain's Men spoke in performance. He includes prose character sketches of each character. He explains that his first ending for the play did not please the audience and then prints both the original and revised endings. Jonson puts his printed text in dialogue with his theatrical "text," and he even puts alternative versions of his own nature in dialogue with one another by figuring himself both in Asper and in Macilente. In the first version of *EMO*, the Queen appeared onstage to impose her authority on Macilente; Cynthia and Augustus play analogous roles in *Cynthia's Revels* and *Poetaster*. Jonson resists but also embraces authority.

31. All citations of *The Staple of News* refer to *The Cambridge Edition of the Works of Ben Jonson*, ed. David Bevington, Martin Butler and Ian Donaldson, 7 vols., vol. 6, 1–158, ed. Joseph Loewenstein.

32. Stephen Wittek, *The Media Players: Shakespeare, Middleton, Jonson and the Idea of News* (Ann Arbor: University of Michigan Press, 2015), 61. Jonson's earlier references to "news" are detailed in Mark Z. Muggli, "Ben Jonson and the Business of News," *SEL* 32 (1992): 323–40.

33. See the listing in Wittek, 109–11. In an argument often based on these items of "news," Alan B. Farmer proposes that *Staple* in print affiliates itself with the Protestant side in the Thirty Years War. See "Play-Reading, News-Reading and Ben Jonson's *The Staple of News*." Catherine Rockwood believes *Staple* in performance parodies *A Game at Chess* to show the foolishness of choosing a single side in the religious conflict. See "'Know Thy Side': Propaganda and Parody in Jonson's *Staple of News*," *ELH*, 75, no. 1 (Spring, 2008): 135–149.

34. After describing Middleton's play, unlike Jonson's, as criticizing censorship, Lena Steveker asserts, "*A Game at Chess* functions as a news play which stages the tensions between state authority and the news business of its time. While Jonson's play criticizes public theater as a place where 'common follies' such as fashion and news—which the play conceptualizes as just another form of fashion—prevent audiences from benefiting from the educational potential of the stage, Middleton's play conceptualizes public theater as an adequate and indeed necessary medium for disseminating political news" (229). Lena Steveker, "English News Plays of the Early 1620s: Thomas Middleton's *A Game at Chess* and Ben Jonson's *The Staple of News*," in Simon F. Davies and Puck Fletcher, eds., *News in Early Modern Europe: Currents and Connections* (Leiden: Brill, 2014), 215–29.

35. The Latin is from Horace's *Art of Poetry*, the translation is Jonson's own. Cambridge ed., 2 Intermean, note 15.

36. Denys Van Renen tries to explain the apparent contradiction by focusing on the debates in the 1620s about the role of gold (Pecunia is, after all, the Princess of the Mines) in overseas trade. Van Renen says that "in *Staple*, Jonson stages Malynes's and Misselden's debate over whether merchants or the monarch drive the economy and the circulation of goods and moneys." Broadly speaking, Pennyboy Senior is on the side of Malynes in thinking gold—Pecunia—should be kept at home; Cymbal and the Staple are on the side of Misselden in favoring circulation and overseas commerce. But this schematizing unconvincingly values Pennyboy Senior and flattens the vitality of the play. Denys Van Renen, *The other exchange: women, servants, and the urban underclass in early modern English literature* (Lincoln: University of Nebraska Press, 2017), pp. 24–33.

37. Lynn S. Meskill, *Ben Jonson and Envy*, 193.
38. Ibid., 194.
39. Indeed, Steggle says that *Staple* unequivocally rejects print in favor of theater. See *Wars of the Theaters,* 108.
40. I presented an early version of this essay at a conference, "Ben Jonson: Literary Transactions across Cultural Environments," organized at the University of Würtzburg in 2017 by Professor Isabel Karremann, now Chair for Early Modern Literature at the University of Zurich. Later, Adam Zucker of the University of Massachusetts at Amherst and William N. West of Nothwestern offered invaluable advice.

Works Cited

Barton, Anne. 1984. *Ben Jonson, Dramatist.* Cambridge: Cambridge University Press.
Bednarz, James. 2001. *Shakespeare and the Poets' War.* New York: Columbia University Press.
———. 2020. "John Marston and the Revolution at Paul's Playhouse (1599–1601)," *MP* 118 (1): 1–24.
Bowers, Cynthia. 2007. "'I Will Write Satires Still, in Spite of Fear': History, Satire and Free Speech in *Poetaster* and *Sejanus*." *Ben Jonson Journal* 14 (2): 153–72.
Boys, Jayne E. E. 2011. *London's News Press and the Thirty Years War.* Woodbridge: The Boydell Press.
Bruster, Douglas. 2000. "The Structural Transformation of Print in Late Elizabethan England." In *Print, Manuscript, Performance: The Changing Relations of the Media in Early Modern England,* ed. Arthur F. Marotti and Michael D. Bristol, 48–89. Columbus, Ohio: Ohio State University Press.
Burrows, Ian. 2017. "'[Overhearing]':Printing Parentheses and Reading Power in Ben Jonson's *Sejanus*"." *Early Theatre* 20 (2): 99–120.
Castro-Ibaseta, Javier. 2015. "Sonnets from Carthage, Ballads from Prison: Entertainment and Public-Making in Early Modern Spain." In *Forms of Association: Making Publics in Early Modern Europe*, ed. Marlene Eberhart and Paul Yachnin, 133–52. Amherst: University of Massachusetts Press.
Clare, Janet. 2014. *Shakespeare's Stage Traffic: Imitation, Borrowing and Competition in Renaissance Theater* . Cambridge: Cambridge University Press.
Dekker, Thomas. 1953. *The Dramatic Works of Thomas Dekker.* Ed. Fredson Bowers. 4 vols. Cambridge: Cambridge University Press.
Doty, Jeffrey S. 2017. *Shakespeare, Popularity and the Public Sphere.* Cambridge: Cambridge University Press.
———, and Musa Gurnis. 2018. "Theatre Scene and Theatre Public in Early Modern London." *Shakespeare* 14 (1): 12–25.
Eberhart, Marlene, Amy Scott and Paul Yachnin. 2015. "Introduction." In *Forms of Association: Making Publics in Early Modern Europe*, ed. Paul Yachnin and Marlene Eberhart, 1–16. Amherst, MA: University of Massachusetts Press.
Farmer, Alan B. 2006. "Play-Reading, News-Reading and Ben Jonson's *The Staple of News*." In *The Book of the Play: Playwrights, Stationers and Readers in Early Modern England,* edited by Marta Straznicky, 127–58. Amherst: University of Massachusetts Press.
Habermas, Jürgen, trans. Thomas Burger with the assistance of Frederick Lawrence. 1989. *The Structural Tranformation of the Public Sphere: An Inquiry into a Category of Bourgeois Society.* Cambridge, MA: MIT Press.

Halasz, Alexandra. 1997. *The Marketplace of Print: Pamphlets and the Public Sphere in Early Modern England.* Cambridge: Cambridge University Press.
Hoy, Cyrus. 1980. *Introductions, Notes and Commentaries to texts in "The Dramatic Works of Thomas Dekker,* ed. Fredson Bowers." 4 vols. Cambridge: Cambridge University Press.
Jonson, Ben. 2012. *The Cambridge Edition of the Works of Ben Jonson.* Edited by David Bevington, Martin Butler, and Ian Donaldson. 7 vols. Cambridge: Cambridge University Press.
Knutson, Roslyn Lander. 2001. *Playing Companies and Commerce in Shakespeare's Time.* Cambridge: Cambridge University Press.
Lake, Peter. 2016. *How Shakespeare Put Politics on the Stage: Power and Succession in the History Plays.* New Haven: Yale University Press.
Lake, Peter and Steven Pincus, eds. 2007. *The Politics of the Public Sphere in Early Modern England.* Manchester: Manchester University Press.
Lenthe, Victor. 2017. "Ben Jonson's Antagonistic Style, Public Opinion and *Sejanus.*" *SEL* 57 (2): 349–68.
Levy, F. J. 2000. "Staging the News." In *Print, Manuscript and Performance: The Changing Relations of the Media in Early Modern England,* ed. Arthur F. Marotti and Michael D. Bristol, 252–78. Columbus: Ohio State University Press.
Mah, Harold. 2000. "Phantasies of the Public Sphere: Rethinking the Habermas of Historians." *Journal of Modern History* 72 (1): 153–182.
Mears, Natalie. 2005. *Queenship and Political Discourse in the Elizabethan Realms*. Cambridge: Cambridge University Press.
Meskill, Lynn S. 2009. *Ben Jonson and Envy.* Cambridge: Cambridge University Press.
Muggli, Mark Z. 1992. "Ben Jonson and the Business of News." *SEL* 32: 323–40.
Mullaney, Steven. 2013. "What's Hamlet to Habermas? Spatial Literacy, Theatrical Publication and the Publics of the Early Modern Public Stage." In *Making Space Public in Early Modern Europe: Performance, Geography, Privacy,* ed. Angela Vanhalen and Joseph P. Ward, 17–40. New York: Routledge.
Munro, Lucy. 2020. "'As it was Played in the Blackfriars': Jonson, Marston and the Business of Playing." *ELR* 50 (2): 256–95.
Publicover, Laurence. 2017. *Dramatic Geography: Romance, Intertheatricality, and Cultural Encounter in Early Modern Mediterranean Drama.* Oxford: Oxford University Press.
Rickard, Jane. 2012. "A Divided Jonson?: Art and Truth in *The Staple of News.*" *ELR* 42 (2): 294–316.
Rockwood, Catherine. 2008. "'Know thy Side': Propaganda and Parody in Jonson's *Staple of News.*" *ELH* 75 (1): 135–49.
Rodgers, Amy. 2018. *A Monster with a Thousand Hands: The Discursive Spectator in Early Modern England.* Philadelphia: University of Pennsylvania Press.
Sanders, Julie. 1998. *Ben Jonson's Theatrical Republics.* Houndmills: Palgrave.
Shakespeare, William. 2016. *The Norton Shakespeare, 3rd Edition.* Ed. Stephen Greenblatt et. al. New York: W. W. Norton.
Sinfield, Alan. 2000. "*Poetaster,* the Author, and the Perils of Cutural Production." In *Material London, ca. 1600,* edited by Lena Cowen Orlin, 75–90. Philadelphia: University of Pennsylvania Press.
Slights, William W. E. 1994. *Ben Jonson and the Art of Secrecy.* Toronto: University of Toronto Press.
Smuts, R. Malcolm. 2019. "Jonson's *Poetaster* and the Politics of Defamation." *ELR* 49 (2): 224–47.

Steggle, Matthew. 1998. *Wars of the Theaters: The Poetics of Personation in the Age of Jonson.* Victoria, B.C.: English Literary Studies, University of Victoria.
Steveker, Lena. 2014. "English News Plays of the Early 1620s: Thomas Middleton's *A Game at Chess* and Ben Jonson's *The Staple of News.*" In *News in Early Modern Europe: Currents and Connections*, ed. Simon F. Davies and Puck Fletcher, 215–29. Leiden: Brill.
Van Renen, Denys. 2017. *The other exchange: women, servants and the urban underclass in early modern English literature.* Lincoln: University of Nebraska Press.
Vivier, Eric D. 2017. "Judging Jonson: Ben Jonson's Satirical Self-Defense in *Poetaster.*" *The Ben Jonson Journal* 24 (1): 1–21.
Warner, Michael. 2005. *Publics and Counterpublics.* New York: Zone Books.
Wilson, Bronwen, and Paul Yachnin. 2010. *Making Publics in Early Modern Europe: People, Things, Forms of Knowledge.* New York: Routledge.
Wittek, Stephen. 2015. *The Media Players: Shakespeare, Middleton, Jonson and the Idea of News.* Ann Arbor: University of Michigan Press.
Zucker, Adam. 2020. "Pedantic Ben Jonson." In *Ben Jonson and Posterity*, edited by Jane Rickard and Martin Butler, 44–62. Cambridge: Cambridge University Press.

Who told on Samuel Daniel? Robert Cecil, Ben Jonson, and the Non-Scandal of *The Tragedy of Philotas*

John Pitcher

After the second sounding, ENVIE.

Jonson, *Poetaster*

The last thing the poet and historian Samuel Daniel (1562–1619) would have wanted was to be remembered for a scandal. Some of his famous contemporaries, Ben Jonson among them, appear to have enjoyed notoriety, or at least pretended not to care what people said about them. This is not what Daniel felt. The irony is that today he is read and studied as often for the topical significance and supposed scandal of his 1605 play *The Tragedy of Philotas* as for the literary achievements of his poems, verse epistles, and neo-epic on kingship and usurpation, *The Civil Wars*. The reason the moderns have neglected Daniel—unjustly, according to Coleridge, Daniel's warmest admirer—is a subject for other occasions. One aim here is to set out a fuller context for *Philotas* and to correct misunderstandings about what happened before and after the performance of the play, indeed why it was performed at all—and to examine what the consequences were for Daniel himself. At one point after the performance, he did fear the worst: that the play in print would be publicly suppressed and he would be shamed and turned out on his ear without a penny. However, the evidence suggests, to the contrary, that it was in part *because* of the *Philotas* upset that Daniel's circumstances changed for the better.

This essay offers a new conversation about *Philotas*,[1] in the period between 8 January 1604 and 31 August 1605, the dates of Daniel's major court successes in the service of James I's consort, Anne of Denmark. It re-examines the evidence for modern working assumptions—that Daniel deliberately licensed dangerous public stage plays, for instance—and suggests that one intervention in particular, by Robert Cecil, was decisive in advancing and protecting Daniel's historical writing, and in securing a place for him in the Queen's court. The new conversation also brings into play for the first time

43

the full extent of Ben Jonson's enmity towards Daniel, which, it is suggested here, went well beyond rivalry over patrons and literary models: Jonson wanted to supplant and eliminate Daniel, get rid of him in the way that an informer or an undercover man might. We shall see that there was indeed an informer in this matter, and whoever he was, it was his account of *Philotas* that shaped the case against Daniel (framed him, one might say) with the Privy Council—which is the case literary scholars are still discussing (and accepting) today. To challenge this, the conversation includes a section on contemporary uses of the *Philotas* story. Was it inherently dangerous? What did Montaigne or the Elizabethan intellectuals Henry Howard and Francis Bacon make of it, or the ousted court favorite Walter Raleigh who had been imprisoned on trumped up charges? Modern scholarship has been preoccupied with showing that *Philotas* was Daniel's partisan allegory or commentary, written for the stage, on the rebellion, trial and execution of Robert, Earl of Essex.[2] The new conversation suggests another way of thinking about this— that the play was meant at first for the study or the briefing meeting or the council table. It was not intended for (as Daniel thought of it) the gross and trivial public theater. Not that this would free the play from other accusations that it was contentious. Did the informer detect in it a potential libel against living great men, *scandalum magnatum*, one of whom was (the very much alive) Robert Cecil?

An enemy

So far as we know, the first masque Daniel wrote for the court was *The Vision of the Twelve Goddesses*, performed in the Great Hall at Hampton Court Palace on 8 January 1604, the year before the staging of *Philotas*. Daniel was paid £40 for the *Vision*, which included six weeks in attendance at Hampton Court.[3] Presumably he was in charge of the music, singing and acted roles, and liaised with the dancing masters who instructed the maskers (the new Queen and her ladies) in their complicated dance steps. The text of the masque was short, under 120 lines of verse including two songs, something like a libretto for an opera. The ceremonial processions and dances took up much of the playing time. The theme of the *Vision*, anticipating the upcoming peace talks with top-level Spanish negotiators, was armed peace with honor. It was the first large-scale masque at the Jacobean court, presented under the auspices of the Queen, and commissioned by her favorite, Lucy, Countess of Bedford. From the point of view of the Spanish and foreign dignitaries, it was a success. The theme of peace achieved through female intervention (the Queen and her ladies), and Daniel's treatment of it, evidently satisfied most of the participants and spectators. The elite and semi-elite, including insiders who had been at the performance, wanted a printed record of this prestigious event. An unauthorised text and description was published within days of its being performed. Daniel issued an authorized text in response, which began with a letter he wrote to Lady Bedford by way of an apologia and a rebuttal of the "captious Censurers" who had criticized the masque.

Chief among Daniel's captious critics was Ben Jonson. As early as 1599, Daniel had defeated Jonson in the contest for Lady Bedford's favor. In person and in his public theater play *Cynthia's Revels* Jonson had promoted himself to the Countess as an inventor of masques who would glorify her at court, so her selection of Daniel for the first of the Queen's masques must have been galling. Jonson was confident—and modern literary historians agree with him—that he could better any entertainment Daniel wrote for the court. Jonson's sense of grievance got the better of him on the night of the performance, when he and a reckless but able young acolyte, Sir John Roe, interrupted the masque in some way, probably by shouting out what they thought was wrongheaded and unsophisticated about it, and why Daniel should never have been chosen to write it.[4] They were both "thrust out," but they must have expected to be and probably relished being excluded. Even four centuries after the event, Jonson's interruption looks like a publicity stunt, designed to ridicule Daniel in front of his sponsors, and so magnify Jonson's own superior theatrical talent. Jonson would have known what was going to be in the masque because the boy actors who sang and had speaking roles (rehearsed in the weeks of preparation) were his own favorites. They would have told Jonson everything in advance, including Daniel's idea behind the *Vision*, its "device" or "conceit," as well as its staging.

Modern scholars have concluded, perhaps too readily, that Jonson's criticism hit home with the Queen and Daniel's patrons. Important people heeded Jonson's words, it is claimed, and gave him, rather than Daniel, the commission for the next big masque at court, for the following Christmas season (*The Masque of Blackness*, performed in January 1605). However, there was no sign of disfavor towards Daniel at the time; quite the opposite. A royal patent was issued on 4 February 1604, stipulating the creation of a company of boy actors, under the protection of the Queen, to be called the Children of the Queen's Revels.[5] This patent licensed the Children to perform at court or in the public theaters, under the management of four individuals from the theater world. Two of these, Thomas Kendall and Robert Payne, had been involved in Daniel's masque in January (the others were Alexander Hawkins and Edward Kirkham, the Yeoman of the Revels). Kendall had supplied some of the masque costumes and Payne brought seven (unnamed) boy singers and actors to Hampton Court and tended to them. The February patent further stipulated that the Company were to perform only plays approved and allowed by Samuel Daniel.

A patent and an agreement

In line with the provision for Daniel in the patent, the four managers of
the Children agreed to pay him from 28 April 1604 an annuity or annual fee
of £10, secured by a £100 bond in the event of a default. Some years later,
as we learn from a lawsuit in 1609,[6] what Daniel was supposed to do for this
£10 a year was disputed by the parties. The managers claimed the payment
was for the work of approval and allowance; Daniel maintained it was for
the "paines" he had taken in obtaining the patent—it was his finder's fee, in
other words, a gift from the Crown, specifically from the Queen.

Literary historians have sided with the managers over this. They imagine
Daniel reading the Company's playscripts, perhaps even attending plays in
rehearsal, before giving his assent, a signed approval on the script. They
point out that this is what Edmund Tilney, the Master of the Revels, did with
the generality of public stage plays presented to him for license, without
which a play could not be performed lawfully. They argue that the provision
for Daniel in the patent was in fact an encroachment on Tilney's licensing
monopoly, though it was only a very small slice of it. This has led critics to
blame Daniel for poor judgment in approving controversial plays acted by
the Children—altogether mistakenly with plays such as *The Malcontent* and
Eastwood Ho, which were not even in the Company's repertoire in the twelve-
month period Daniel was "licenser" (that is, 28 April 1604 to 28 April 1605).
Daniel's most notable misjudgement, the critics say, was over his own play,
Philotas. He approved this for performance, but because it was tendentious
and politically risky, the argument runs, he specifically asked Tilney to read
it too, as an "insurance policy" in case parallels with the Essex case were
detected.[7]

This is the received explanation. An alternative view is that what Daniel
said was true: he never read any of the Company's plays for approval or
expected to. He was not paid to read them, and the payment for reading and
allowance remained the perquisite of Tilney as Master of the Revels, who
charged acting companies per play. Daniel's "allowance" or assent, specified
in the patent, was in this interpretation a formality, merely a confirmatory
signature. Monopolies and patents came in different forms with different
purposes at this date,[8] but the provision for Daniel, an unencumbered gift
with no real duties, only provided him with an income indirectly, the £10 per
annum the managers agreed to pay him—nothing was specified for reading
playscripts, and nothing was paid from the Queen's exchequer.[9] If this explanation is correct, Tilney read *Philotas* in the normal course of things, not as
a special one-off because Daniel was apprehensive ahead of its being performed. Tilney would have been paid for reading Daniel's play as he was for
the other Children's plays he read during 1604–5.

Something else in the 1609 law case, Kirkham *versus* Daniel, adds to this argument that Daniel never formally read or "allowed" the Children's plays. On 28 April 1605, when Daniel assigned his rights in the agreement with the managers, he passed the £10 annuity and £100 default bond to John Gerard. (What Gerard paid Daniel for this is not known.) The patent issued in February 1604 was still in force as regards the named managers, Kirkham and the others, but the stipulation that Daniel was the Company's "licenser" would lapse. There is no sign that Gerard "allowed" any plays; his was solely a financial investment in the annuity and the bond. However, *someone* continued to license the Children's plays for performance after 28 April 1605 and that was Tilney. Famously, Tilney did not license *Eastward Ho*, the Children's satirical play acted without allowance very likely in August 1605 when the King and the whole court were away from the capital in Oxford (see below)— but this infringement only confirms what was supposed to happen. Tilney remained the real overseer of the boy actors' plays before, during, and after Daniel's brief sinecure as their "licenser."

The deal with the managers of the Company was a disaster for Daniel. Their business model could never produce enough money to satisfy everyone (producers, actors, and authors), let alone an extra "licenser." To start with, it appears there were too few new plays. In the twelve months to April 1605—when Daniel relinquished his license—the number of known new plays was perhaps as few as five (two by Marston, who had a small share in the Company, two by Chapman, and Daniel's *Philotas*)[10]. In the same period, so far as we know, the Children may have performed no more than a dozen or so times. There were probably unrecorded second performances and revivals of older plays, but the Company's dealings with Daniel make one wonder whether there were many of these. The partners expected to make money out the enterprise—Kendall, a haberdasher, rented out and adapted clothes as costumes, for instance—but the profit was probably small. A few calculations show this. Assuming the maximum audience at the Blackfriars was 500–600, as historians of the theater think, and the minimum price of a seat was 6d, the best the Company could hope for from a performance was £15 plus the extra takings from the pricier seats, say £20 in all. In reality the takings may have been smaller on quiet days, as low as £10. The Company was paid £20 for two performances at court in January 1605, where the payees were the disgraced impresario Henry Evans and Daniel,[11] so £10 per performance may have been a decent outcome at the Blackfriars. But this was a gross sum. Before the shareholders got anything, the actors had to be paid, plus incidental costs, plus whatever the Company had to pay the author, plus any fixed fees. One fixed fee of £10 was to their "licenser" Daniel, paid as fifty shillings per quarter, irrespective of the plays performed, Even if the Children did not perform for a full six months because of the "pestilence," the managers were obliged to pay Daniel at the rate of 16s.8d per month.

Daniel's necessities

The first 50 shillings payments were due on 24 June and 29 September 1604, but before the next quarter-day the arrangement appears to have changed. From the 1609 lawsuit, we learn that on 25 October Daniel and Kirkham, the lead manager-partner in the Company, agreed in principle to convert the £10 per annum payment to 5 shillings per week to Daniel for (this is crucial) any week in which the Company actually performed. It is not clear whether the 5 shillings arrangement ever began, or how Kirkham persuaded Daniel to accept a reduction in fee—perhaps that the takings were not what the Company expected at the outset. Perhaps there were too few new or reprised plays, or too few regular patrons, or the Blackfriars was forced to shut too many times because of the plague (notwithstanding the "pestilence" provision in the agreement). Whatever the reason, paring down his fee came at the worst time for Daniel. According to Kirkham, in the wording of the 1609 lawsuit, Daniel would 'importune and Request the said Kyrkham and Kendall to pay to him his mony before the day did come that the same was due and somtymes to pay the same to others to whom the said Danyell did stande indebted.' These were Daniel's circumstances in late 1604, the earliest date *Philotas* was acted: he was regularly asking for his fee ahead of the due date, or that his creditors be paid; and the people with whom he had the 'licenser' agreement were looking to cut his fee. When Daniel came to explain why *Philotas* had been acted on stage, he insisted "my necessitie . . . hath driuen me," "my necessities ouer-maistred mee"; and "[I was] driuen by necessity to make vse of my pen." He swore that when he read parts of the play in private to his patron Lord Mountjoy, he had had no intention of having it played in public. Certainly, when he first thought of a tragedy about Philotas, he had anticipated having it performed, but only in a private home in the city of Bath, by the sons of "Gentlemen," that is, well-bred young amateurs acting or reciting the play to people similar in rank—gentry, clerics, and functionaries like Daniel himself.

Most modern critics have concluded that Daniel's presenting of *Philotas* on the public stage was planned all along, a vehicle for the commentary on Lord Essex he was aiming at. To believe this, we need to ignore the evidence he was in dire straits financially; and to explain what he says about "necessities" as an excuse he dreamt up when the performance backfired. This is not really believable, and it also obscures what else Daniel may have meant by "necessity." This is normally taken to mean the equivalent of "I was so hard up I had to finish the play and sell it to the Company." Necessity and necessities can certainly mean this, but Daniel may have intended something more vague—"I was forced by circumstances," rather than just "I was desperate for money," though he certainly was (see *OED* 'Necessity', *n*. 9). Perhaps he wanted to blur over the dispute with Kirkham about his role as "licenser" and his fee. Or he was unhappy that he had succumbed to pressure Kirkham put on him to finish *Philotas* for the stage. He had started writing the play for young gentlemen in Bath, Kirkham might remind him: surely it could not be difficult to complete it for another set of high-quality boys, the Company's Children, whose regular London audience was professional and at least middling sort.

Perhaps Daniel did not intend the play for the public stage, but was it not inevitable that the subject matter would be inflammatory? It showed a vainglorious king and his advisors in a very bad light, and a favorite snared by his enemies but also by his own misplaced confidence and sense of self-worth. Daniel must have been aware that the story of Philotas was dangerous, and that it glanced at the Essex rebellion and his execution. It is not clear, however, as the following brief survey shows, that the subject was connected exclusively with the coup Essex attempted and its consequences.

The exemplary story of Philotas

Daniel had the Philotas story in mind well before he wrote the play and was obliged to have it performed—as early as the mid-1590s when, by virtue of his connections with Charles, Earl of Devonshire (i.e., Mountjoy), he was within the orbit of the Essex circle, the courtiers, writers, and scholars gathered around Robert, Earl of Essex (1563–1601). The idea of writing about Philotas occurred to him, Daniel said, in 1596 or 1597. In the *Apology*, probably written around April 1605, at the time of his letters to Robert Cecil and to Devonshire (see below), Daniel went out of his way to fix the date by which he decided to write a tragedy on the subject:

> aboue eight yeares since, meeting with my deare friend *D. Lateware*, (whose memory I reuerence) in his Lords Chamber, and mine [i.e., Mountjoy], I told him the purpose I had for *Philotas*, who sayd that himselfe had written the same argument, and caused it to be presented in S^t. *Iohns* Colledge in *Oxford*, where as I after heard, it was worthily and with great applause performed.[12]

Daniel's friendship with the cleric, poet and Fellow of St John's, Dr Richard Latewar (1559/60–1601) may have dated from the time they overlapped at Oxford in the early 1580s. By 1596 they were Mountjoy's men; Latewar his chaplain, and Daniel his prized client, the most significant literary talent associated with Essex House. Latewar had conceived of a tragedy in Latin about Philotas, along with other tragedies from classical mythology, in the 1580s.[13] The production at St John's may have been staged or revived much later, as late as the mid-1590s, not long before Daniel spoke with Latewar in Mountjoy's "Chamber." There is thus an intriguing possibility that both men were at work on Philotas plays while they were in Mountjoy's service, and in proximity to the Earl of Essex himself. (Latewar had a further connection through his friend John Buckeridge, another Fellow of St John's, who became Essex's chaplain in 1595). It is conceivable that Essex's situation around 1596, after the raid on the Spanish port of Cadiz, lent itself to ideas about Alexander's favorite Philotas and his path to tragedy.

Philotas' predicament was certainly in the mind of another of Essex' clients, Lord Henry Howard (1540–1614) around the same time. Howard—the future Earl of Northampton, the Privy Councillor who investigated Daniel in 1605—was one of Essex's most ardent supporters in the 1590s, at least until the end of the decade. In a letter he wrote to Essex in August 1597, to assure him of his unswerving loyalty, Howard made a striking allusion to Philotas, by way of a comparison. "If euer," he wrote, "I find change whear I desir most to establish permanente contente the last wurdes that I to y^u shall vtter I shall conclude wth that brefe sentence of Philotas at his end"

> O simplex et singularis amor
> O nimuim sincera fides
> O veri consilij periculosa libertas
>   vos me perdidistis

Howard pointedly adapted the moment in Curtius' history of Alexander when Philotas, on trial for his life, declared he had been unfairly misjudged.[14] It was true, Howard admitted, that Philotas expressed himself candidly and critically when Alexander grew to believe he was the son of a god, but it was love for Alexander, not disloyalty, that made him be truthful. He, Howard, was doing the same as Philotas had in Curtius' account:

> it may be said, I also wrote that I pitied those who had to live under a man [Alexander] who believed himself the son of Jupiter. *O loyalty to friendship, O dangerous freedom in giving true counsel, it is you that played me false!* It was you that impelled me not to keep silent about what I thought.[15]

Howard, perhaps in pique, cast himself as a latter-day Philotas, in danger of being sacrificed if the frank counsel he had given Essex were used to accuse him of being disloyal. This passage confirms one thing: that the history of Philotas, as insouciant favorite or confessed traitor, was not *inescapably* provocative and inflammatory. It was what was made of it that mattered—its intent and how "mannerely" or well-behaved the treatment was, in its language in particular.[16]

Around the time Howard wrote his letter, another of Daniel's contemporaries, Francis Bacon (1561–1626), was examining the ancient histories of Alexander. Bacon wrote about the sources twice, first in relation to Plutarch's *Life of Alexander*, second about Curtius' *History* as well as Plutarch's *Life*. Bacon wrote the first as a set of private "how-to" notes headed "A direccion for the readeinge of histories with profitt." He showed what insightful sayings might be taken from Plutarch's life, as well as notable examples of virtue and vice. One vice was Alexander's "tirranie when he was present at the torture of Philotas."[17] Bacon's second piece was the letter of advice he wrote to Fulke Greville, probably around 1596, on "research techniques" in reading histories.[18] This time the "how-to" advice was for the research assistants Greville planned to employ. The ancient historians Bacon recommends are ones we might expect—Tacitus, Livy, and Thucydides—but it is interesting that when he sets out the questions that need to be asked, he begins with Alexander "out of Curtius, or Plutarch," as though this is what was uppermost in his mind at the time. Under the heading of "Periods, or Revolucions of States," two reasons he gives for the "Loss of the Grecian Monarchy" were "the Uncertainty of Succession," and "the Equal Greatness of divers Grandeis." It has been suggested Bacon wrote this in the late 1590s when he and Greville were in the Essex House circle. Daniel was a client of Greville's who had a direct connection through Mountjoy into the intellectual and political milieu of Bacon, Latewar, and Howard, all connected to some degree with Essex. Did the topic of Philotas and Alexander become one of the regular think pieces, subjects to be debated pro and contra, in Essex House? Is this where Daniel's tragedy began its life—as part of a briefing conversation within the Essex set, possibly even an informal colloquium?

We should not rush to position Daniel among the Essex advisors. A number of these were Oxbridge dons who put their learning at the Earl's disposal. They argued for interpretations of ancient history that would guide the Earl in his dealings with the Queen or with enemies at court. Others around him were "martialists," or advocates of continuing war with Spain and assistance to England's allies, the Dutch, to resist Spanish hegemony. Still others were lawyers or former diplomats like Anthony Bacon. In modern parlance, the Essex advisors weaponized scholarship. Daniel by contrast was not an academic but a poet and intellectual, an observer of his times and a champion of letters—certainly more a Modern than an Ancient in the battle of the books. He admired Essex greatly, but his outlook was probably more internationalist (an ancestor of Daniel's patron, Mountjoy, had been the patron of Erasmus in England), and he was not a proponent of more war with Spain.[19] In *Musophilus*, written *c.* 1597, he was critical of the universities and Reformation zeal. It was characteristic of him that he should be drawn to the moral and intellectual complexities of the Philotas case—Alexander and his courtiers were double dealers but so was Philotas in his not revealing that there was indeed

a real plan to kill the king, even if he were innocent of it. The genesis of
Daniel's play, begun on the sidelines of Essex House, may have been an
exemplary history of a compromised favorite, who like Essex trusted too
much in his talents, his family and his place with the monarch. What the play
became, at least how the Blackfriars' informer reported it, is the subject below.

The Essex advisors were Daniel's contemporaries, scholars and statesmen
whom he knew personally and was in conversation with. The most powerful
influence on him, however, was from a contemporary he never met in person,
namely Montaigne. In the matter of Philotas, as in many things, it was Montaigne who shaped Daniel's outlook and writing, from the mid-1590s onwards.
Montaigne referred to Philotas twice in the *Essays*, first in the short essay in
Book II, published in 1580, "Of Conscience," where he considered the use
of torture to establish guilt or innocence. "To say truth, it is a meane full of
vncertaintie and danger" he wrote, "What would not a man say, nay, what
not doe, to avoide so grievous paines and shunne such torments?" He was
thinking in particular of the tortures inflicted on Philotas while Alexander
watched him, concealed from sight: "Many thousands have thereby charged
their heads with false confessions. Amongst which I may well place *Phylotas*,
considering the circumstances of the enditement that *Alexander* framed against
him, and the progresse of his torture."[20]

Montaigne did not believe Philotas and Parmenio had planned to overthrow
Alexander—Philotas only confessed to avoid more horrible pain. What was
doubtless at the back of Montaigne's mind, and perhaps in Howard's mind
too, was the ancient negative view of Alexander, found in Seneca and Lucan
as well as in the historian Curtius, that the king became a cruel and murderous
tyrant when corrupted by Persian custom.

In his other mention of Philotas, Montaigne addressed a familiar part of
Alexander's history, his glorification as a god (in the same passage in Curtius
that Howard alluded to), but he used it in a particular way. The discussion is
in the final essay of Book III, "Of Experience," in one of the last sentences
in the *Essays* as a whole. Montaigne reflects on the delusion among ancient
philosophers that the body and soul can be separated. It is madness, he says,
to believe we can escape from our bodies by thinking super-celestial thoughts.
"I finde nothing so humble and mortall in *Alexanders* life," he concludes, "as
his conceipts [fancies] about his immortalization." It was Philotas who called
Alexander out over this foolishness, and "by his answere quipped at him very
pleasantly and wittily." Philotas congratulated Alexander by letter

and rejoyced that the Oracle of *Iupiter Hammon* had placed him amongest the Gods;
to whom he answered, that in respect and consideration of him [Alexander] he was
very glad; but yet there was some cause those men should be pittyed that were to
live with a man and obay him, who outwent others, and would not bee contented
with the state and condition of mortall man.[21]

Philotas saw through Alexander's vanity as a man—he was just flesh and blood—as much as through his puffed-up pretensions as a king. Montaigne's subtext (visible in "Of Conscience") was that Philotas' wit and candor cost him his life, and an agonizing death, but still he made Alexander look preposterous and, the way things went in the trial, horribly cruel too.[22]

Thus, among educated Elizabethans, including ones who read Montaigne, the history of Philotas could mean different things and serve different ends. The modern view is that Daniel intended his play as a series of parallels between Essex and Philotas, but to what end? If Alexander was ungrateful to Philotas and misjudged him (recall what Howard says), did this implicitly criticize Queen Elizabeth for similar treatment of Essex? If Alexander was shown as cruel and criminally overgrand (as in Montaigne), was Daniel accusing the Queen of being a despot and self-deluded? Is that what the informer told the authorities he had seen at the Blackfriars performance? Daniel's own defense, in his letters and the *Apology*, is not much help in this respect. He had such a fright at being accused—whatever the accusation—that his only line in response, which he kept repeating, was that there was nothing new under the sun, history repeats itself, and any parallel was accidental. But Philotas had incriminated others when he was tortured, and in 1601 so had Essex, to the point of implicating even his sister Penelope Rich. Was Daniel denouncing the great men around Elizabeth (Cecil and others) who had tried to finish off Essex, using judicial torture, to ensure he could never make a comeback?

Some years later, this is certainly what one elite contemporary thought was Daniel's motive for writing the play. This was Sir Walter Raleigh, who in 1603 had himself been outmanoeuvred at court and convicted of treason. Raleigh had given evidence against Essex when the Earl was prosecuted in 1601, so he knew from the inside what had to be done to destroy an enemy. Imprisoned in the Tower, a decade later, he included a chapter in his *History of the World*, "*A conspiracie against* ALEXANDER. *The death of* PHILOTAS *and* PARMENIO." Raleigh was sure he knew what the chief prosecutor, Alexander's minster Craterus, was thinking. Raleigh turned first to Curtius' history, but then to what Daniel had made of it in his play:

Curtius giues a note of *Craterus* in this businesse; How hee [Craterus] perswaded himselfe, that hee could neuer finde a better occasion to oppresse his priuate enemie [Philotas], than by pretending pietie and dutie towards the King. Heereof a Poet of our owne [Daniel] hath giuen a note as much better as it is more generall in his *Philotas.*

> See how these great men cloathe their priuate hate,
> In these faire colours of the publike good,
> And to effect their ends, pretend the State,
> As if the State by their affection stood,

> And arm'd with power and Princes jealousies,
> Will put the least conceit of discontent
> Into the greatest ranke of treacheries,
> That no one action shall seeme innocent;
> Yea valour, honour, bountie, shall be made
> As accessaries vnto ends vnjust:
> And euen the seruice of the State must lade
> The needfull'st vndertaking with distrust,
> So that base vilensse; idle Luxurie,
> Seeme safer farre, than to doe worthily, &c.[23]

Raleigh quoted this from a printed edition of *Philotas*,[24] from the Chorus at the end of act 3.3, which follows immediately after Craterus has coerced the other lords into agreeing that Philotas should be tortured. Philotas will incriminate himself about something or other, Craterus urges in a recognizably Machiavellian way, whether or not Philotas is truly part of the "plot." The torture "will force out some such thoughts of his | As will vndoo him."[25]

Raleigh evidently suspected Daniel knew what had happened with Essex when he was tortured, since the poet could have learned of it from conversations with his patron Mountjoy. This was the raison d'être of the play, Raleigh thought—that everyone, even the Chorus of soldiers, history's unimportant underlings, believed it was Craterus' ambition and hate that destroyed Philotas. And for Craterus and Philotas, an observer only needed to move from past to present and read them as the opposing figures, Cecil and Essex.

If Raleigh was right, then Daniel's "application" of the Craterus-Cecil parallel in *Philotas* was an open-and-shut case of defaming a nobleman, what was known as *scandalum magnatum*, still a high crime at this date.[26] Is this what the informer at the Blackfriars alleged was wrong with the play, that it contained a personal attack on Robert Cecil, the first minister of state? Was this a different but even worse charge than the supposed parallels between Philotas and Essex, pressed by the Privy Council? One way to weigh this is to look for evidence that Cecil himself took offense over *Philotas*. Once the play had been acted, did Daniel suffer from an investigation into his conduct, led by Cecil and the Privy Council?

The performance of *Philotas*

At this point we can move to the moment Daniel was denounced. *The Tragedy of Philotas* was acted before King James at court on 3 January 1605, so the modern account of the play goes, and the parallels between Essex and Philotas were noticed. The Privy Council called Daniel in, and from his various responses, according to the prevailing narrative, we gain an insight into the censorship of public stage drama at this date. Robert P. Adams writes that the play was "suppressed and Daniel was called to account by the authorities." Andrew Gurr adds that in 1604 "the Privy Council punished Daniel for representing Essex in *Philotas*."[27] However, neither of these claims, and others like them, is true.[28] It is not even true that *Philotas* was acted at court.

Two letters Daniel wrote about *Philotas* have survived. The first is to Robert Cecil (1563–1612) addressing him by his 1604–5 title Viscount Cranborne; the second, written soon afterwards, is to Daniel's patron, Charles Blount, 8th Baron Mountjoy (1563–1606),[29] whom Daniel addresses as the 1st Earl of Devonshire, the title conferred on him in 1603.[30] After he had written the letters, Daniel used phrases and ideas from them in a short piece in prose entitled *The Apology*. It appears he intended to attach this to the end of a printed text of *Philotas*, but in the event it did not appear until four years after Daniel's death, in the 1623 collection, *The Whole Workes of Samuel Daniel Esquire in Poetrie*.[31] Thus, when *Philotas* was first published, in an octavo edition in 1605, the *Apology* was not included. Instead, the text of the play was prefaced with a poem in which Daniel dedicated the tragedy to the eleven-year old Prince Henry, King James' heir. Daniel published a slightly revised text of *Philotas* in a 1607 collection of his poems and plays, and in this version, he made important changes to the poem to the Prince.[32]

The view that *Philotas* was acted at court in January 1605 is an old one, but it is not credible. It is based on a payment of £20 from Queen Anne's exchequer to Daniel and to Henry Evans, the disreputable theater impresario, on 24 February 1605. This was "for twoe Enterludes or plaies presented before the Kinges Matie by the Quenes Ma^ts Children of the Revells the one on New-yeres daie at nighte 1604 [i.e., 1 January 1605] and the other on the third daie of Januarie followinge."[33] The first of the unnamed plays performed by the Children of the Queen's Revels was almost certainly George Chapman's comedy *All Fools*, and it has been assumed, because Daniel was one of the payees for the two plays together, that the unnamed play on 3 January was *Philotas*.[34]

This does not square with what Daniel says explicitly about the performance—that *Philotas* was acted on the public stage. In the 1605 verse dedication to Prince Henry, Daniel regrets that because of the play he has been "*mistaken by the censuring Stage*," and in the letter to Cecil he says that in writing *Philotas* he "sought to reduce the stage from idleness to those grave presentments of antiquitie vsed by the wisest nations." This palpably refers to the public stage, a place of censure and idleness, as Daniel saw it (i.e., of impudent political criticism and trivial pastimes), and not to a performance at court. In the *Apology* Daniel explains that by using

> my pen, and the Stage to bee the mouth of my lines, which before were neuer heard to speake but in silence, I thought the representing so true a History, in the ancient forme of a Tragedy, could not but haue had an unreproueable passage with the time,

and the better sort of men, seeing with what idle fictions, and grosse follies, the Stage at this day abused mens recreations.[35]

Nothing in this points to the court as the venue for *Philotas*. There is a slim chance the play was acted before the king on 3 January as well as on the Blackfriars public stage, but to believe this, even as a possibility, we would need to know, on other grounds, that part of the £20 paid to Daniel and Evans in January 1605 was for *Philotas*. The truth is different and simpler. In December 1604 Evans fell out with his partners, Kirkham and the others, to the extent of locking them out of the theater. To be paid the £20 from the exchequer, Evans was forced to surface as a payee alongside Daniel (the only person other than Kirkham and the others specified in the patent).

No evidence has been found to determine exactly when *Philotas* was performed. Daniel wrote his letter to Cecil, at some date between 20 August 1604, when Cecil was made Viscount Cranborne, and 4 May 1605, when he became Earl of Salisbury. The letter is endorsed "1605 | Mr Samuel Daniel | to my Lord," perhaps in the hand of Cecil's secretary, Sir Walter Cope. Daniel's publishers, Simon Waterson and Edward Blount, entered *Philotas* in the Stationers' Register on 29 November 1604, when printing of the play may have begun (see below). The SR entry shows there was a full manuscript of *Philotas*, possibly ready for performance, by the end of November 1604 at the latest.

Within this period of eight months (September 1604 to April 1605), Chambers thought a performance in later 1604 would best fit the date Daniel said he was writing the *Apology*,[36] that is, "about foure years" after the Essex rebellion in February 1601, "the Shrouetide of that vnhappy disorder."[37] The date may have been a few months later, however, when Daniel assigned his rights established in the patent, 28 April 1605. The argument below is that it was the Privy Council's reaction to the performance that led Daniel to get out of the agreement with the Children's Company.

Philotas was undoubtably acted by the Children of the Queen's Revels at the Blackfriars. We saw earlier that Daniel's connection with the boys and their managers began in late 1603 with his masque, *The Vision of the Twelve Goddesses*. The Company's indoor home venue, the Blackfriars, was smaller, posher, and more expensive than the big open-air theaters like the Globe, but Daniel would have thought the Blackfriars was equally "public" and trashy. There was an obvious risk with the boys. What made them exciting and watchable made them dangerous. Jonson and Marston, who wrote for the previous boys' company, the Children of the Chapel, liked to mash up genres and modes with new ideas and literary theories—comedy with satire, tragedy with comic farce, satire with tragicomedy, masque with old-fashioned character types—and they joined slick smuttiness to morality stories and social commentary. Nothing changed much in the year, 1604 to 1605, when Daniel was designated their "licenser." The upmarket audiences, made up of London lawyers and professionals, would-be's and well-off hangers-on, were tickled pink with the Blackfriars innovations, experiments and brushes with sexual and moral norms, but they never paid enough—with bums on seats—to keep the company playing for more than a couple of seasons, and even then, only half of any one year.[38] Moreover, the boys would never shut up. Sooner or later their poets had them say something too risqué or politically out of turn, or they libelled somebody, and the company was shut down or disbanded—only to pop up again, like rogues in a Jonson comedy, with a new manager and name, as happened with the patent in February 1604.

The Blackfriars had never seen anything like Daniel's *Philotas*. Many lines ended in a rhyme (couplets, cross rhymes, stanzas, and whole sections in rhyme), and there was a formal neo-classical Chorus of four interlocutors—three Greek soldiers and a Persian captive—together with a Nuntius or Messenger who communicated with them. Some of the audience who had seen college academic plays may have been familiar with these conventions, but many people watching were probably baffled. As Daniel intended, the play was unlike anything being acted on the London stage. However, the report that came out of the Blackfriars was not about Daniel's neoclassicism or subtle use of sententiae, or his success (or failure) in recreating an ancient Chorus; but was instead a narrowly political comment. The person who told on him to the Privy Council said there were conspicuous parallels between Philotas the conspirator and the late Lord Essex the "conspirator."

The part that the "reporter," or informer, played in denouncing Daniel has not been examined before, though it is of importance. The informer was the chief witness for the investigation or (as it might have become) prosecution of Daniel, since it is unlikely that members of the Privy Council themselves ever saw the play. Who was he, this "reporter" at the performance? Was he a Concerned Citizen or an Alarmed Advocate? Did he have any motive other than telling the truth?

Daniel explains himself to Cecil

The informer's allegation triggered a series of communications, two of which we still have: Daniel's 1605 letters, written in quick succession, first to Cecil (as Cranborne), then to Mountjoy (as Devonshire). The informer contacted the Privy Council, or perhaps Cecil himself, by letter or word of mouth, and this prompted a message of some kind to Daniel, most likely from the Privy Council. We can infer this from the letter to Cecil, framed as a reply—there is a complaint about this, my Lord, and I respond to what you have heard—as well as an upfront acknowledgment of fault and error followed by a defense (motive, context, a plea of innocence and a wish to clear his name). Daniel does not

refer to the Earl of Essex explicitly, but he knows he must explain why he
chose this particular subject for a tragedy:

> my necessitie I confess hath driuen mee to doo a thing vnworthy of mee, and much
> against my harte, in making the stage the speaker of my lynes, which never here-
> tofore had any other theater then the vniuersall dominions of England

> [in] this tragedie of Philotas . . . I sought to reduce the stage from idlenes to those
> grave presentments of antiquitie vsed by the wisest nations

> [I took] no other forme in personating the Actors that performd it, then the very
> Idea of those tymes, as they appeared vnto mee both by the cast of the storie and
> the vniuersall notions of the affayres of men, which in all ages beare the same
> resemblances, and are measured by one and the same foote of vnderstanding

> my lord let no misapplying wronge my innocent writing, which in respect of myne
> owne reputation, vndertaking such a subiect, I must not make frivolous, or vnlike
> my stile, vnderstanding the world & the probable course of those tymes.

In the final portion of the letter, Daniel asks Cecil and "my Lord of Northampton" (Henry Howard, Earl of Northampton) that he be allowed to withdraw
the book and himself, to avoid any scandal over the "misapplying" or mis-
conception of his play. All this has the appearance of Daniel's writing to
Cecil because he has been told to, perhaps in a letter from the Privy Council
as a whole (Cecil and Northampton were its most powerful members, alongside Mountjoy). Did the letter come as a request to Daniel to attend the Privy
Council to answer for his choice of Philotas in general terms? It is well
known that the Privy Council Registers for this period (1602 to 1613) were
destroyed in a fire at Whitehall, but abstracts of some of the contents have
survived, made by one of the Council clerks. There is no mention of Daniel
in any of the abstracts, but we can see what Privy Council messages were
like from examples around this time. One abstract, listed under 21 July 1606,
relating to a courtier called William Windsor, illustrates the type of letter
that might have been sent to Daniel:

> A letter to Sir William Windsor to apeare before the Lordes, to answere to some
> matters concerning his majesties service appertaininge to himself &c.[39]

A summons sent to Daniel from the Privy Council ("the Lordes") would
probably have included or been accompanied by an interrogatory list of questions, of the sort used in cases from the most serious to the relatively trivial.
In the letter Daniel wrote to Mountjoy, he says that particular questions were
put to him in his interview (what the questions were, is considered below).

Daniel, perhaps in response to a written question about the dissemination of the play, confirmed to Cecil that a text had already been printed. Daniel insisted he was innocent of any wrongful intention in the play, but he agreed, if it

> shall seeme sknendulous [*sic*] to any by misconceiuing it, and y*our* ho*nour* [i.e., Cecil] be so pleased I will finde the meanes to let it fall of it self, by *with*drawing the booke & mee to my pore home, pretending some other occasion, so *that* the suppressing it by autoritie might not make the world to ymagin, other matters in it then there is.

At this date the word "booke" could be used of a manuscript, so it is not impossible Daniel meant the theater manuscript (or copies of it) used at the Blackfriars: he would quietly slip out of London, making some excuse, taking this manuscript "booke" with him. Much more likely he had in mind the copies of the octavo edition already typeset and printed by the printer George Eld. As noted above, the play was entered in the Stationers' Register on 29 November 1604, the point at which printing probably began. In this interpretation, the "booke" Daniel refers to is Eld's printed text of *Philotas*, already stored in a warehouse by (say) February 1605, waiting to be bound in as part of the collection of Daniel, *Certaine Small Poems with the Tragedy of Philotas* (STC 6239). If Cecil wished it, Daniel assured him, all physical trace of *Philotas* could disappear, so there would be no need for the Privy Council to ban the play from being read.

There is something more in Daniel's talk of scandal and misinterpretation. The word "scandalous" meant what was offensive, disgraceful, or infamous, but also what in speech and writing was a libel or defamatory; "misconceiuing" meant mistaking someone's meaning or intention, or entertaining wrong ideas. On the surface Daniel says "if the play appears offensive to anyone because they have misread it," but equally he could mean "if anyone (deliberately) misconstrues the play as defaming you (my Lord Cranborne)"—that is, Daniel might suspect, or been told, this is what was alleged he had done in *Philotas*, insulted and libeled Cecil via the character Craterus. Perhaps this is what the informer accused him of, in addition to charges about the Philotas Essex parallels. The curious, uncorrected slip in "sknendulous, a momentary loss of attention and mix up of minims, hints he may have had *scandalum magnatum* in mind, though he does not say it explicitly—after all, as we saw, this is what Raleigh in the *History* thought Daniel was aiming at, a libel on Cecil. This possibility takes us back to the earlier sentence, "good my lord let no misapplying wronge my innocent writing," which sounds more urgent and insistent if we think Daniel had realized someone had been *deliberately* misapplying the play so as to discredit him.

Daniel should have known better as regards *scandalum magnatum*. The
Jacobean lawyer who defined the term, Dr John Cowell, was a friend of
Daniel's whom he met regularly in London along with Camden: their meetings
may have been famous.[40] Whatever Daniel wrote about a favorite in the ancient
past—a favorite whose trial and fate had been manipulated by Alexander's
chief minister—he must (we think) have known he was running a risk. Perhaps, because he was a bit donnish and too trusting, Daniel misjudged the
support his sponsors would give him (Mountjoy especially) and underestimated
how an enemy might pounce on his mistakes.

An interview or two

Daniel closed his letter to Cecil defeated. In the final paragraph he referred
to another key player on the Privy Council alongside Cecil. This was the
nobleman we encountered before in relation to the Philotas story, Lord Henry
Howard, by this date Earl of Northampton. Daniel petitioned them jointly

> (seeing the tyme will yeald me no grace nor comfort & *that* my studies, my faculties
> are vnnecessarie complements of the ~~tyme~~ season) to bestow some small viaticu*m*
> to carry me from the world where I may bury my self, & my writings out of the
> way of envie

We will come to see that the use of "envie" here is freighted with an extra
layer of meaning; more broadly, the letter also begs the question of how many
messages Daniel received. Did Cecil with his ally Northampton write to the
poet telling him he was about to be summoned formally by the Privy Council?
They would both be present at his interview, but he might wish to advise
them what he had to say about his play, and what he had meant by it. Why
had he written and staged it in public? Was there anything dangerous in it,
or harmful to the kingdom or to the reputation of anyone? Daniel had important noble friends at court (Lord Mountjoy, for instance): had they known
about his play before it was acted? Was it wise for him, a gentleman and
scholar, to be so connected by money to tradesmen, actors, and the underclass
from the common stage?

If it were put like this, their preliminary message could be full of insinua-
tions and traps (Daniel fell into one trap when he mentioned his patron Mountjoy in the Privy Council interview). The poet thought the only thing left to
him was get out of London. He had no supporters ("no grace nor comfort"),
and no one cared for his writing. He wanted to disentangle himself from the
whole business, but he had no means, not even for travel. Might he beg money
("some small viaticu*m*") to get back to his "pore home" in Somerset?

Daniel said he wanted to get 'out of the way of envie'. It is possible he simply meant his poetry had become odious and unpopular (see "envy," *OED sb*. 1c; Latin "Invidia"), but more likely that others felt extreme hostility and ill will towards him. They had misapplied his play and misconceived the meaning, because of envy or rivalry. Perhaps Daniel had no one in mind in particular, but it is worth noting, as a point to come back to, that the figure of Envy (with the alternative Latin name "Livor") had actually appeared on the public stage, spectacularly, only a year or so earlier in a Blackfriars play performed by the boys who acted *Philotas* in 1605—that is, in the same venue, with the same actors and much the same audience (lawyers, professionals, functionaries). The play was *Poetaster or the Arraignment* and its author was Ben Jonson. In *Poetaster*, Envy-Livor is a threat before the play proper begins, which Jonson protects himself against with an armed Prologue. But did Daniel come to think that in his case, in respect of *Philotas*, it was Jonson himself who was the true figure of danger and envy?

Daniel reported the interview with the Privy Council in his letter to Mountjoy. Like the one to Cecil, this second letter is undated, but Daniel wrote it, he said, after he had "fully satisfyde my L*ord* of Cranborne '[i.e. Cecil]' in 'this matter of Philotas.'" This last detail allows us to piece together a plausible timeline:

The informer tells Cecil and the Privy Council about *Philotas* at the Blackfriars Cecil and Northampton invite Daniel to respond prior to the Privy Council Daniel writes to Cecil and Northampton (as described above) The Privy Council, including Cecil and Northampton, interview Daniel Cecil is "satisfyde" by the Privy Council interview, or when he sees Daniel alone Mountjoy learns of Daniel's responses to the Privy Council and is furious Daniel writes to Mountjoy defending what he said in the interview Daniel writes the *Apology* and calls Craterus "one of the most honest men"

At this date the Privy Council comprised 20 and more noblemen and officers of state. Not everyone attended the meetings, though at this date Cecil and Northampton were usually there. Mountjoy was evidently not present—perhaps he stayed away because his poet and client was to be interrogated—but Daniel's answers, some of them probably to a written list of questions, put the Earl in a difficult situation. "I tolde the Lordes," Daniel admitted to Mountjoy, "I had written"

3 Acts of this tragedie the Christmas before my L. of Essex troubles
I saide the maister of the Revells [Edmund Tilney] had pe*rv*sed it
I said I had read some parte of it to y*our* hon*our* [i.e., to Mountjoy]
I did not say yo*w* incouraged me vnto the p*r*esenting of it

This was highly damaging to Mountjoy. Daniel revealed he had read some of the play to him—he did not say which parts—so the Privy Council wanted to know if his lordship had urged him to stage it in public, with its critical portrayal of Craterus (Cecil) and the recognizable parallels with Essex as a favorite and in his state trial for treason. If it were shown that one peer (Mountjoy) had defamed another (Cecil) it was, in theory, a matter for Star Chamber (*scandalum magnatum*). However, it is hard to believe Cecil really believed Mountjoy was trying to get at him through the play; at this point, they were concluding the Anglo-Spanish peace and they each had too much to lose in a squabble, including fat Spanish pensions. But putting Daniel on the spot was a useful way to remind Mountjoy of his vulnerabilities—he had nearly been caught up in Essex's rebellion plot and had survived only because of Cecil's support and because his army won in Ireland. Moreover, Daniel himself might be useful in a small way.

Cecil manages Daniel

Daniel probably never regained Mountjoy's full trust after the Privy Council interview. At the end of 1605 the nobleman was overwhelmed by a real scandal of his own making—his marriage to Penelope Rich—and he died suddenly only a few months later. The loss of Mountjoy's favor was a personal catastrophe for Daniel but, revealingly, other than that he seems not to have suffered on account of *Philotas*. He had feared Cecil might have the "booke" of the play suppressed, banned, or burnt, but instead it was published six or seven months later in 1605, dedicated to the heir apparent, Prince Henry. The plans went ahead that had been made for Daniel to be a key player at the visit of the royal family to Oxford in late August. It was his play, *Arcadia Reformed*, that was acted at Christ Church before the Queen and Prince; it was his book of poetry that was accepted into the Bodleian when the King visited the Library; it was Daniel whom the dons at Christ Church asked to join them whenever he wished, because of his great service to the College and the University as a whole (the details are below).

We can make an informed guess about how Cecil managed things. None of it is certain but it is consistent with later events. Cecil may have seen Daniel alone, following the Privy Council interview. Perhaps he told Daniel he had never thought he intended anything scandalous, certainly not about him personally. Then Cecil talked about money. Daniel must give up this wretched company of players: it had been a mistake from the beginning. He should sell his rights in the agreement—this would bring him money—and in due course a route to a respectable office in the Queen's court would be available. Daniel did sell his rights to John Gerard on 28 April 1605; and subsequently he was made a Groom of the Queen's Chamber, with a salary of £60 per annum.[41]

Then there was the question of what Daniel should do next. The discerning men and women at court—the Queen, Mountjoy, Lady Bedford—praised Daniel's poetry, but also his ability as an historian. He was a master of prose, and his zeal for England and its kings was unrivalled. It was his, Cecil's, hope that soon there would be a history of the nation, of the kind that Lord Keeper Egerton (another sponsor of Daniel's) and Sir Francis Bacon wished for.[42] Now His Majesty had founded the kingdom of "Great Britain," it was time to write the history of England through its monarchs, from the Conquest to the death of Queen Elizabeth. The history would need tact as well as insight. Might he, Daniel, undertake this? He evidently did. Back home in Somerset, Daniel began his account of Conquest England. The surviving manuscripts show the history was to have been dedicated to Cecil, who died only weeks before it was published in 1612.[43]

Why would Cecil overlook dangerous stuff in *Philotas* (especially parallels with Craterus), which so unsettled Mountjoy and which was obvious to Raleigh? There may have been a number of reasons. Not allowing Daniel's play to be published or suppressing it might draw more attention to the Black-friars performance. Cecil could imagine what the audience of benchers and lawyers would make of parts of the play in which Craterus (Cecil) sucked up to Alexander (King James)—but if so, so what? Clever types would soon lose interest in this particular slander and be on to the next (as they were, in *East-ward Ho*, performed by the boy actors the following August: see below). It was true Daniel was only small fry, but he was the Queen's small fry, and Cecil would want to keep her Majesty on side. Cecil was in charge of her court, and she was one key to the future, in her son Prince Henry. Best to encourage the Queen in her cultural projects with the other women courtiers who admired Daniel's writing and character.[44] As regards the future, in time Daniel might turn out to be Mountjoy's weak spot, so why not keep the poet in play for now? The possibility of a history of England was a bonus. Cecil could be Daniel's barely visible patron, in control of state papers and documents that needed to be read, particularly if and when Daniel's history approached the reign of the late Queen. (Cecil famously refused Fulke Greville access to Elizabeth's state papers, but he could be sure Greville's client Daniel would be easier to manage.)

There was a further reason why Cecil might downplay the supposed scandal in the play. How much trust could he place in the informer who had made the allegation(s)?[45] No doubt Cecil was familiar with the Philotas story in Curtius (as Henry Howard and others were), but the informer might stress that Daniel had emphasized anew how Craterus, Alexander's chief minister, was self-serving, cruel, and ruthless—to the extent that he had a woman brought to torture, something not dwelt on in the sources. The application of the story to the Essex revolt and trial was clear, according to the informer, but Daniel's play also showed the lower orders, in a Chorus, presuming to be critical of their masters in a manner that was certainly not "mannerly." The ancient historians had reported nothing of this. Such additions were scandalous in themselves, the informer might urge.

This is the point at which the identity of Cecil's snitch becomes significant. It is arguable that the identity of the informer was just as important as Daniel's initial "intention" when he wrote and presented *Philotas*. Whatever Daniel intended, the informer shaped the meaning—we might say manipulated or framed it—from what he saw acted at the Blackfriars.

The informer

It may seem impossible to know who told on Daniel so long after the event. The audience at the Blackfriars *Philotas* may have numbered 600 (most of them men, many under thirty). One might disaggregate the 600 into groups of Blackfriars regulars—the audience of students, lawyers, toffs, and citizens in one group, and the people who entertained them—actors, writers, crew, in the other. But even viewed like this the informer remains hidden. Given what audiences paid for pricey seats at the Blackfriars, though, he was either of some means (a bencher, perhaps a gentleman) or he knew the players, or was perhaps one of them. It is not entirely impossible he was upper class or gentry, with a head full of plays, or a fashionista who loved being looked at, and paid for a stool on the stage while plays were acted. But gentry, well-off, and professional types knew the Blackfriars' reputation and they went there in order to be "scandalized"—titillated by a bit of clever scandal—not to find reasons to complain to the authorities.

The informer becomes more visible if we ask why he was at the performance. Was it his routine job to go to the public theaters and report on what was disruptive, irreligious, or anti-establishment—a surveillance man? This might mean he had contacts among government people who paid him to scan for allusions, open or veiled, to topical events and people—the incarceration of Raleigh in The Tower, or the King's policy on tolerating Catholics and promoting Scottish courtiers, or the story of how Essex, the late Queen's favorite, had been done down by his enemies, who had become members of the King's council. This would make the informer an undercover agent— Shakespeare's phrase for such men was "speculations intelligent"—in this case reporting to the Privy Council what the stage world was daring to say about the upper crust.

Perhaps he never reported systematically, and never got a penny for his information. He did it because he was indebted to a protector, or because of "duty" to his nation and the king. However, we can now make more guesses about him. He was most likely non-elite, a servant not a master, but he was known at the Blackfriars, perhaps to the actors, and he could communicate with great men. He may have had contact with Cecil already or was known to the Privy Council as an informer. This narrows down the 600 quite a lot and lets us to look for him from different angles.

In US criminal law, and in modern crime fiction, one method of investigation is to ask three things of a crime and a suspect. Did he or she have the means, motive, and opportunity? We have already referred to one suspect, a rival and an enemy of Daniel's, whose profile fits that of the unknown informer to a remarkable extent. This suspect is of course Ben Jonson, a younger man than Daniel by ten years, and someone who had to work even harder than Daniel to find a niche in the social world of Elizabethan England. The way he did this—by making himself a hybrid of autodidact scholar, dramatist, theater critic and social celebrity—tells us about the "means" by which he could have made allegations about the performance of *Philotas*.

Jonson did not so much inhabit the world of the theater as make it a place for his ambitions and self-realization. He spread himself wherever he could, in writing for and being seen in every theatre there was, roofless amphitheater stage, private theater auditorium or open-court space. He knew everyone in the theater and made sure everyone knew him. In the satirical comedy of 1601, *Poetaster*, he identified himself with the central character of the play— he was the Horace of the Elizabethan age, whom (he said) the hack writers, Dekker and Marston, had disparaged out of envy. Jonson conducted his side of the contest with them in the Blackfriars, with the Children of the Chapel as the actors. He enjoyed writing for the Children, but it was for the adult actors (the Chamberlain's, later King's Men, Shakespeare's company) that he wrote his most ambitious early plays, *Every Man in his Humour* in 1598 and *Sejanus* in 1603–5. These were his attempts to write comedy and tragedy according to the principles and examples of the ancients, unadulterated by the clumsy accretions and indecorum of the Elizabethan stage (Shakespeare was guilty of this, Jonson thought). In all, it is hard to think of anyone more caught up than Jonson in the writing and acting of stage plays and in the world of contemporary theater.

There was no limit to Jonson's ambitions, in terms of the dramatic forms he was sure he would excel in, and the high social circles he felt he should be invited to join. This was clear in another of his satirical comedies acted in 1600 by the Children, *Cynthia's Revels*. In the latter part of this he introduced a masque-like section that trailed, not very subtly, the masques he planned for the court (as the future "revels"), if only Lady "Arete," Queen Cynthia's most brilliant attendant, would support him. This was Jonson's bid for the patronage of a real-life noblewoman at Queen Elizabeth's court, Lucy, Countess of Bedford (1581–1627), a rising *grande dame* of poetry and the arts. The attempt to move between the common theater and the intellectual salon did not come off fully for Jonson, who blamed his lack of success on the favor Lady Bedford bestowed on Daniel. "LVCY the bright," Jonson called the Countess, whom he would continue to praise, even "though shee haue"

> a better verser got,
> (Or *Poet*, in the court account) then I,
> And, who doth me (though I not him) enuy.[46]

Jonson did not need to name Daniel. He said the same things for the next 20 years, even when Daniel was on his deathbed (in 1619 he said the "verser" Daniel was "at jealousies" with him, that he was "honest" but "no Poet" and so forth). We saw earlier how Jonson's pent-up resentment and enmity showed themselves at Daniel's masque in January 1604. A year later Jonson got what he wanted, and he, not Daniel, was feted as the deviser of the annual entertainment for the Queen, with his *Masque of Blackness*. The recognition was evidently not enough for Jonson. On 2 February 1605, the King's Men (Shakespeare's Company) performed at court a revised version of *Every Man in his Humour*—in which Jonson changed to a jeer his original (faintly) friendly remark about Daniel's sonnets *To Delia*.[47]

Something else must have infuriated Jonson, namely the patent that made Daniel a licenser of the Children's plays and brought him the £10 annuity. The dramatist Dekker claimed that Jonson, among his other pretensions, wanted to be Master of the Revels.[48] How was it, Jonson might ask, that Daniel, who was openly dismissive about the public stage and knew nothing about it, had been given this new office, consanguine with the Revels job? Why should Daniel oversee the boy players, when it was he, Jonson, who wrote comedies for them and nurtured them? When he heard the boys were to act in an ancient tragedy by Daniel at the Blackfriars—they would tell Jonson this as they had told him about Daniel's Hampton Court masque—the news must have piqued his interest. Daniel's tragedy, he learnt, had a formal chorus, and much of it was written in cross rhymes and long passages of joined-up stanzas, elements Jonson had already decided were unsuitable in any higher genre of English poetry.

All this makes it difficult to believe Jonson was not at the Blackfriars to see *Philotas*. He hated Daniel for (as he saw it) Daniel's undeserved advancement and reputation among the upper class. Moreover, this was the first time Daniel had ventured into his (Jonson's) territory, the popular theater, and he was writing in a form, neoclassical tragedy, that Jonson wanted to show he was the master of in *Sejanus*. Why would Jonson *not* be at the performance, if only to see Daniel the "*Poet*" fail?

We would have to pause at this point—acknowledging that Jonson's being at the performance was only possible—were it not for another piece of evidence. We saw earlier, in the letter to Cecil, how Daniel, to avoid an impending scandal, offered to withdraw himself and the "booke" of *Philotas* to his "pore home,"

> pretending some other occasion, so *that* the suppressing it by autoritie might not make the world to ymagin, other matters in it then there is.

By "suppressing it by autoritie," Daniel had in mind the kind of public order the Privy Council might make to impound and destroy printed copies of the play not yet on sale. The alternative, that he meant the manuscript(s) used at the Blackfriars, is not really credible. To begin with, the idea of withdrawing a book applies more obviously to printed books then to a theater manuscript. Moreover, the Council's banning of a private manuscript would undoubtedly "make the world to ymagin, other matters in it then there is." It would encourage whoever missed the performance of a suppressed play to seek out surreptitious manuscripts. By "withdrawing" the book Daniel meant arranging for the printed copies to be pulped.

But the copies of *Philotas* were not destroyed. Rather, they were attached, in line with the original plan for the book, as the final section of Daniel's 1605 collected edition, printed in the same octavo format, entitled *Certaine Small Poems lately printed: with the Tragedie of Philotas.* Daniel's publisher, the bookseller Simon Waterson, owned the shorter ('*Small*') poems in this edition, but he published *Philotas* jointly with another bookseller, Edward Blount. There is evidence that the composite edition, *Small Poems* with *Philotas*, did not go on sale until autumn 1605, in September or even later.[49] However, according to what Daniel wrote to Cecil, the *Philotas* part had been printed, some months earlier, perhaps by the time of the performance in March or April. Since the stationer Eld printed both parts of the book, it is fair to suppose that the copies of *Philotas* were stored during 1605, while the remainder of the book was being finished.

The *Philotas* copies were adjusted in one respect, however, as the preliminaries on signature A were printed on a different stock of paper. Blank leaves A1 and A2, the title- page of *Philotas* (A3r), the dedication to Prince Henry (A4r-A5v) the Argument (A6r-A7v) and the Names of the Actors (A8r) (i.e. a list of characters)—these were all printed on a single sheet on paper different from the remainder of the play. It was usual for prelims to be printed last, but the very different paper in sig A suggests it was not only printed after sigs B-E, but somewhat later. In the lines to Prince Henry, Daniel alluded obliquely to the Blackfriars performance, so the verse dedication was almost certainly added after the text of the play had been printed—hence the need to replace sig. A.

In the letter to Cecil, Daniel offered to make the printed text of *Philotas* disappear. He appears to respond to two questions: was this play acted and is it already in print? This will make us ask how Cecil could know about the book as well as the performance. The answer of course is that the informer supplied the information on both counts. Not only did he see *Philotas* at the Blackfriars, he knew that George Eld had printed the book, which was intended for sale in the Blount and Waterson bookshops. Given what is argued above, it will come as no surprise to learn that in late summer 1605 Eld printed Jonson's tragedy, *Sejanus*, a deluxe quarto edition, on high quality paper. The bookseller Blount at first owned the copyright of *Sejanus*, but he sold it to Thomas Thorpe in August 1605, just before Eld began printing. The Thorpe-Blount-Eld edition had Jonson's annotations in the margins, citing ancient authorities. *Sejanus* was Jonson's first venture into presenting his plays as modern book classics. He knew the micro-society of the London book trade the way he did the theater—what was new or coming, what the competition was, and what was inflammatory. Once again it is impossible to believe Jonson was unaware of things so pertinent to him, that a rival's neoclassical tragedy, the Blount-Eld *Philotas*, had been printed and published by the same people at the same time as the *Sejanus* edition. Who else but Jonson would be as informed about the performance as well as the book—and so ready to use the information against Daniel?

Jonson knew the book trade and the public theater, and he also knew the underworld of surveillance and spying.[50] In 1597, he wrote a seditious or at least slanderous play with Thomas Nashe, and he was informed on—probably by the serial liar, William Udall, who made his living by snitching on suspects and making up stories to incriminate them. The accusations against Jonson led to a spell in jail but he was soon released, in part because Robert Cecil, in charge of the investigation, did not trust Udall.[51] Jonson's conversion to the Catholic faith around this time complicated things. Agents posing as Catholics, one of them possibly the notorious double agent Robert Poley, were put into prison with Jonson, to get him to implicate himself out of his own mouth. Jonson made a great deal of this episode in later life—how tight-lipped he had been and how he hated spies and undercover machinations—but his own experience of being informed against, and how to do it properly, would have been very useful if he decided to accuse an enemy of a state or personal slander.[52] Because Jonson was himself denounced and lied about does not prove he told on Daniel, but it does not exonerate him either.

Jonson's subsequent dealings with Robert Cecil were ambiguous to say the least. Cecil commissioned Jonson to write various celebration pieces, but he very likely put him to other uses as well—suborning him to spy on or inform against his Catholic co-religionists, for instance, in the crucial days before the Gunpowder Plot in November 1605.[53] Modern suspicions that Jonson turned his writing against Cecil have reached a new level recently, with the claim that the keenest satirical target in *Volpone* (written early 1606) was Cecil, whom Jonson showed up in all his duplicity and avarice.[54] Just before this, in September 1605, Cecil helped Jonson get out of jail again when he was imprisoned over the scandal of *Eastward Ho*, an event related (it is argued below) to the successes Daniel enjoyed once he too had been helped (in his case, endorsed) by Cecil.

In all of this, one thing is certain: Jonson had a tested line of communication with Cecil, which would have allowed him to articulate a case (or invent one) against Daniel. Jonson's motive was clear: envy and enmity; his means were the people of the theater and the world of books; and the "opportunity" presented itself because Daniel, forced by his "necessities," had crossed onto Jonson's home turf, where the inhabitants were shady, quarrelsome businessmen on the make—like those in Jonson's city comedies. Whatever you did there, someone would lie about it or try to cheat you.

In Arcadia

It is not possible to prove Jonson was the informer, or that he tried to finish off Daniel. All the same, Jonson's biography in the half year following the Blackfriars *Philotas* becomes more intelligible if we factor in a measure of frustration, to the point of his making a mistake, at the incredible string of successes Daniel had in 1605.

The key event of summer 1605 was the visit of the royal family to Oxford. Planning and budgeting for the event began early in the year. Christ Church built a neoclassical theater in its hall, in part to a design by Inigo Jones, for a succession of plays in Latin by different dons to be performed before the king. There was only one play in English, intended for the Queen and Prince in the same venue, and that was the tragicomedy, *Arcadia Reformed*, by Daniel, who was an Oxford alumnus. While this was being acted, the King visited the newly opened Bodleian Library, probably at the time Daniel presented to the Library a special copy of his magnum opus, his *Works* of 1601. These were all firsts of one kind or another. Daniel's tragicomedy was the first English play modelled on the Italian masters, Tasso and Guarini. Daniel was the first living English poet to give the title *The Works* to a collection of his poetry. Daniel's *Works* was the first book of contemporary English poetry accepted into the Bodleian.[55]

Arcadia Reformed was a major success. When it was published in 1606 the book was dedicated to the Queen with a new title, *The Queen's Arcadia*—a mark of her approval and advancement (Daniel was made a Groom of the Queen's Privy Chamber in 1607). Contemporaries—not merely the nobility and university and city dignitaries—evidently thought highly of the play. In *The Tempest*, for instance, Shakespeare drew on (and perhaps silently acknowledged) Daniel's borrowings and inspiration from Montaigne.[56] The dons at Christ Church, where the play was acted, were grateful too. They invited Daniel into their number, as far as they could any outsider, in the first instance paying personally for his entertainment in college, "in consideration of certain good and liberal service done" by Daniel, "the excellence of which we cannot forget was of great use and honour not only to our [Christ] Church but to all the great Academy."[57]

These rewards and opportunities (the tragicomedy, the Bodleian presentation) were planned months ahead. In any interview Cecil had with Daniel in (say) April, all that was needed was for Cecil to confirm the Oxford arrangements, because the Privy Council (in reality, Cecil) had concluded that the suspicions about *Philotas* were ill founded. There was no dark talk about Daniel at court and no sign of scandal; it appears that only Mountjoy was put out by what Daniel had said. Perhaps the Blackfriars informer was disappointed, though, at the lack of reaction to his report of sedition and slander in *Philotas*. If the informer was in fact Jonson, he might well have felt chagrin as well—chagrin at not being invited by anyone to any of the Oxford big occasions, the Latin plays, the entertainments, the academic speeches and receptions. Jonson's notable absence from these, given how assiduous he was at self-promotion, is telling. Evidently, the cognoscenti as well as the professors could happily do without him, while they happily applauded Daniel's play at Christ Church.

When the royal family visited Oxford in August 1605, the whole court, with the whole upper echelon of London society, decamped with them. Lower level city professionals remained (lawyers, merchants) who wanted entertainment, the category of regulars at the Blackfriars. This was the moment that Jonson, together with Chapman and Marston, supplied the satirical comedy *Eastward Ho* for an unlicensed Blackfriars performance by the Children of the Queen's Revels. *Eastward Ho* contained satire on the King's selling of knighthoods, and his favoritism towards Scottish courtiers, and Jonson and Chapman ended up in jail because of it. Jonson petitioned Cecil and Lady Bedford, and he and Chapman were released after six weeks without the severe physical punishment they expected. The play was banned but a censored, revised text appeared in September 1605—printed by the ubiquitous George Eld, who had begun printing *Sejanus*.

The satire in *Eastward Ho* was reckless and overconfident. The Children risked a performance without a license from Tilney, which Jonson and the others evidently hoped they could get away with. Perhaps Jonson looked at Daniel's recent history and thought, "the acting of a seditious play, *Philotas*, has done him no harm." More likely, he could not bottle up his frustration and envy at Daniel's successes in Oxford. He was happy to respond in kind with a sharper, rival city play, acted by the Children with whom Daniel had severed connections.

Perhaps there were feelings of envy in respect of *Sejanus* as well. Blount had registered the tragedy as his in November 1604, but he had been slow to get it into print. Did Jonson badger Blount?—either publish it or sell it to another publisher. Thomas Thorpe bought the play from Blount in August, and printing began in September, presumably when Jonson was let out of jail. Did he want an immediate success of his own—a special learned book, informed by the Ancients, printed on special paper—to reply to Daniel? The Thorpe *Sejanus* was a step upward, but Jonson had to admit in the Preface that his play lacked one thing the Ancients required, a Chorus. This, he said, was because the manner and verse forms of a Chorus were so difficult

> as not any, whome I haue seene, since the *Auncients*, (no not they who haue most presently affected Lawes) haue yet come in the way off.

By the phrase "they who haue most presently affected Lawes," Jonson meant "modern writers who have most recently attempted or theorized about a Chorus." Some of this was almost certainly directed at Daniel, who had written a sophisticated Chorus for his closet drama *The Tragedy of Cleopatra* and had discussed the verse forms suitable for tragedy and for a Chorus.[58] Jonson's chief objection, however, was that a formal Chorus could never find favor with audiences in the public theaters:

> Nor is it needful, or almost possible, in these our Times, and to such Auditors, as commonly Things are presented, to obserue the ould state, and splendour of *Drammatick Poemes*, with preseruation of any popular delight.

In this context, it is worth emphasizing that at this time the *only* play on the English public stage in which there was a neoclassical Chorus was *Philotas*. Perhaps this does indirectly confirm that Jonson saw Daniel's play performed at the Blackfriars in 1605.

No scandal

Much of this essay has been concerned with things that did not happen. *Philotas* was *not* acted at court, and Daniel was *not* paid from the exchequer for presenting it there. The patent of February 1604 stipulated that the Children could only perform plays with the "approbation and allowaunce" of Daniel, but it did *not* say that the Company would pay him to read and examine the plays (Daniel's rebuttal of this was successful in a lawsuit in Chancery). The role of "licenser" required Daniel's signature, nothing more, and he only held the office for 12 months. Daniel did not, as modern academics think, act as a censor and allow a stream of seditious plays on the stage, whether by design or incompetence. Daniel was desperately short of money throughout this period, and there is no reason to doubt that this is why he reluctantly sold his play for presentation by the Children at their Blackfriars venue.

There are some things that did happen, however, which have not merited discussion before now. Someone saw the play at the Blackfriars and reported that there was scandalous stuff in it. The informer communicated this to Robert Cecil and the Privy Council, who in turn formally requested that Daniel answer the charges in person, probably with a list of questions that would be put to him. It was alleged Daniel contrived parallels between the plot, trial, and execution of Philotas and comparable events leading up to the execution of Robert, Earl of Essex. The Blackfriars spy may have made even more damning accusations, that Robert Cecil was defamed in the play—this is certainly what his enemy Walter Raleigh thought. Prior to the Privy Council interview, Daniel wrote a letter of apology and defense to Cecil and Northampton. Evidently, he suspected he was the victim of deliberate "mis-applying" and "misconceiuing," something he was more certain of in *The Apology*. "I could not imagine that Enuy or ignorance," he said, "could possibly have made the story of Philotas, "to take any particular acquaintance with vs." This was disingenuous—Elizabethans often drew parallels between ancient histories and their own—but Daniel was right to see "Enuy" in the allegations he was facing.

Daniel's choice of "Enuy" suggests he may have suspected his accuser was Ben Jonson. This was Jonson's go-to word when he referred to his rivals. They were all envious or jealous of him, he said, indeed their envy was so palpable that the embodiment of Envy itself menaced him in public on stage (see the epigraph to this essay). At different times he said Daniel envied him and was "at jealousies" with him. Daniel saw, as critics have for centuries, that Jonson thrived on castigating and belittling opponents, channelling his own jealousy and attributing it to them.[59] Evidence looked at earlier shows that Jonson envied Daniel on many counts—his connections among statesmen and scholars and at Oxford, and his reputation with the Queen and her ladies. Recent findings suggest that money too might have been a factor. Jonson had a financial stake in the Children of the Queens Revels at the time Daniel was paid a fee as their "licenser," which Jonson probably thought, as the managers did, was unearned.[60]

This essay has argued it was Jonson who made the allegations against Daniel. No one else is put forward as the informer, if only because, so far as we know, Daniel had no other real enemies, except possibly one or two people connected to Jonson (Sir John Roe, for instance). It remains to be seen if the case against Jonson convinces, but there can be no doubt he had the means, motive and, through his connections with the theater and book trade, the opportunity and inside knowledge to inform on Daniel. Whoever the informer was, though, what he said against Daniel and *Philotas* failed completely. There was no scandal and no repercussion in Daniel's standing at court. His book was not banned or censored; indeed, it was published with a dedication to the heir apparent. When one prominent contemporary, a lawyer and a recorder in London, annotated the play he noted no connections or parallels with the rebellion of Essex or covert attacks on Cecil.[61] Daniel's career as a writer was not tarnished (within a year he had published the first fully fledged tragicomedy in English, endorsed by the court), but rather amplified, as an historian. From this time on, with Cecil's patronage, Daniel proceeded to write in prose the first modern history of mediaeval England and its kings.

The essay also suggests that the public staging of *Philotas* was a blunder, a forced error, on Daniel's part, but not a political attack. The argument is that at Essex House in the mid-1590s Daniel had a reputation as someone who could think unpalatable political thoughts and think around a thorny problem. For example, in Daniel's poem *The Civil Wars*, Richard II was a legitimate king of England, but he was a spoiled despot. Bolingbroke might be right to replace him, in the interests of good government, but the usurpation would change not just the detail of who was king but the political order as a whole.[62] Informed historical reasoning like this, offered as counsel, pro and contra, was what in the 1590s Daniel brought to the table of peers and statesmen. Mountjoy and Greville were his sponsors, but also Essex himself—in *The Apology* Daniel said he had been "perticularly beholding" to the Earl's "bounty." Within the Essex circle, the history of Philotas, like that of Richard II, would offer different avenues of opinion and advice: should a favorite reveal his private thoughts, were Crown prosecutions just rigged show trials, were a prince's motives ever understandable, even to himself?

Daniel was telling the truth when he explained why he wrote *Philotas*. "First," he said, "the delight I tooke in the History it selfe as it lay, and then the aptnesse, I saw it had to fall easily into act, without interlacing other inuention then it properly yeelded in the[ir] owne circumstances, were sufficient for the worke,[63] and a lawfull representing of a Tragedy." Daniel drew from within the history of Philotas an ineluctable tragedy (i.e., a "lawfull" one, shaped by the laws of tragedy). As Aristotle had said (in the *Poetics*), history only told what happened, tragedy what might happen.[64] The counsellors at Essex House might advise Essex this way or that, but Daniel saw—another unpalatable thought—that the Earl's history, like that of Philotas, had within it an inexorable tragedy that must unfold itself. It was that insight that gave the play its resonance and political relevance.

Appendix

1. Daniel's undated autograph letter to Sir Robert Cecil (as Viscount Cranborne), written on the first page of a folded sheet of four pages: Hatfield House, Cecil Papers 191/123.

Addressed 'To the right honorable my worthy good *L*ord the Lord Vicont Craneborne'

Right honorable my good *L*ord
my necessitie I confess hath driuen mee to doo a thing vnworthy of mee, and much against my harte, in making the stage the speaker of my lynes, w*hich* never heretofore had any other theater then the vniuersall dominions of England, w*hich* so long as it shall keepe the tongue it hath, will keepe my name & travayles from perishing. And for this tragedie of Philotas, wherein I sought to reduce the stage from idlenes to those grave p*r*esentments of antiquitie vsed by the wisest nations, I *pro*test I have taken no other forme in personating the Acto*rs that per*formd it, then the very Idea of those tymes, as they appeared vnto mee both by the cast of the storie and the vniuersall notions of the affayres of men, w*hich* in all ages beare the same resemblances, and are measured by one and the same foote of vnderstanding. No tyme but brought forth the like concurrencies, the like interstriuing for place and dignitie, the like supplantations, rysings & overthrowes. so *that* there is nothing new vnder the Sunne, nothing in theas tymes *that* is not in bookes, nor in bookes that is not in theas tymes. And therefore good my lord let no misapplying wronge my innocent writing, w*hich* in respect of myne owne reputation, vndertaking such a subiect, I must not make frivolous, or vnlike my stile, vnderstanding the world & the probable course of those tymes. But yf it shall seeme sknendulous [*sic*] to any by misconceiuing it, and y*our* ho*nour* be so pleased I will finde the meanes to let it fall of it self, by wi*th*drawing the booke & mee to my pore home, p*r*etending some other occasion, so *that* the suppressing it by autoritie might not make the world to ymagin, other matters in it then there is. Onely I would beseach my Lord of Northampto*n* & y*our* ho*nour* (seeing the tyme will yeald me no grace nor comfort & *that* my studies, my faculties are vnnecessarie complements of the ~~tyme~~ season) to bestow some small viaticu*m* to carry me from the world where I may bury my self, & my writings out of the way of envie, & liue in some other kind, more agreeing to my harte & the nature of my studies. and where yf yo*w* will doo me good I will labo*r* to doo yo*w* all the hono*ur* & service I may.
and be most faithfully y*our* hono*urs* in all humilitie, Samuel Danyel.

2. Daniel's undated autograph letter to Charles Blount, 8th Baron Mountjoy (as 1st Earl of Devonshire), written on the first page of a folded sheet of four pages: TNA (PRO) SP 14/11, fos. 7 & 8.
Addressed 'Master Samuell Daniell to my Lord of Deuonshire'

My Lorde
Vnderstanding yo*ur* ho*nour* is displeased w*ith* mee, it hath more shaken my harte then I did thinke any fortune could have donne, in respect I have not

deservd it, nor donne or spoken any thing in this matter of Philotas vnworthy of yow or mee. And now having fully satisfyde my Lord of Cranborne I crave to vnburthen me of this imputation with your honour and it is the last sute I will ever make. And therfore I beseach yow to vnderstand all this great error I have committed.

first I tolde the Lordes I had written 3 Acts of this tragedie the Christmas before my Lord of Essex troubles, as diuers in the cittie could witnes. I saide the maister of the Revells had pervsed it. I said I had read some parte of it to your honour and this I said having none els of powre to grace mee now in Corte & hoping *that* yow out of your knowledg of bookes, & fauour of letters & mee might answere that there was nothing in it disagreeing nor any thing as I protest there is not, but out of the vniuersall notions of ambition and Envie the perptuall arguments of bookes & tragedies. I did not say yow incouraged me vnto the presenting of it yf I should I had bene a villayne for *that* when I shewd it to your honour I was not resolud to have had it acted, nor should it have bene had not my necessities overmaistred mee. And therefore I beseach yow let not now an Earle of Devonshire overthrow what a Lord Mountioy hath donne, who hath donne mee good and I have donne him honour. The world must, & shall know myne innocencie whilst I haue a pen to shew it. and for *that* I know I shall liue inter historiam temporis as well as greater men, I must not be such an abiect vnto my self as to neglect my repution [*sic*], and having bene knowne throughout all England for my virtue I will not leave a stayne of villanie vppon my name whatsoever error els might skape me vnfortunately thorow mine indiscreation, & misvnderstanding of the tyme. wherein good my Lord mistake not my harte that hath bene & is a syncere honorer of yow and seekes yow now for no other end but to cleare it self, and to be held as I ame (though I never more come nere yow) your honours pore follower & faithfull Servant, Samuel Danyel

Notes

1. The Elizabethans knew about Philotas from Plutarch, *Life of Alexander* and Quintus Curtius, *History of Alexander*, VI.6–7 (Curtius was translated from Latin into English by John Brende in 1553). Philotas, an elite Macedonian cavalry commander under Alexander the Great, was the son of Parmenio, the foremost general in Alexander's wars. After the conquest of Persia, Philotas was accused of conspiring against Alexander. He was tried and convicted (Craterus was one of the prosecutors), tortured to reveal the extent of the conspiracy, and then stoned to death by Alexander's soldiers. Parmenio was murdered on Alexander's orders. Commentators in the ancient world believed Philotas was innocent, and that Alexander fabricated the charges against him. In Daniel's tragedy the focus is on the alleged plot and the trial. A recent discussion of the play is Alzada Tipton, '"What hath been his mind?": Motivation, History, and Theater in Samuel Daniel's *Philotas*,' *Studies in Philology* 117 (2020): 40–75.

2. The most cogent essay along these lines remains Hugh Gazzard, ' "Those Graue Presentments of Antiquitie": Samuel Daniel's *Philotas* and the Earl of Essex,' *Review of English Studies* 51 (2000): 423–50.

3. John Pitcher, 'Samuel Daniel's Masque *The Vision of the Twelve Goddesses*: Texts and Payments,' *Medieval and Renaissance Drama in England* 26 (2013): 17–42.

4. Martin Butler discusses Jonson's interruption in *The Stuart Court Masque and Political Culture* (Cambridge: Cambridge University Press, 2008), 34–39.

5. Enrolled copy of letters patent, TNA (PRO) C 66/1614, m. 31; printed in E.K. Chambers and W.W. Greg, *Malone Society Collections*, I.3 (1909), 260–84 (267–68). A notice of the license for the Company is among the State Papers, endorsed on the reverse 'xxxj° die Ian: 1603' (i.e., 31 January 1604), TNA (PRO) SP 38/7/65.

6. Information about *Kirkham v. Daniel* is in the Bill of Complaint started in Chancery by Kirkham against Daniel on 4 May 1609, and the response to the Bill from Daniel. (See the documents in R. E. Brettle, 'Samuel Daniel and the Children of the Queen's Revels, 1604–5', *Review of English Studies* 3 (1927): 162–68. Financial details of the agreement are referred to in the exchanges.) One thing is certain from this lawsuit: the April 1604 agreement was concluded so far as Daniel was concerned one year later on 28 April 1605. This was when, for an unknown payment, he transferred his rights in the agreement to one John Gerard. Kirkham began the Bill of Complaint to prevent Gerard from suing him for the £100 bond (Gerard had not been paid the annuity for some while). Kirkham knew Daniel had sold his interest in 1605, but he used the poet as a stalking horse to obtain an injunction against Gerard. Daniel in his counterpetition explained that after 28 April 1605 he had nothing more to do with Kirkham and the bond, and, we must assume, the Children of the Queen's Revels. There is no recorded decision, so perhaps Kirkham's case collapsed.

7. Richard Dutton, *Mastering the Revels: The Regulation and Censorship of English Renaissance Drama* (Basingstoke: Macmillan, 1991), 167. Dutton amplifies his views on Daniel in 'The Revels Office and the Boy Companies, 1600–1613: New Perspectives', *English Literary Renaissance* 32 (2002): 324–51 (325 and 334–36).

8. For the larger picture, see Harold G. Fox, *Monopolies and Patents: a Study of the History and Future of the Patent Monopoly* (Toronto: University of Toronto Press, 1947).

9. In short, Daniel's role was an anomaly created for his sake, not for the sake of the Children's plays or the theater. The role looks like a temporary measure or experiment in outsourcing some of the costs of the new Queen's court. The first Grooms of the Queen's Privy Chamber, John Florio and Daniel Bacheler, were appointed in summer 1604, two years before Daniel was made a Groom (though he received two gifts of £10 from the Queen's exchequer in 1605–6: see below n.41).

10. It is hard to know for sure which of the Children's plays were performed for the first time in the year to April 1605, and which older plays may have been revived. Evidence of second or more performances is limited. Works consulted: Lucy Munro, *Children of the Queen's Revels: a Jacobean Theatre Repertory* (Cambridge: Cambridge University Press, 2005); Robert Meriwether Wren, 'The Blackfriars Theatre and its Repertory, 1600–1608,' Princeton University PhD, 1965; R.A. Foakes, 'Tragedy at the Children's Theatres after 1600: a Challenge to the Adult Stage,' *The Elizabethan Theatre II*, ed. David Galloway (London: Macmillan, 1970), 37–59.

11. For the £20 payment for court performances, see n. 33.

12. Quoted from *The Tragedy of Philotas by Samuel Daniel*, ed. Laurence Michel (New Haven: Yale University Press, 1949), 155–56.

13. Karl Josef Höltgen, 'Richard Latewar Elizabethan Poet and Divine: with three unpublished Poems,' *Anglia* 89 (1971): 417–38 (426).

14. D. C. Andersson, *Lord Henry Howard (1540–1614): An Elizabethan Life* (Cambridge: Boydell & Brewer, 2009), 118.

15. Quintus Curtius, *History of Alexander* (VI.10.26–7): 'enim scripsi misereri me eorum quibus vivendum esset sub eo qui se Iovis filium crederet. *Fides amicitiae, veri consilii periculosa libertas, vos me decepistis!* vos quae sentiebam ne reticerem, impulistis!' (emphasis added).

16. On well-behaved language in particular, see Debora Shuger. *Censorship and Cultural Sensibility: The Regulation of Language in Tudor-Stuart England* (Philadelphia: University of Pennsylvania Press, 2006).

17. David M. Bergeron, 'Francis Bacon: An Unpublished Manuscript,' *Papers of the Bibliographical Society of America,* 84 (1990): 397–404.

18. Vernon F. Snow, 'Francis Bacon's Advice to Fulke Greville on Research Techniques', *Huntington Library Quarterly*, 23 (1959–60): 369–78.

19. As noted above, the theme of his 1604 masque *The Vision of the Twelve Goddesses*, just before formal negotiations with the Spanish, was armed peace with honor.

20. John Florio's 1603 translation: *The Essayes*, II.5, p. 214.

21. Florio: *The Essayes*, III.13, 664.

22. Discussed by David Quint in *Montaigne and the Quality of Mercy* (Princeton NJ: Princeton University Press, 1998), 34–41.

23. Raleigh, *History of the World*, 1614, 198–201 (Part I, Book 4, Chapter 2.17–18).

24. In STC 6239 (1605), STC 6240 (1607), STC 6263 (1607) or STC 6242 or 6243 (1611).

25. Craterus says 'If that he be not found t'have dealt in this, | Yet this will force out some such thoughts of his,' | As will vndoo him: for you seldome see | Such men arraigned, that euer guiltesse be.', quoted from *Philotas*, ed. Michel, 131, ll.1102–5 (the Chorus that Raleigh quotes from begins on 1110).

26. In England, commoners who defamed peers and senior officers of state could face a criminal trial or be sued for damages under fourteenth-century statutes relating to *scandalum magnatum*. This was a legal privilege that set the peerage apart from the rest of society. In 1607 Dr John Cowell, Professor of Civil Law at Cambridge, defined *scandalum magnatum* in his legal dictionary, *The Interpreter*, Cambridge, 1607, 3N2v. The term, according to Cowell, is 'the especial name of a wrong done to any personage of the land, as Prelates, Dukes, Earles, Barons, and other Nobles: and also of the Chanceler . . . by false news: or horrible & false messages, whereby debates and discords betwixt them and the commons, or any scandall to their persons might arise.'

27. Robert P. Adams, 'Despotism, Censorship, and Mirrors of Power Politics in Late Elizabethan Times,' *Sixteenth Century Journal*, X.3 (1979): 5–16 (8); Andrew Gurr, *Playgoing in Shakespeare's London*, 2nd edition (Cambridge: Cambridge University Press, 1996), 151.

28. For example, on the British Library website, in a 2017 essay, 'Subversive theatre in Renaissance England,' Eric Rasmussen and Ian De Jong make the bolder but unsubstantiated claim that when 'Daniel was appointed as the official licenser' of the Children's plays, dramatists 'flocked to this company where they (rightly) assumed that a sympathetic fellow writer would be more likely to allow subversive plays to be staged than a rigorous government censor.'

29. The letter to Cecil is in Hatfield House, the one to Mountjoy in the State Papers: they are printed in H. Sellers, 'A Bibliography of the Works of Samuel Daniel,

1585–1623: with an Appendix of Daniel's Letters,' *Proceedings and Papers of the Oxford Bibliographical Society* 2 (1927–30): 29–54 (51–52). The letters are not well known, and there is no digital text of them, so in the Appendix, there are lightly edited texts, with contractions expanded and minor adjustments in punctuation, interlineation, and layout. The letters are quoted from the Appendix below.

30. Blount is familiar as Mountjoy, the Lord Deputy of Ireland who defeated the Irish and Spanish forces at the Battle of Kinsale in southern Ireland in December 1601.

31. STC 6238, sigs. 2E5-6. *The Apology* was probably found among Daniel's papers at his death by his brother John Danyel (?1564–?1626) the celebrated composer for the song and lute.

32. Unfortunately, the standard edition, Michel's *The Tragedy of Philotas* (see n. 12), is not reliable, especially in court history and textual matters: see the review by Harold Jenkins, *Modern Language Review*, 45 (1950): 243–44. For convenience, the *Apology* and dedication poem are quoted from Michel, 155–57 and 97–99 (Michel inexplicably conflates the original and revised dedication poem: see p. 158).

33. The payment, dated 24 February 1605, was recorded in the account of the Treasurer of the Queen's Chamber, Sir John Stanhope: TNA (PRO) E 351/543, m. 137. Printed in Harold Newcomb Hillebrand, *The Child Actors* (Urbana: University of Illinois, 1926), p.190, n. 42; and in E. K. Chambers and W. W. Greg, "Dramatic Records in the Declared Accounts of the Treasurer of the Chamber 1558–1642," *Malone Society Collections* 6 (1961): no. 137a, 41.

34. This misunderstanding is at the heart of Michel's edition: *Philotas*, 36, n.1.

35. Michel, 156.

36. E.K. Chambers, *The Elizabethan Stage*, 4 vols. (Oxford: Clarendon Press, 1923), 3:276.

37. For a clear outline of all the evidence relating to *Philotas*, see Martin Wiggins in association with Catherine Richardson, *British Drama 1533–1642: A Catalogue*, 11 vols. (Oxford: Oxford University Press, 2011–), 5:142–45.

38. That is, the normal Blackfriars playing season: for details, see Robert Meriwether Wren, 'The Blackfriars Theatre and its Repertory', 23–25.

39. From the abstracts of the Privy Council registers made (in 1610?) by the scribe and antiquary, Ralph Starkey: Add MS 11402, fo. 114r.

40. For *scandalum magnatum*, see n. 26. According to Thomas Fuller, 'M^r. *Daniel* would lye hid at his Garden-house in *Oldstreet*, nigh *London*, for some Months together, (the more retiredly to enjoy the Company of the *Muses*,) and then would appear in publick, to converse with his Friends, whereof D^r. *Cowel*, and M^r. *Camden* were principal', *The History of the Worthies of England* (London, 1662), 3rd part, 28–29.

41. Daniel was first described as a Groom of the Queen's Chamber in 1607 on the title page of the collected edition, *Certaine Small Workes*, STC 6240. The first known payment of £60 was in 1614/15: TNA (PRO) SC 6/JasI/1650, fo. [12v]. The Queen gave Daniel two separate gratuities, £10 each, during the year 1605/6: British Library MS Add. 27404, fos. 38r, 40r.

42. See Bacon's 1605 letter to Egerton, quoted in Virgil B. Heltzel 'Sir Thomas Egerton as Patron', *Huntington Library Quarterly*, 11 (1948): 105–27 (121–22).

43. See Rudolf B Gottfried, 'The Authorship of *A Breviary of the History of England*', *Studies in Philology*, 53 (1956): 172–90; and the Breviary and Conquest history manuscripts listed under Samuel Daniel, DaS 31–39, in the online *Catalogue of English Literary Manuscripts 1450–1700*, (www/celm-ms.org/uk), compiled by Peter Beal.

44. Among them at this date were the Countesses of Bedford, Hertford and Cumberland: see John Pitcher, 'Samuel Daniel (1562/1563–1619), poet and historian', *Oxford Dictionary of National Biography* (2004).

45. And also, Cecil might ask, just how close were the alleged parallels between Philotas (at worst, a secret plotter who took no action) and Essex (the leader of an armed uprising in the streets)? See the shrewd remarks by Kevin Curran, 'Treasonous Silence: "The Tragedy of Philotas" and Legal Epistemology', *English Literary Renaissance*, 42 (2012): 58–89 (especially 61–62)'.

46. Jonson refers to Lady Bedford as Lucy "the bright" in the verse epistle he wrote to Elizabeth, Countess of Rutland, for New Year's Day 1600, ll. 68–70. For a discussion of the quarrel between the poets, see John Pitcher, 'Daniel *versus* Jonson: Books, Beasts and Birds', *Review of English Studies*, 73 (2022): 1–22.

47. The original version and revision can be compared in the parallel-text edition *Every Man in his Humour*, ed. J. W. Lever (London: Edward Arnold), 1971, 270–73.

48. Noted in Richard Dutton, *Shakespeare, Court Dramatist* (Oxford: Oxford University Press), 2016, 90

49. Evidence for this date is set out in John Pitcher, '"After the manner of Horace": Samuel Daniel in the Bodleian in 1605,' *Papers of the Bibliographical Society of America*, 113 (2019): 149–86 (175–80).

50. Bill Angus discusses Jonson's dramaturgy in the context of the culture of surveillance and spying in '"Masters both of arts and lies": Metadrama and the Informer in *Poetaster* and *Sejanus*', in *Metadrama and the Informer in Shakespeare and Jonson* (Edinburgh: Edinburgh University Press, 2016), 115–35.

51. See Misha Teramura, 'Richard Topcliffe's Informant: New Light on *The Isle of Dogs*', *Review of English Studies*, 68 (2017): 44–59 (especially 53–58).

52. In 'Jonson's *Poetaster* and the Politics of Defamation', *English Literary Renaissance*, 49 (2019): 224–47, R. Malcolm Smuts shows that on the public stage Jonson mocked and defamed contemporaries beneath a mask of pretended 'critical detachment' (see especially 245–47).

53. The evidence is summarized in Richard Dutton, *Ben Jonson, Volpone and the Gunpowder Plot* (Cambridge: Cambridge University Press, 2008), 22–24.

54. This is Dutton's argument in *Volpone and the Gunpowder Plot.*

55. See Pitcher, "After the manner of Horace," 160–65.

56. Warren Boutcher argues this in *The School of Montaigne in Early Modern Europe*, 2 vols. (Oxford: Oxford University Press, 2017), 2:258–71.

57. For the recognition by Christ Church, see John Pitcher, "Samuel Daniel: New and Future Research," *Oxford Handbooks Online* (Oxford: Oxford University Press, 2017).

58. See Pitcher, "After the Manner of Horace," 180–83.

59. For an insightful modern study, see Lynn Meskill, *Ben Jonson and Envy* (Cambridge: Cambridge University Press, 2009).

60. See Lucy Munro, ' "As it was Played in the Blackfriars": Jonson, Marston, and the Business of Playmaking,' *English Literary Renaissance*, 2020 (50): 256–95 (especially 269 and 288).

61. This was Anthony Benn, who annotated a copy of the 1605 edition. See John Pitcher, 'Samuel Daniel and the Authorities', *Medieval and Renaissance Drama in England*, 10 (1998): 113–48.

62. A point made in Alexandra Gajda, *The Earl of Essex and Late Elizabethan Political Culture* (Oxford: Oxford University Press, 2012), 216–55 (especially 250–51).

63. The 1623 text is slightly faulty at this point ([2E5r]), where it reads "yeelded in the owne circumstances, we were sufficient for the worke." (The Michel edition ignores misprints.)

64. The interplay in *Philotas* between ancient history and tragedy, at the level of form and general rule, remains unexamined. Two articles that show how a discussion might begin are Richard Stoneman, "Alexander, Philotas, and the Origins of Modern Historiography," *Greece and Rome* 60 (2013): 296–312; and Brett Roscoe, 'On Reading Renaissance Closet Drama: A Reconsideration of the Chorus in Fulke Greville's *Alaham* and *Mustapha*', *Studies in Philology*, 110 (2013): 762–88.

Plagues, Plays, and Pictures

Fran Teague

Whosoever loves not picture is injurious to truth, and all the wisdom of
poetry.

(*Discoveries*, 1641)[1]

The Plague

As the twenty-first century world responds to our own plague, we re-examine
early modern plagues with new insights. The comedy series *Upstart Crow*
broadcast a Christmas special in December 2020 entitled "Lockdown Christmas 1603." Trapped in London lodgings, Will and Kate have the same feelings
as their viewers in COVID confinement: a deep desire to throttle those with
whom you live and a yearning to rejoin a community. The satire throughout
burlesques December 2020 with lines like these: "As the government's leading
alchemists say, 'Follow the superstition'" or "What's the point of wearing
your plaguey beak around your neck? It's a plaguey beak, not a scarf!"
Through the problems of *Upstart Crow*'s quarantine, Will struggles with
creating a great play. While the episode shows Kate inadvertently muttering
her way through "Tomorrow and tomorrow and tomorrow," as Will jots her
words down to create *Macbeth*, the other play that the historical Shakespeare
wrote during the plague years of 1607–9 was *Lear*. He was not alone in writing
a brilliant plague play.[2]

Ben Jonson wrote *The Alchemist*, widely considered his finest comedy, an
assessment due in part to Coleridge's declaration that it had one of the three
most perfect plots in literature (CWBJ, 3:543). In the world of *Upstart Crow,*
plague quarantine is comic, but in Jonson's world, as he well knew, plague
was terrifying. He had lost children and friends to the plague. Jonson's daughter Mary had died in 1601, and while we cannot be sure her death was because
of the plague, it seems likely. As Tom Cain has shown, her death deeply
affected Jonson's work. His first son died of plague in 1603, or the pest as
Jonson called it when talking to William Drummond.

When the King came in England, at that time the pest was in London. He being in the country at Sir Robert Cotton's house with old Camden, he saw in a vision his oldest son. then a child and at London, appear unto him with the mark of a bloody cross on his forehead, as if it had been cutted with a sword; at which, amazed, he prayed unto God; and in the morning he came to Mr Camden's chamber to tell him, who persuaded him it was but an apprehension of his fantasy, at which he should not be disjected. In the mean time comes there letters from his wife of the death of that boy in the plague. He appeared to him, he said, of a manly shape, and of that growth that he thinks he shall be at the Resurrection. (CWBJ 5:373)

Both Cain and Ian Donaldson suggest that Jonson had the plague himself in 1602/03.[3] In 1605/6, Jonson had close contact with the disease again, when Sir John Roe, a close friend, died of plague in Jonson's arms.

Sir John Roe was an infinite spender, and used to say, when he had no more to spend he could die. He died in his arms of the pest, and he furnished his charges, £20; which was given him back. (CWBJ 5:369)[4]

Rebecca Totaro follows W. David Kay in suggesting that Jonson's mother and stepfather died of the plague in 1609, the year before *The Alchemist* was produced. Trying to imagine what anyone in London faced with the plague— loss, grief, fear, a present filled with enforced isolation, but without hope of a cure or safer future—one can understand the writers who created serious works. As Totaro points out, however, such works are rarely theatrical.[5] Yet Jonson made comedy about the plague. In this essay I want to examine several comic elements in the play, particularly the way that Jonson might have thought about them as he wrote the play for production. I am particularly interested in issues of trickery, comic technique, and hidden narratives.

As he wrote, the first thing Jonson must have considered is that his play could not be performed as long as the plague was in London. His response was to write the plague into his play, for the three cheats at the center of the play operate from a respectable house in the Blackfriars because its owner Lovewit has fled London to escape the plague. Their various schemes collapse upon Lovewit's unexpected return.

Many critics have described the way that the metaphor of the plague works throughout the play. But the play also uses "the material threat of the plague" (14), as Christopher Foley has suggested.[6] Traces of that anxiety also run throughout the play, mirroring the way that the poor (like servants and scoundrels) were trapped in London, while the well-to-do (like Lovewit) could afford to leave the city and the plague behind. When Lovewit returns, the dialogue, as Foley points out, directly discusses the plague. Face improvises a lie that the buttery cat has had the plague, and Lovewit is alarmed by this ridiculous excuse: "Hence Lovewit's directive to Face/Jeremy moments later to 'Breathe less, and farther off,' despite the fact that his servant claims that he 'had it [i.e., the plague] not' (5.2.15)" (516). Other passages in the play address the ways that seventeenth-century Londoners responded to the plague, both in social tensions and in attempts to control and treat disease (much as *Upstart Crow* did).

Reading this passage after the COVID lockdown, one recognizes the exchange between Face and Lovewit as a parallel to the experience of standing next to someone who isn't wearing a mask or who is coughing. "Breathe less and farther off" is an imperative that works as well in the twenty-first-century grocery store line as in the seventeenth century. That doubleness of meaning, both metaphoric and material, suddenly becomes too obvious to have missed. But other aspects of the play remain invisible today. We no longer consider the way the play uses the practices that were once considered essential for controlling the supernatural—alchemy, astrology, fairies—in the way that Jonson's audiences did or as Jonson himself did.

Like the plague, the metaphor of alchemy is often considered in discussions of *The Alchemist*. Critics note the dramatic irony. Despite the play's talk about how alchemy can control threats to health and offer power and control, the sole result of all the *venter tripartite*'s promises offer is trash since they, like Chaucer's canon's yeoman, are cheats. Editors look to the past, carefully tracking passages that echo Geoffrey Chaucer's "The Canon's Yeoman's Tale" about fraudulent alchemists, and to the future, pointing to *Mercury Vindicated from the Alchemists at Court* (1616), in order to establish Jonson's scorn for alchemy. As Michael Flachmann writes:

> The mass of scholarship on Jonson's *The Alchemist* has invariably agreed upon two points: (1) that the author intended to satirize alchemy as a transparent, chemical con-game and (2) that the pseudo-scientific subject provided a rich source for the diction, puns, metaphors, similes, and topical references that Jonson delighted in using to dazzle his audience. (259)[7]

I resist that statement, however, because it results from our own attitudes, not Jonson's. Today a serious interest in alchemy and the Philosopher's Stone is likely to elicit scorn accorded subjects like perpetual motion machines and the flat earth theory.

Jonson's attitude toward alchemy was probably similar to Chaucer's. As Robert C. Evans has established, Jonson was an admirer of Chaucer, although he had reservations about the Middle English language that Chaucer used. Evans notes, however, that

> Chaucer is one of the authors cited most frequently in Jonson's *Grammar*, . . . and Chaucer, Gower, and Spenser are three of the four exemplary English poets honored by being presented . . . as characters in *The Golden Age Restor'd*. . . . Jonson's personal copy of Chaucer suggests that in some instances at least he read his predecessor with care. (325)[8]

In writing "The Canon's Yeoman's Tale," Chaucer certainly did not disdain alchemists: he disdained confidence tricksters. That claim is borne out by recent work by Euan Roger, who argues that he has identified the man, William de Brumley, on whom the Canon's Yeoman was based.[9] In tracing that identification, Roger also notes that in a court case for counterfeiting brought against de Brumley, expert testimony on certain coins was provided by three men: the Master of the Royal Mint, the alderman in charge of the Royal Exchange, and a prominent goldsmith. The group is impressively high-powered, and Chaucer would likely have known all three. Roger points out, however, that those expert witnesses did not express skepticism about alchemy (although they did about de Brumley's coins). He remarks of the case,

> Alchemical counterfeiting, rather than the more straightforward crime of coin clipping, appears to have been treated as a matter of interest, and may have been considered as a means of expanding, or protecting, England's wealth, although the laxity of de Brumley's fine may indicate that it was not considered as dangerous as regular counterfeiting. Alchemy was also interesting in general terms, surrounded by mystery and the potential to make money from base materials. As the *pars prima* of the Canon's Yeoman's Tale demonstrates, Chaucer had an active interest in alchemy, which may have predated or been stimulated by the news of William de Brumley.

Chaucer's interest in alchemy was not one of scorn, but of professional interest. As comptroller of Customs for London, he needed to stay abreast of financial news, both of counterfeiting and of research into alchemy.

Ben Jonson had fewer financial interests than did Chaucer, but in his role as masque-maker along with Inigo Jones, he too expresses contempt for cheats, counterfeit alchemists. In *Mercury Vindicated from the Alchemists at Court* (1616), Mercury's first speech leaves no doubt the gang that has captured him at Vulcan's behest includes no true alchemists. He declares, "The whole household of 'em are become alchemists, since their trade of armour-making failed them, only to keep themselves in fire for this winter" (CWBJ4: 435). Mercury goes on to scorn them for their consumption of whiskey and their ignorance of alchemy. Furthermore, Mercury says, they treat him badly and believe that simply by using a furnace they have earned "the title of philosophy, that creature of glory." Once Mercury calls in Nature and Prometheus along with twelve handsome men to dance before the court, the fraudulent alchemists are banished. The text of the masque is clear: the problem is not with alchemy, which is appropriate to true philosophers, but fraud.

As a court masque, *Mercury Vindicated* praises the power of the monarch and the court, and that praise is cleverly couched within the metaphor of alchemy during the performance. Arguably, the metaphor should be understood not as performed, but rather as performative, transforming the individuals present, and potentially transforming the readers who studied Jonson's text of the masque. John Shanahan argues that the conclusion of the masque shows the process in action, much as Jonson's earlier play, *The Alchemist*, shows a vision of what science might look like:

> Like Lovewit returned home to claim the spoils at the close of *The Alchemist*, the King's presence at the masque moves all from chaos to harmonious concord. Functioning something like a Utopian idyll to *The Alchemist*'s gritty realism, the *Mercury Vindicated* masque also portrays a scenario of unauthorized empirical work redeemed by a choice of dramatic form and a more sophisticated audience. (56)[10]

Shanahan's discussion of the way that the transformation fails in *The Alchemist* depends on this recognition: what turns trash to treasure in *The Alchemist* is not the false alchemist's failed efforts, but rather the true theatrical art that turns a tale of fraud into something that offers the Horatian promise of both worthy lesson and pleasant entertainment. Taking this argument a step further, Katherine Shrieves argues that in the masque

> Mercury mocks the impossibility of success in either the alchemists' or courtiers' endeavors, yet his complaint suggests that there is genuine transformative power that should only be wielded by the king. The alchemists and deceptive courtiers fail not because transmutation is impossible, but because their base motives render them unworthy of success. (72)[11]

In short, one cannot find anything in either of Jonson's works about alchemy that suggests he scorns alchemy or alchemists. Even in Epigram 6, "To Alchemists," a reader notes the ambiguity of what Jonson says: "If all you boast of your great art be true, / Sure, willing poverty lives most in you" (CWBJ 5:117). A true philosopher would willingly live in poverty, while a false one does not speak truly of his art. Certainly one can argue that Jonson is skeptical about most alchemical schemes and that he consistently scorned fraud. All the same, one might reasonably ask whether Jonson ever wrote directly and approvingly of an alchemist.

He did. The most prominent alchemist that Jonson admired was his close friend, Sir Kenelm Digby, who would serve as Jonson's literary executor. Jonson praises Digby highly in the poems he wrote about him. The *Oxford Dictionary of Biography* notes that "Digby set himself the task of examining on mechanical principles the concepts of current Paracelsian chemistry, especially alchemy and the 'universal spirit' giving life to all things." One of the Founder members of the Royal Society, Digby "became a member of the chemical committee. His personal distinction added lustre to the new body, whose patron, Charles II, was himself a chemist in the Paracelsian tradition."[12] But I am not the first to note that Jonson's attitudes toward alchemy are less dismissive than some have said. In his biography of Jonson, Ian Donaldson remarks, "Jonson had a sceptical fascination with the arts that had so entranced

John Dee, and owned a copy of *Liber sacer*, also known as the *sworn Book of Honorius* (one of the key texts for ritual magic in pre-Reformation England) that had previously been in Dee's possession" (*Life* 247).[13]

This skeptical interest was closely linked to Jonson's attitude toward astrology. His beloved schoolmaster, William Camden, believed in astrology, and Jonson could set a horoscope himself, as he told Drummond, but did not believe them. (He also told Drummond of an adventure in which he had dressed as an astrologer to deceive a lady). His ability to draw a horoscope suggests he had at one point been favorably inclined toward astrology, but had changed his mind at some point. His belief in the supernatural existed, however, if we can trust his account of the vision he had of his dead son.

We have come full circle, it seems: Jonson's son probably died of the plague, and the time of the plague makes people credulous about what may or may not be true. Consider the President Trump's suggestion that injecting disinfectants like Lysol or bleach is sound health advice rather than incredibly dangerous. Consider the common belief that wearing a mask (or being vaccinated) protects you from becoming sick, rather than saving other people from you. For Jonson, other people's credulity produced great comedy since he had his greatest success writing about tricksters and those tricked.

Donaldson says, "By the end of the seventeenth century the entire system of astrology would be largely discredited; but in Jonson's day the issue was more finely poised" (59). Later audiences might watch *The Alchemist* as a sort of burlesque about people who believe utter nonsense because of ignorance and stupidity. In 1610, Jonson's audiences watched characters like Mammon and Tribulation Wholesome who were themselves sharp enough to follow Subtle's arguments about alchemy and greedy enough to believe in the cheaters' empty promises. If epidemics breed anxiety, then they also breed credulity. And from the pest an artist like Ben Jonson creates a brilliantly funny play.

The Play

The play is a comic masterpiece because it is relentless. As the introduction in the *Cambridge Ben Jonson* notes,

Farce—and *The Alchemist* is the greatest of all English farces—depends on speed, on a pace that accelerates mercilessly as the action becomes ever more complicated; and the risk of an entrance at the wrong moment that will overturn the drama's mechanism increases to a hysterical point. As Face changes costume at ever-increasing speed, he despondently yearns, in the midst of an exchange with Subtle so fast that there are fourteen speech heading in seven lines, for a new technology for clothing: 'Oh, for a suit/To fall now, like a curtain: flap' (4.2.6–7). (CWBJ 3:545)

This analysis, phrased so skillfully to imitate the action it describes, reminds us that farce is typically episodic. Structurally the play is, as Coleridge said, a perfect plot, perhaps the finest example of the trickster tricked plot type in drama. The various gulls trek into the house, get cozened, race off to do what the cheats suggest, and return to the house. Each return, of course, cranks the comic tension higher and higher as the play moves toward its final explosion—offstage in the alchemy laboratory (if it, indeed, exists) and onstage as Lovewit returns and the subplots must conclude almost simultaneously.

The structure gives the illusion of speed, but also of barely contained energy as people race in and out. As more and more characters are drawn in, the room becomes increasingly crowded. The time-place setting also allows the playwright to draw the audience's attention back to the plague—both by the play's topicality and by the insistence on time passing in a safe, but claustrophobic room surrounded by dangerous territory, something any community living through an epidemic learns to consider. Set in the Blackfriars, *The Alchemist* was produced in the playhouse there only after the plague had shut London theaters and forced the company to tour.

Opening in Oxford, the company's first production startled university audiences by the play's impropriety, since jokes about the Anabaptists scandalized at least one viewer (*CWBJ* 3:544). Once the play moved to London and Blackfriars theater, the audience might, as critics like Donaldson and Foley have suggested, have also laughed anxiously at plague jokes made about life in Blackfriars. Moreover, Rebecca Totaro notes that in a time when bad air was considered the cause of the plague, "The play proper opens with a fart."

These transgressive jokes—about Anabaptists, plague, the neighborhood, and flatulence—are not the only uncomfortable topics that elicit laughter. Topical references to Mistress Amo, Madame Caesarean, and "And madam with a dildo writ o' the walls," along with near-miss sexual adventures like Mammon's interrupted seduction of Dol or Dame Pliant's many would-be husbands shock laughter out of the audience. In a play built around cozeners, the transgressive humor—scatological, sexual, sacrilegious—always suits the characters making the joke or those at whom the joke is aimed. The play's language does not depend solely on shock value, however, since some of the finest lines evoke amusement because of their ridiculousness.

Often these moments veer into the domestic (as did the interests of many people during quarantine). A pattern of jokes about food and clothing runs throughout. Some jokes are business depending on the constant costume changes, like Face's yearning for a drop-down suit. The repeated switches among the men wearing the Spanish suit as a preliminary to seducing Dame Pliant is another. Others are verbal. While Subtle does his alchemist's patter with Face as Lungs, Surly listens to the alchemical jargon, and then has a fine comic aside.

> Sub.   Ha' you set the oil of *Luna* in *kemia*?
> Face. Yes, sir.
> Sub.   And the philosopher's vinegar?
> Face.   Ay.
> Sur.   We shall have a salad.
>
> (2.3.99–101)

The anticlimax of "salad" after the "oil of Luna" and "philosopher's vinegar" technobabble invites the audience's laughter. If Face's performance as Lungs here is monosyllabic, he waxes more heartily later in the play when, as the Captain, he deals with Drugger.

> Sub.   'Tis good tobacco, this! What is't an ounce?
> Face. He'll send you a pound, Doctor.
> Sub.   O, no.
> Face.   He will do't.
> It is the goodest soul. Abel, about it.
> [*Aside to him*] Thou shalt know more anon. Away, be gone.)
>   [*Exit Drugger.*]
> A miserable rogue, and lives with cheese,
> And has the worms. That was the cause indeed,
> Why he came now. He dealt with me, in private,
> To get a med'cine for 'em.
>
> (2.6.76–83)

Tribulation Wholesome in the midst of a speech about human sinfulness, throws in this *non sequitur* rhetorical question, "Where have you greater atheists than cooks?" (3.1.21). The gifts that the Fairy Queen sends poor Dapper also follow this note of ridiculous domesticity: Subtle tells Dapper,

>   She now is set
> At dinner in her bed, and she has sent you,
> From her own private trencher, a dead mouse
> And a piece of gingerbread, to be merry withal
>
> (3.5.63–66)

The abrupt tone shift, from the delicacies on the Fairy Queen's private trencher to the dead mouse, is closely followed by the gingerbread gag—in both senses. As he is carried away to the privy, Subtle becomes the footman and Face the major-domo to set up another comic tone shift thanks to a painfully juvenile pun:

Sub.	Where shall we now
	Bestow him?
Doll.	I' the **privy**.
Sub.	Come along, sir,
	I now must show you Fortune's **privy** lodgings.
Face.	Are they perfum'd? and his bath ready?
Sub.	All
	Only the fumigation's somewhat strong. (3.5.78–81, emphasis mine)

Perhaps the funniest example of this domesticity pattern comes as a fashion comment. Ananias enters when Kastril is attacking Surly, who is disguised in the seductive Spanish suit.

Ana.	What is the motive?
Sub.	Zeal, in the young gentleman,
	Against his Spanish slops—
Ana.	They are profane,
	Lewd, superstitious, and idolatrous breeches.(4.7.47–49)

This speech, so characteristic of Ananias and such an unexpected detection of sin, derails the quarrel. When Ananias goes on to proclaim, "Thou look'st like the Antichrist in that lewd hat," Surly surrenders, "I must give way" (4.6.55–56). Kastril, of course, takes all the credit for overcoming Surly.

Finally all this humor is set against the great comic catalogues that burst forth throughout the play. The volleys of insults in the opening, Dol's tortuous twisting of Hugh Broughton's religiosity, Subtle's alchemical and astrological maundering, and Mammon's list of earthly delights for Surly and Dol all rattle by to great effect, much like patter songs in a Gilbert and Sullivan operetta. The sound builds, as in *Epicoene* at the end of Act 3 when all the characters invade Morose's silent home—and with the noise comes laughter.

The Pictures

The Alchemist's language and gags arrive so quickly that the audience (like the confidence tricksters and their gulls) can hardly catch its breath. Even as we laugh, we know we are missing some point of comedy as the language unreels. Yet Jonson also builds in stage pictures with the performer's bodies. These stage pictures are less easily spotted: I am not aware of any comments on them, although I suspect most people who have staged the play will have noted them. The stage pictures may well have been private jokes or tricks that the playwright tucked in for his own or the actors' amusement. They may be accidental or unconscious creations. But they are part of the play.

The play's opening scene features the first trick on the audience. Onstage the viewers see three actors, one playing a bearded captain (who is about to shave at the end of 4.7), another playing an attractive woman (2.3.225, 3.3.42, 5.4.22), and the third an old man (4.3.10, 79). Since plays did not come with programs in the seventeenth century, Jonson's audience would have no idea who these characters were. They heard language pouring forth, the two men shouting at each other in argument, as the woman showed distress and tried to calm them. The audience could initially think that they were seeing a lover quarrel with his sweetheart's father or older brother. These speeches, often broken off, are fast, larded with personal insults, and remarkably uninformative unless one already knows something about the play. After assuming they are watching a pair of sweethearts and a blocking figure to that romance, the audience realizes that something else might be happening when the insults become sufficiently salty. At the peak of the argument, the soldier unsheathes his sword, and the older man waves a container of liquid, presumably something noxious. Clearly, the audience might expect that the play will continue with a fight, perhaps a murder! A stage direction following line 155 tells us that Dol steps in: "*She catcheth out Face his sword: and breaks Subtle's glass.*" The woman suddenly snatches up the soldier's sword and the glass of liquid and threatens both the men while berating them.

Although the stage direction suggests that Dol should break Subtle's glass, no acting company wants broken glass on stage during a performance because of the danger to the actors. We have always known that Jonson's printed texts differ from their productions, and here we see evidence of how a scene might change. Jonson tricks his audience by showing them one stage picture (sweethearts and blocking father), then another (men turn violent), before Dol intervenes and finally performs the truth: three cheats quarrel until the strongest, a woman, prevails over the two men. In five or ten minutes, the audience has had to adjust its expectations twice. The shifting narratives gull the audience.

Jonson may also build into the play an iconographic reference as well. As Jackson Cope suggested over fifty years ago, Jonson stages a bit of business in *Bartholomew Fair* that presents Ursula the Pigwoman as the allegorical figure of Discord.[14] Might Dol's stage business of snatching up the sword and the glass serve a similar purpose? I think so. In looking for an image of an armed woman holding a glass, I found the goddess Soteria, or safety, who is often coupled with another goddess, Peira, or Danger. Moreover, these two goddesses are ones Jonson knew from an earlier work, the presentation of speeches to King James as he entered London for as king. Stephen Harrison had constructed elaborate and enormous arches of triumph, and James stopped at each arch, he heard speeches in his praise. Jonson had written speeches for several of the arches to welcome the monarch. One was the arch at Temple Bar (fig. 1), featuring the image of Soteria setting her foot on Peira (fig.2).[15]

Figure 1. The Temple Bar Arch. Soteria and Peira are in the bottom niche on the left. By permission of the Folger Shakespeare Library, Washington, DC.

Figure 2. Detail, showing Soteria and Peira from the Temple
Bar Arch. By permission of the Folger Shakespeare Library,
Washington, DC.

Of these two figures Jonson wrote:

SOTERIA,

> or Safety, a damsel in carnation, the colour signifying cheer, and life; she sat high; upon her Head she wore an antique helm, and in her right hand a spear for defence, in her left a cup for medicine; at her feet was set a pedestal upon which a serpent rolled up did lie. Beneath was

PEIRA,

> or *Danger,* a woman despoiled and almost naked, the little garment she hath left her of several colours, to note her various disposition. Besides her lies a torch out and a sword broken, the instruments of her fury, with a net and wolf's-skin, the ensigns of her malice, rent in pieces. The word,

TERGA DEDERE METUS.

*Lib.*12.*Ep.*6

> Borrowed from Martial and implying, that now all Fears have turned their backs and our safety might become security, danger being so wholly depressed and unfurnished of all means to hurt.
> (CWBJ 2:449–50)

While Soteria should have a spear and pedestal with coiled serpent, Dol has a sword and cup of some vile substance. But Dol, while concerned about Safety, is unlike Soteria by being a crook, not a goddess. Sadly, she does not recognize her dual identity as Peira as well, but by play's end she becomes the second goddess, Peira. Dapper and Face have just left Subtle and Dol, dressed for the Fairy Queen scene. When Face returns, he makes sure of the loot, and then turns his companions out of the house. As Face taunts his partners, he jokes about Dol's clothing:

> All I can do
> Is to help you over the wall, o' the back side,
> Or lend you a sheet to save your velvet gown, Doll.
> Here will be officers, presently . . . .
> (5.4.132–34)

From a strong woman armed with a sword and a glass to a woman in despoiled clothing, Dol descends, just as Face goes from a fine bearded Captain to a clean-shaven servant, and all three go from safety to danger. I am perhaps over-reading a stage direction, but the possibility certainly exists that Jonson included these moments as an inside joke for those familiar with Cesare Ripa's *Iconologia*.

Finally, critics have drawn attention to the ending of *The Alchemist* because it concludes with Lovewit taking advantage of both the tricksters and their victims. He keeps all their ill-gotten gains, marries the pliant widow, and has his servant Jeremy kick out Dol and Subtle. To be sure, Jeremy has the play's last words:

> Gentlemen,
> My part a little fell in this last scene,
> Yet 'twas decorum. And though I am clean
> Got off from Subtle, Surly, Mammon, Dol,
> Hot Ananias, Dapper, Drugger, all
> With whom I traded, yet I put myself
> On you, that are my country: and this pelf,
> Which I have got, if you do quit me, rests
> To feast you often, and invite new guests.
>
> (5.5.157–65)

His part fell for he is once again a servant, but no one seeks to arrest him. Indeed, the pelf or loot remains for him to use to defray the household expenses, such as those incurred by inviting the audience to a feast. The conclusion, unlike those of Jonson's other major comedies—*Volpone, Epicoene,* and *Bartholomew Fair*—does not include a public revelation of fools and tricksters, much less consequences for bad behavior. Rather the master proves as great a rascal as his manservant. I want to suggest that this moment is the play's final trick. Just as the play began with a stage picture that audiences understood in one way, only to realize they had misunderstood it, so too does this scene fail to resolve into a neat meaning. This point is not original, since critics have tried to make sense of the ending speech, usually by pointing out that Jeremy is metatheatrically all the other roles he has played in the comedy. Other critics note that the Blackfriars audience has been tricked into coming into the King's Men's new playhouse after an outbreak of the plague in London. That unwise action on the audience's part is interpreted as a trick the company plays on its neighbors who had tried to block the playhouse's opening or a trick on the audience itself by persuading them to ignore the threat to their health. I propose a simpler interpretation.

An old man, a pretty and pliant young wife, and a clever servant living together in a single household does not end the plot, but rather starts a new one—or one as old as Plautus or a medieval fabliau. The old husband will soon be a cuckold, either because Dame Pliant will sleep with the clever servant (as in a fabliau) or Jeremy will act as a go-between for Dame Pliant and a young lover (as in Plautus). That stage picture is the final joke of the comedy. Written in the midst of an epidemic by a man who had watched people that he loved die from plague, *The Alchemist* celebrates laughter, life, and desire.

Notes

1. Quotations from Jonson are all from the Cambridge edition of *Ben Jonson's Works* (CWBJ), eds. David Bevington, Martin Butler, and Ian Donaldson (Cambridge: Cambridge University Press, 2012). Information about Jonson's life comes from Ian Donaldson, *Ben Jonson A Life* (Oxford: Oxford University Press, 2011), cited as *Life*. The epigraph is from *Discoveries*, CWBJ, 7:550.

2. For more information on the episode, see https://www.bbc.co.uk/programmes/m000qrsx.

3. Tom Cain, "Mary and Bedford Jonson: A Note," *Ben Jonson Journal*, 14, no. 1: 82; *Life*, 181.

4. For information on Roe's death, Alvaro Ribeiro, "Sir John Roe: Ben Jonson's Friend," *The Review of English Studies*, New Series 24, no. 94 (1973): 153–64. Accessed July 4, 2021. http://www.jstor.org/stable/514684.

5. Rebecca Totaro, *Suffering in Paradise: The Bubonic Plague in English Literature, from More to Milton* (Pittsburgh:Duquesne University Press, 2005), 110.

6. Christopher Foley, "Breathe Less, and Farther Off," *Studies in Philology*, 115, no. 3: 505–23. Accessed July 4, 2021. https://www.jstor.org/stable/10.2307/90022564.

7. Michael Flachman, "Ben Jonson and the Alchemy of Satire." *Studies in English Literature, 1500–1900* 17, no. 2 (1977): 259–80. https://www.jstor.org/stable/450136.

8. Robert C. Evans, "Ben Jonson's Chaucer," *English Literary Renaissance* 19, no. 3 (1989): 324–45. https://www.jstor.org/stable/43447715. Reading this article, I vaguely recalled a *carpe diem* poem about Chaucer's reputation in early modern England, and I am grateful to Miriam Jacobson and Megan Cook for helping me to identify Edmund Waller's "Of English Verse." Jonson owned a copy of *The workes of our Ancient and learned English Poet, Geofrey Chaucer. . . .* Impensis Geor. Bishop: London, 1602, according to David McPherson's "Ben Jonson's Library and Marginalia: An Annotated Catalogue," *Studies in Philology* 71, no. 5 (1974): item 39.

9. Euan Cameron Roger, "Chaucer's *Pars Secunda* Canon: A New Identification," *The Chaucer Review* 54, no. 4 (2019): 464–81. I am grateful to Susan Cerasano who pointed out to me that Marion Turner's *Chaucer: A European Life* (Princeton: Princeton University Press, 2019) discusses Chaucer's attitude toward gold, particularly its association with desirable women (246, an association relevant to *Volpone*), and Chaucer's anxiety about gold coinage (246–49).

10. John Shanahan, "Ben Jonson's *Alchemist* and Early Modern Laboratory Space, *Journal for Early Modern Cultural Studies* 8, no. 1 (2008): 35–66. https://www.jstor.org/stable/40339589.

11. Katherine Shrieves, "Spiritual Alchemy through Embodied Hieroglyphs in Jonson's *Mercury Vindicated from the Alchemists at Court*," *Journal for Early Modern Cultural Studies* 14, no. 3 (2014): 55–82. https://www.jstor.org/stable/jearlmodcultstud.14.3.55.

12. Michael Foster, "Digby, Sir Kenelm (1603–1665), natural philosopher and courtier." *Oxford Dictionary of National Biography.* 23 Sep. 2004; Accessed 25 Jun. 2021. https://www.oxforddnb.com/view/10.1093/ref:odnb/9780198614128.001.0001/odnb-9780198614128-e-7629.

13. David McPherson's catalogue of Jonson's books lists half a dozen mystical or occult books; see items 4, 32, 77, 111, 131, 160. I must also mention that the Fairy Queen who entrances poor Dapper may well be based on several cases of fraudsters who made promises of gold from the fairies to folks who invested their wealth and dignity in the project only to be cheated. An excellent survey of these tricks can be found in Thomas Willard, "Chapter 20. Pimping for the Fairy Queen: Some Cozeners in Shakespeare's England," *Crime and Punishment in the Middle Ages and Early*

Modern Age, edited by Albrecht Classen and Connie Scarborough (Berlin, Boston: De Gruyter, 2012), 491–508. https://doi.org/10.1515/9783110294583.491. Willard discusses a pamphlet about the inimitable Judith Philips, noting that

> The Hampshire man [she was cheating] had to let her saddle him up and ride him around a tree behind his house. He then had to wait, with the saddle still in place, while she met inside with the Queen of the Fairies. Needless to say, she disappeared, taking his best candlesticks and silverware. (493)

One wants to believe that Jonson had read and relished this account.

14. Jackson Cope, "*Bartholomew Fair* as Blasphemy," *Renaissance Drama* (1965), 8, 127–52. The discussion of Ursula as Discord occurs 142–45.

15. The image of the Temple Bar gate comes from the Folger Shakespeare Library LUNA Catalogue entry for Stephen Harrison's *The Arch's of Triumph erected in Honour of the High and Mighty Prince, Iames* (File Name 46582), and I use that image as licensed under the Creative Commons Attribution-ShareAlike 4.0 International License (CC BY-SA 4.0) by the Folger.

Bibliography

Cain, Tom. "Mary and Bedford Jonson: A Note." *Ben Jonson Journal* 14, no. 1 (2007): 79–87.

Cope, Jackson. "*Bartholomew Fair* as Blasphemy." *Renaissance Drama* 8 (1965): 127–52.

Donaldson, Ian. *Ben Jonson A Life*. Oxford: Oxford University Press, 2011.

Evans, Robert C. "Ben Jonson's Chaucer." *English Literary Renaissance* 19.3 (1989): 324–45. Accessed July 4, 2021. https://www.jstor.org/stable/43447715.

Flachman, Michael. "Ben Jonson and the Alchemy of Satire." *Studies in English Literature, 1500–1900* 17, no. 2 (1977): 259–80. Accessed July 4, 2021. https://www.jstor.org/stable/450136.

Foley, Christopher. "Breathe Less, and Farther Off." *Studies in Philology* 115, no. 3: 505–23. Accessed July 4, 2021. https://www.jstor.org/stable/10.2307/90022564.

Foster, Michael. "Digby, Sir Kenelm (1603–1665), natural philosopher and courtier." *Oxford Dictionary of National Biography*. Accessed 25 Jun. 2021. https://www.oxforddnb.com/view/10.1093/ref:odnb/9780198614128.001.0001/odnb-9780198614128-e-7629.

Harrison, Stephen, et al. *The Arch's of Triumph Erected in Honor of the High and Mighty Prince. Iames. the First of That Name. King, of England. and the Sixt of Scotland at His Maiesties Entrance and Passage through His Honorable Citty & Chamber of London. Vpon the 15th. Day of March 1603. Invented and Published by Stephen Harrison Ioyner and Architect: And Graven by William Kip*. By Iohn VVindet, printer to the honourable citie of London, and are to be sold at the authors house in Lime-street, at the signe of the Snayle, 1604. STC 12863a. LUNA: Folger Digital Image Collection, file 46582. Accessed August 18, 2021. http://luna.folger.edu.

Jonson, Ben. *Cambridge Edition of the Works of Ben Jonson*. Bevington, David, Martin Butler, Ian Donaldson, gen. eds. 7 vols. Cambridge: Cambridge University Press, 2012. *The Alchemist*. Ed. Peter Holland and William Sherman. Vol. 3. *Discoveries*. Ed. Lorna Hutson. Vol. 7. *Epigrams*. Ed. Colin Burrows. Vol. 5. *Informations to William Drummond of Hawthornden*. Ed. Ian Donaldson. Vol. 5: *The King's*

Entertainment. Ed. Martin Butler. Vol. 2. *Mercury Vindicated from the Alchemists at Court.* Ed. Martin Butler. Vol. 4.

McPherson, David. "Ben Jonson's Library and Marginalia: An Annotated Catalogue." *Studies in Philology* 71, no. 5 (1974), Texts and Studies, 1–106. Accessed July 4, 2021. https://www.jstor.org/stable/4173858.

Ribeiro, Alvaro. "Sir John Roe: Ben Jonson's Friend." *The Review of English Studies* New Series, 24, no. 94 (1973): 153–64. Accessed July 4, 2021. http://www.jstor.org/stable/514684.

Roger, Euan Cameron. "Chaucer's *Pars Secunda* Canon: A New Identification." *The Chaucer Review* 54, no. 4 (2019): 464–81. Accessed July 4, 2021. https://muse.jhu.edu/article/734841.

Shanahan, John. "Ben Jonson's *Alchemist* and Early Modern Laboratory Space." *Journal for Early Modern Cultural Studies* 8, no. 1 (2008): 35–66. Accessed July 4, 2021. https://www.jstor.org/stable/40339589.

Shrieves, Katherine. "Spiritual Alchemy through Embodied Hieroglyphs in Jonson's *Mercury Vindicated from the Alchemists at Court.*" *Journal for Early Modern Cultural Studies* 14, no. 3 (2014): 55–82. Accessed July 4, 2021. https://www.jstor.org/stable/jearlmodcultstud.14.3.55.

Totaro, Rebecca. *Suffering in Paradise: The Bubonic Plague in English Literature, from More to Milton.* Pittsburgh: Duquesne University Press, 2005.

Turner, Marion. *Chaucer: A European Life.* Princeton: Princeton University Press, 2019.

Willard, Thomas. "Pimping for the Fairy Queen: Some Cozeners in Shakespeare's England," *Crime and Punishment in the Middle Ages and Early Modern Age*, edited by Albrecht Classen and Connie Scarborough (Berlin, Boston: De Gruyter, 2012), 491–508. Accessed July 4, 2021. https://doi.org/10.1515/9783110294583.491.

Jonson's Beard and Shakespeare's Purge:
Hamlet, Parnassus, and the Poet's War

Steve Roth

In the Christmas season of 1601/1602, probably at New Year's (Leishman 24–26, and note to ll. 1065–72), students of St. John's College, Cambridge presented an entertainment to their compatriots in the college's great hall: *The Return from Pernassus, Or the Scourge of Simony.* (This its published title; in manuscript it's *The Progresse to Parnassus.*) It was the final work in a trilogy presented at St. John's Christmas-season celebrations starting in 1598/1599 or 1599/1600. (I will refer to it here as *Parnassus* or *II Returne,* and to its prequels as *Pilgrimage* and *I Returne.*) A thorough *drama à clef* depicting and parodying the London literary scene, *Parnassus* is best known among Shakespeareans for its on-stage depiction of Chamberlain's Men Richard Burbage and William Kempe (by those names), and for its repeated references to William Shakespeare, Ben Jonson, and other dramatists and literateurs of the day—both their persons and their works. Despite energetic speculations over many decades, it's not known if the plays were by a single author or multiple, or who he or they may have been.

One passage of Kempe's from the play has always attracted the most attention (1766–773; emphasis added):

> Few of the university men pen plaies well, they smell too much of that writer Ovid, and that writer Metamorphoses, and talk too much of Proserpina & Juppiter. Why heres our fellow Shakespeare puts them all down, I and Ben Jonson too. And *that Ben Jonson is a pestilent fellow, he brought up Horace giving the Poets a pill, but our fellow Shakespeare hath given him a purge that made him beray his credit.*[1]

There has been much discussion of that pill, purge, and bewrayal, and their relation to the 1598–1601 "poet's war" or *poetomachia* (so-styled by Thomas Dekker in his "To the World," prepended to *Satiro-mastix* in the 1602 quarto). That contention concluded with *Satiro-mastix* and Ben Jonson's *Poetaster*— both composed and produced in 1601 (spring or probably fall), registered in Nov and Dec 1601, respectively, and both published in 1602.[2]

To encapsulate the critical thinking about *Parnassus*'s pill, purge, and bewrayal:

All commenters agree that the pill refers to a scene in Jonson's *Poetaster*, in which Horace (figuring Jonson) gives Crispinus (figuring John Marston) a pill that causes him to vomit up a whole lexicon of identifiably Marston-esque verbiage (v.iii.498–564).

Various have averred[3] that Shakespeare's purge of Jonson was delivered in *Satiro-mastix* (which also figures Jonson as Horace, and "untrusses" him), played by the Chamberlain's Men at the Globe in the fall of 1601—the theory being that the *Parnassus* author simply conflated Shakespeare with his company. While plausible, this is unsatisfying for obvious reasons: 1. Shakespeare doesn't administer the purge; his company does. 2. As Bednarz (22) points out, there is no purge. "Horace is never literally purged in *Satiro-mastix*. He is 'untrussed' (or stripped bare), threatened with whipping, and crowned with nettles." He adds in a footnote [283], "Horace/Jonson is threatened with a purge, but none is given."

Bednarz and his predecessors (e.g., Fleay, Smeaton, Small, Elton, Potts) have argued that the purge was administered in *Troilus and Cressida*—that Ajax ("a jakes") is at least partially a purgative send-up of Jonson. Bednarz has argued this most convincingly, in a much larger context of Shakespeare's engagement throughout the poetomachia, in multiple plays.

Brooke (383–86) is singular, I believe, in suggesting that the purge was administered in *Hamlet*—though he suggests it happened in now-lost lines from a production acted at Cambridge (per *Hamlet*'s Q1 title page). He suggests that the lines were intentionally omitted from Q2 of 1604 because of "Restraint by Authority"—as Jonson's Apologetical Dialogue was omitted from the 1602 quarto of *Poetaster* (it's included in the 1616 folio version), and as the "little eyases" reference to the poetomachia (2.2.338–63) was (in Brooke's view) omitted from Q2 *Hamlet* of 1604. The lost lines were omitted from F1 *Hamlet*, he believes—despite the inclusion of the eyases passage—out of deference to Jonson, who was a dominant dramatic éminence grise by 1623, and was contributing a fulsome eulogy of Shakespeare to the volume.

Jonson's self-bewrayal has been little discussed, but Roth (2002b) has argued that it occurred in the ill-tempered "Apologetical Dialogue," added to *Poetaster* after its first playings. The dialogue is absent from the 1602 quarto edition, and an appended "To the reader" explains that it was "restrained by authority." A different "To the reader" in the 1616 folio (which does include the dialogue) gives us our name for the dialogue, and says it "was only once spoken upon the stage." That edition's dedication to Richard Martin gives thanks for Martin's defense of Jonson in legal proceedings apparently brought against him for presenting the dialogue: "this peece . . . for whose innocence, as for the Authors, you were once a noble and timely undertaker, to the greatest Justice of this kindome . . . which so much ignorance, and malice of the times, then conspir'd to have supprest." That Jonson himself spoke the dialogue on stage is suggested in the 1602 quarto's "To the Reader" (emphasis added): "thinke charitably of what thou has read, till thou maist *heare him speake what hee hath written*." (Penniman 167) Jonson represented himself as a character in his own *poetomachian* works multiple times—as Asper in *Every Man Out of his Humour* (1599, Chamberlain's), Criticus/Crites (Q/F) in *Cynthia's Revels* (1600, Children of the Chapel), and Horace in *Poetaster* (1601, Children of the Chapel). The Apologetical Dialogue is the only instance in which the character is "Author."

The theories about *Troilus* as the site of the purge have much merit which I won't essay to impugn here. (The armed prologues in both *Poetaster* and *Troilus* constitute especially convincing evidence.) The purge could have been administered in more than one play. But I would like to suggest an explanation that may serve to crowd out or supplement that position: that Shakespeare administered his purge of Jonson in *Hamlet*—and *pace* Brooke, in *Hamlet* as we know it.

Dating *Hamlet*

This suggestion is supported, firstly, by the chronology. *Poetaster* was presented by the Children of the Chapel at Blackfriar's before 25 September, 1601. *Satiromastix* was completed after 14 August and played before 24 October (Bednarz 272)—first by the Paul's Boys, then by the Chamberlains' Men at the Globe. (This sequence is attested by Tucca's "Epilogus"; see note 13.) According to almost all editors and commentators, *Hamlet* was presented largely in its extant form in the months immediately following.

Fleay, Penniman, Small, Chambers, Wilson, Honigman, Jenkins, Hibbard, Edwards, (Gary) Taylor, Ioppolo, Thompson & Taylor, and Bednarz, among many others, all agree that *Hamlet*'s F1-only "eyrie of children, little eyases" passage (2.2.340; also Q1's "humour of children" adumbration) refers to the poetomachian contentions that culminated with *Poetaster* and *Satiromastix*, and that that passage, at least, was composed in the Fall of 1601. Despite much other suggestive evidence, none of it sets a definitive *terminus post quem* prior to this date for the first performances of the Shakesperean *Hamlet* as we know it in F, Q2, and portions of Q1.[4]

The consensus on the eyases passage has been questioned by Roslyn Knutson (1995), who suggests the passage was composed between 1606 and 1608. To condense her positive argument for those dates (21): "If . . . [three speculative surmises are all true,] . . . it is plausible . . ." The argument is far from definitive. The autumn 1601 date for the passage remains decidedly plausible, and most still think it is the most plausible.

Further support for this dating arises in Gonzago's "full thirty times" speech, which so obviously draws on *Alphonsus, King of Aragon*, revived by The Admiral's Men in August 1601. Two other passages in *Hamlet* echo the *True Tragedy of Richard III*, which the Admiral's may have had in production at the same time. (All discussed at more length below.)

Sohmer (1996, supported by Roth 2002a) has suggested even more specific dating for the internal action in *Hamlet* (and perhaps even a date for its 1601 season opening), based on calendrical evidence: the ghost's four appearances on the ramparts are identified with the nights of Friday 30 October through Monday 2 November 1601—the Feast of Marcellus, All Hallows Eve, All Saints', and All Souls'. (The latter three are all deeply associated with ghostly appearances, and remembrance of the dead. *Viz:* the ghost's "Remember me," thrice echoed by Hamlet.) That dating also sets up a telling conjunction between the King's murder and the death of Shakespeare's father John just under two months prior ("But two months dead, nay not so much, not two" 1.2.138). Multiple editors (most recently Thompson and Taylor [36]) have found intuitive appeal in the coincidence of Shakespeare's father's death, the litany of half a dozen dead fathers in *Hamlet*, and *Hamlet*'s final composition date.

That coincidence, the scholarly consensus on the eyries/eyases passage, and that passage's "inside-baseball" commentary on the *poetomachia* that culminated in late 1601 (which was then commented upon in *Parnassus* at the turn of the year), plus the *Alphonsus* and *True Tragedie* allusions, all position the play's final composition at the very culmination, and in the very thick of, the poetomachia's intensely rivalrous self-commentary on Eliza-thethan theater and drama—in the fall of 1601. The present discussion both relies on and further supports that dating, demonstrating responses in *Hamlet* to tragic and poetomachian material and events prior to October/November, 1601—often immediately prior.

A Poetomachian *Hamlet*?

Hamlet delivers a dense, complex, very funny web of topical, theater-insider allusions that extend well beyond the eyases passage, encompassing the whole, central "players" portion of the play. According to Rosencranz in that "eyases" passage, and both Jonson ("Author") and Histrio in *Poetaster,* such railleries at least contributed to a play's commercial success in those poetomachian days. In Josiah Penniman's words (1897, 105):

> Jonson states [in the Apological Dialogue to *Poetaster*] that these satirical plays were profitable to the writers. The plays 'gave them meat' and 'got them clothes,'

and this was their end in writing them. Histrio says (III. 1) that the reason for hiring Demetrius (Dekker) to bring in Horace (Jonson) and his gallants in a play [*Satiro-mastix*] is that 'it will get us a huge deal of money . . . and we have need on't.

This is not to suggest (as Brooke does, unwisely), that The Chamberlain's Men were driven to provincial touring by competition from the boys' companies. Brooke is on firmer ground when he says:

> Commercially speaking, plays like 'Cynthia's Revels' and 'The Poetaster' can hardly have been very formidable rivals to such notable successes as 'Henry V,' 'Julius Caesar,' and 'Hamlet,' even when we make the greatest possible allowance for the current topical interest of the former. The Blackfriars Theatre also was relatively small, and appears to have been open only one night a week.

For his latter point, Brooke cites Wallace (1908, 104–7), who offers his own translation of passages from the diary of Frederic Gerschow, who attended a performance of the Children of the Chapel at Blackfriars on Saturday, 18 September, 1602. Of the boys he says, "it is required of them to act a play every week." Of equal interest here: the price of admittance was "as much as eight shillings of our [Wallace: Pomeranian] coinage [Wallace: *ca. 12 d.*]". The most expensive gallery seats at the Globe went for half that amount: six pence.

Add to all this: Richard Burbage was landlord to Nathaniel Giles and Henry Evans and their Children of the Chapel Royal at Blackfriars. And the Chamberlain's took up Dekker's *Satiro-mastix* from Paul's Boys, playing it at the Globe. Both suggest rather friendly rivalry.

So yes, the boy's companies were, once a week, drawing away some of the Chamberlain's most profitable customers—the six-penny tenants of the galleries—and given the higher entrance fee, even more of those customers' playgoing budgets. These were also the Globe's best-educated, highest-status customers, in an age when status very much mattered. And they were the bloggers and tweeters (and book buyers) of their day, commonplacing choice phrases in their "tables" and (mis)quoting them to others (see, for instance, Gullio in *I Returne,* and Judicio in *II Returne*), and including them in published literary miscellanies like *Belvedere. (Parnassus* 1.2 consists almost entirely of two wits discussing that work.) But this is insufficient to suggest that the Chamberlain's were forced into provincial touring like the players in *Hamlet.* The "estimation" that Hamlet asks Rosencrantz about was more about the good opinions of worthies and wits like Hamlet and his fellow playgoers of "the City"—the "many wearing Rapiers"—than about enterprise-threatening commercial competition.

The imagery of the players plodding about the provinces has a target, but it is not the Chamberlain's Men. Rather, it's a direct taking-up of similar

JONSON'S BEARD AND SHAKESPEARE'S PURGE

language and imagery from *Satiro-mastix*—language explicitly directed at Horace/Jonson and his time with the Pembroke's Men. It's among many parodic allusions in *Hamlet* to tragedies, especially revenge tragedies, and particularly to tragedies of companies (Pembroke's, Admiral's) that Jonson had a hand in as an up-and-coming actor, script doctor, and playwright. *Hamlet* delivers an extended send-up of Jonson's "tragic flaws" from the preceding months and years. And it does so at the very culmination of the poetomachia.

A Filthy Whining Ghost

Hamlet's (self-)referential commentary did not emerge in a vacuum, of course. Over the preceding decade—from the late-1580s era of *The Spanish Tragedy* and the presumed *Ur-Hamlet* to the time of the Shakespearean *Hamlet*'s first playings at the turn of the century—Elizabethan theater became increasingly self-aware and metadramatic or metatheatrical (or to employ an unfortunately common academic redundancy, "self-reflexive"). The rise of comical satire, and the poetomachia itself, rather epitomize this.[5] In particular, even while revenge tragedies continued as a successful genre, at the turn of the century they were navigating very different cultural territory. The "tragic clichés . . . of the late 1580s and 1590s tragedy—ambitious tyrants, narrating choruses . . . and ghosts," and "its characteristic style: sensational, over-blown (with its howling choruses and shrieking ghosts), and laden with the flashes, bangs and smoke of special effects" (Smith 2010, 88)—were regular objects of ridicule.

That raillery can be scented even as early as Thomas Nashe's 1589 "whole Hamlets, I should say handfulls of tragical speaches" (McKerrow 1905, 315), but at least by 1596 it was being expressed unequivocally and in reference to the ghost in *Hamlet*, in Thomas Lodge's 1596 treatise, *Wit's Miserie and the World's Madness*: "the ghost which cried so miserably at the Theatre, like an oyster-wife, 'Hamlet, revenge.'" (Lodge 1596, 56) The trope arises explicitly in the induction to Jonson's *Cynthia's Revels* (1600); one of the boy players inveighs against another: "the ghosts of some three or four plays departed a dozen years since, have been seen walking on your stage here; take heed boy, if your house be haunted with such hobgoblins, 'twill fright away all your spectators quickly." (Herford and Simpson Vol. 4.) And it achieves something of an apotheosis in the prominently positioned induction to the anonymous *A Warning for Fair Women* (Chamberlain's Men; stationer's register and printed 1599),[6] where a personified "Comedy" asserts that "Tragedy" rather tiringly and predictably depicts (Farmer 2)[7]:

> How some damned tyrant, to obtain a crown,
> Stabs, hangs, empoisons, smothers, cutteth throats;
> And then a Chorus too comes howling in,
> And tells us of the worrying of a cat;
> Then of a filthy whining ghost,
> Lapped in some foul sheet, or a leather pelch,
> Comes screaming like a pig half-sticked,
> And cries 'Vindicat! Revenge, revenge!'
> With that a little rosin flasheth forth,
> Like smoke out of a tobacco pipe, or a boy's squib;
> Then Comes in two or three like to drovers,
> With tailors' bodkins, stabbing one another[.]

Shakespeare himself takes part in that tragic-ridicule tradition via Hamlet's panegyric for the play from which the tragic Hecuba speech is drawn—a speech (about Pyrrhus revenging his father's murder) that is thoroughly Senecan in its description rather than depiction of bloody deeds of the ancients (2.2.437–48):

> I heard thee speak me a speech once, but it was
> never acted, or, if it was, not above once; for the play,
> I remember, pleased not the million. 'Twas caviare to
> the general. But it was—as I received it, and others
> whose judgements in such matters cried in the top of
> mine—an excellent play, well digested in the scenes,
> set down with as much modesty as cunning. I remember
> one said there was no sallets in the lines to make the
> matter savoury, nor no matter in the phrase that might
> indict the author of affectation, but called it an honest
> method, as wholesome as sweet, and by very much
> more handsome than fine.

The play was "set down with as much modesty as cunning"? "No sallets [seasoning] in the lines to make the matter savory"? "No matter in the phrase"? "As wholesome as sweet"? "Very much more handsome than fine"? Given this staccato of ironically lefthanded praise (at best), it seems safer to view this "caviar to the general" passage as a cleverly framed parody of Hamlet and his fellow playgoing wits ("others, whose judgments in such matters cried in the top of mine"), and their elitist, old-fashioned views on playwriting—a parody written by an inveterately populist playwright.

The youthful E. K. Chambers can stand as proxy for others who have come to this view. In his own edition of the play (1895, 151) he suggests: "perhaps we must not confuse Shakespeare with Hamlet; the actor-playwright . . . may be gently satirizing the point of view of the university and court wit and scholar."[8] Or perhaps not so gently: *Parnassus*'s Kempe likewise demeans such wits, and by comparison to Shakespeare: "few of the university men pen plaies well," he says, but "heres our fellow Shakespeare puts them all down" (1766, 1769).

Hamlet's constant invocation of and commentary on increasingly dated dramatic styles, especially tragical ones, almost begs its audience of Elizabethan playgoers to look back on that tragic tradition, including *Hamlet*'s own earlier incarnations (and the ghost's), and the poetomachian contentions that commented upon it—especially on examplars from the immediately preceding months and years, and notably on exemplars in which Jonson was involved.

The ghost's injunction on the ramparts is not just a call to Hamlet; it's a call to playgoers at the Globe: "Remember me."

The Croaking Raven Doth Bellow for Revenge

The notion that *Hamlet* makes fun of old-fashioned tragic plays, players, playing companies, and playing styles is far from new.[9] A prominent representative example is J. D. Wilson's argument in Appendix C of *What Happens in Hamlet* (1951) that the players—with their neo-Senecan Hecuba speech, dumb show, stagey acting, and patches of purple poetry—are among other things a takeoff on Henslowe and Alleyn's Admiral's Men, their repertoire, and even on Alleyn himself.[10]

According to Wilson, Rosencrantz's description of the players as "tragedians of the city" points to the Admiral's Men, whose main stock included Marlowe's tragedies and Kyd's *The Spanish Tragedy,* and whose leading actor, Alleyn, was famous almost solely as a tragedian. Citing Chambers (1923, II: 297, with his five supporting examples), he asserts that that Hamlet's "When Roscius was an actor in Rome" would immediately bring to mind Alleyn: "'Roscius' was the title almost universally conferred at that time upon Alleyn."

William Armstrong has challenged this characterization of Alleyn's acting, and the assertion that *Hamlet* and Hamlet comment upon it. He points out that the "Roscius" moniker was as frequently applied to Burbage, as well as Shakespeare, Tarleton, and others, and points to praise for Alleyn's acting by notables who also express notable distaste for hand sawing and such: Nashe in 1593, Jonson in 1614 and 1616, and Webster in 1612. But with the exception of the Nashe snippet, these encomia are all from later years; Alleyn's style could have changed with an emerging preference for more naturalistic acting. And in any case Armstrong's Roscius contention doesn't address Wilson's other point: that Alleyn was known almost purely as a tragic actor.

Andrew Gurr has refuted Armstrong's arguments based on earlier contemporaneous mentions, concluding that "two distinct kinds of acting did exist among the adult companies in the early seventeenth century." He assigns the more restrained and naturalistic (or sophisticated) style to Shakespeare's company, the more bombastic and stylized to Alleyn and the Lord Admiral's Men. And Armstrong (84) himself makes an important distinction: "a parody of certain phrases is not necessarily a parody of the style of the actor that may have delivered them." Even if Armstrong is right that Alleyn is not a specific target, Wilson is also surely right that *Hamlet* takes aim at playwrights, passages and plays, and rival playing companies who owned those plays— notably the Chamberlains' chief commercial rivals, The Admiral's Men.

Bednarz is also certainly correct (226) in echoing the scholarly consensus: "Hercules and his load too" (2.2.362–63) being carried away by the boys clearly relates the players to the Chamberlain's Men at the Globe, not the Admiral's. But Shakespeare was perfectly capable of glancing in two (or more) directions at once.

Alphonsus

We can see that targeting of the Admiral's in another, little-discussed *Hamlet* parallel to an Admiral's Men's play. A. C. Bradley (409) points out that Gonzago's opening "Full thirtie times" lines (3.2.148 ff):

> Full thirty times hath Phoebus' cart gone round
> Neptune's salt wash and Tellus' orbed ground,
> And thirty dozen moons with borrowed sheen
> About the world have times twelve thirties been
> Since love our hearts and Hymen did our hands
> Unite commutual in most sacred bands.

Closely mimic lines from Robert Greene's *Alphonsus King of Aragon* (Dyce 42–43):

> Thrice ten times Phoebus with his golden beams
> Hath compassed the circle of the sky,
> Thrice ten times Ceres hath her workmen hir'd,
> And fill'd her barns with fruitful crops of corn,
> Since first in priesthood I did lead my life.

Shakespeare further frames this passage as old-fashioned by converting *Alphonsus'* blank verse to rhyming couplets.

This echo is not so surprising. This 1587 play was published in 1599, and the Admiral's Men quite possibly revived it in August 1601. Following Greg, Chambers equates it with the "Mahomet" in Henslowe's papers, because "In iv. I Mahomet speaks out of a brazen head" (III 327), and a 10 March, 1598 inventory of Admiral's property includes "owld Mahametes head." On 2 and

4 August, 1601, we find Henslowe (in three entries) paying for "A parell," "mackynge of diuers things," and "mackynge of crownes & other things for mahewmet." And on 22 August, 1601, he paid forty shillings via Alleyn "for the Boocke of mahemett." (Foakes, 178, 180, 319.)

Alphonsus' triggering conflict is the usurpation of the crown of Aragon by the king's murderous younger brother—displacing his nephew and grand-nephew. Both want revenge and to reclaim the crown. Here Carinus, exiled son of the murdered king, is in conversation with his son Alphonsus. Alphonsus chides his father for inaction, quoting his father's own words back to him (Dyce 9):

> Next to *Alphonsus* should my father come,
> For to possesse the Diadem by right
> Of *Aragon,* but that the wicked wretch,
> His yonger brother, with aspiring mind,
> By secret treason robd him of his life,
> And me his sonne, of that which was my due.
>   . . .
> The ravening bird could never plague me worse;
> For ever since my mind hath troubled been
> Which way I might revenge this traitorous fact,
> And that recover which is ours by right.

Notably, as in *Hamlet*, the usurper gains the crown "by secret treason." This is singular to *Alphonsus* and *Hamlet*; in every previous revenge tragedy, Elizabethan or classical (and in Shakespeare's Belleforest source for *Hamlet*), the fact of the inciting murder is publicly known—though not necessarily (e.g., *Spanish Tragedy*) the culprit (Roth 2004).

So here in *Hamlet* we have the Gonzago duke/king's "Full thirtie times" passage, obtrusively and multiply framed as old-fashioned, adapted from a speech in an old play about a usurping uncle and younger brother, and secret murderer, that had been published in 1599 and delivered in earnest by the Admiral's Men just months before. And the speech being cribbed was written by Greene, who in *Groatsworth of Wit* (1592, republished 1596) had ridiculed Shakespeare ("Shake-scene") for his tragically overblown tragedy (his writing or his acting or both): "he is as well able to bombast out a blanke verse as the best of you." The "thirtie times" passage serves as a complex and telling, if decidedly posthumous, reply to that ridicule. (Greene died in 1592.)

Ben Jonson and The Admiral's Men

So *Hamlet* repeatedly makes allusion to Admiral's tragic properties and playing styles. But what about Jonson? In commenting upon the line in the eyases passage—"the boys' company's do them wrong to make them exclaim against their own succession" (2.2.351–52)—Steevens is probably not far wrong in saying, "I should have been very much surprised if I had *not* found Ben Jonson among the writers here alluded to." (IX 268) But there are further and more specific references to Jonson as actor and author outside the eyases passage.

Our records of Jonson's pre-*Hamlet* career connect him to Henslowe companies and their tragic productions at several turns—as an actor, script doctor, and author. I'll begin, as Jonson apparently did, with Jonson the actor. Fredson Bowers (1937, 392–406) points out only somewhat reductively that everything we know about Jonson's acting career comes from three sources:

- Henslowe's record of July 28, 1597 of a £4 loan to "Bengemen Johnson player," and the receipt on the same day of 3s 9d "of Bengemenes Johnsones Share." (Foakes, 238, 52.)
- Aubrey's anecdote that Jonson "acted and wrote, but both ill, at the Green Curtaine, a kind of nursery or obscure playhouse, somewhere in the suburbs (I thinke towards Shoreditch or Clarkenwell)—from J. Greenhill." (Clark 1898, 12)[11]
- The main source, "references in Thomas Dekker's *Satiro-Mastix*" to Horace/Jonson as a traveling player.

Bowers fails to note another source: a privy council letter of 15 August 1597 pertaining to *Isle of Dogs* (Jonson and Nashe, played by Pembroke's Men at the Swan before 28 July) cites Jonson as being "not only an actor but a maker of parte of the said plaie" (Chambers 1923 iv 323).

The 15 August privy council letter tells us that Jonson was an actor and author with Pembroke's during its run for Francis Langley at the Swan, beginning late February 1597 and ending 28 July with the inhibition on the theaters in response to the *Isle of Dogs* (Chambers 1923 II 132). Henslowe's 28 July entry also confirms Jonson as a player at that time. It may be only coincidence that on that day of the inhibition, we also find Jonson treating with Henslowe for a "share." (The 3s 9d could perhaps just be partial repayment for the 5s loan Henslowe had made him on 5 January.) Five other Pembroke's men (some of whom were former Admiral's men) made sharing convenants with Henslow over ensuing months, and the company started playing with the Admiral's at the Rose on 11 October (Foakes 60), when Henslowe got a new license (and Langley didn't). For a couple of months we find Henslowe combining receipts from Pembroke's and Admiral's, and paying for multiple plays ("books") for use by both companies (Foakes 71–72). By 1 December, he was no longer referring to them as separate companies. (Records of Pembroke peformances do continue, however, into 1600, including even one in London at the Rose 28/29 October, 1600. REED.)

Jonson's time as a traveling player may have been during the 28 July to 11 October inhibition; Pembroke's was paid for at least one provincial performance in that period, in Bristol, between 28 August and 10 September (£2 payment). But two other uncertainly dated performances are recorded 1596–97, in Oxford and Bath, plus six in 1598 (all after 25 June). So Jonson's sojourn could have been before or after Pembroke's 1597 run at the Swan, or both. (REED)

Whatever the precise dates, it's in Tucca's assaults on Horace-cum-Jonson in *Satiro-mastix* that we get a picture of what Jonson's sojourn with Pembroke's was like, and the roles he took. They point repeatedly to the most prominent of 1590s revenge tragedies—*Spanish Tragedy*—which is also most prominently related to *Hamlet*.

The Spanish Tragedy

The parallels and connections between *Hamlet* and *The Spanish Tragedy* are too ubiquitous and have been too widely discussed to require lengthy catalogue here. The play's connections with Jonson, however, do merit detailing. As imparted in Tucca's raillery at Horace in *Satiro-mastix*:

"I ha seene thy shoulders lapt in a Plaiers old cast Cloake, like a Slie knave as thou art: and when thou ranst mad for the death of Horatio : thou borrowedst a gowne of Roscius the Stager, (that honest Nicodemus) and sentst it home lowsie, didst not?" (I.ii.434–40)

"Goe by Ieronimo, goe by;" (I.ii.461)

"that same tiranicall-tongu'd rag-a-muffin Horace." (II.i.5)

"thou putst up a supplication to be a poore jorneyman player, and hadst beene still so, but that thou couldst not set a good face upon't: thou hast forgot how thou amblest (in leather pilch) by a play-wagon, in the high way, and took'st mad Ieronimoes part, to get service among the mimickes: and, when the Stagerites banisht thee into the Ile of Dogs, thou turn'dst ban-dog (villanous Guy) & ever since bitest, therefore I aske if th'ast been at Parris-garden, because thou hast such a good mouth." (IV.i.158–69)

"Dost roare bulchin? dost roare? th'ast a good rouncivall voice to cry Lanthorne and Candle-light." (IV.iii.89–91)

Tucca's "took'st mad Ieronimoes part, to get service among the mimickes" and "thou ranst mad for the death of Horatio" tell us that Jonson played Hieronimo in *Spanish Tragedy*, even that it was his first acting role with the company. A provincial tour with Pembroke's would explain his taking a lead role his first time out; Pembroke's could not have played *Spanish Tragedy* in London—it was an Admiral's property—and one could hardly imagine a noverint player replacing Alleyn in the lead role for the Admiral's on the Rose stage.

Spanish Tragedy ("Jeronymo" and similar in Henslowe's diaries) was revived by the Admiral's on 7 Jan 1597, and played a dozen times over the next two weeks (Foakes, 51–58). Henslowe's "ne" (new) notation on the 7 Jan 1597 *Spanish Tragedy* entry suggests to both Bowers (395) and Chambers (1923, III 396), following Greg, that the play underwent substantial revision at that time. (Foakes [55] says the "ne" designating a new play was "erased at some time" prior to Malone noting the erasure in 1821.) Multiple scholars have suggested (Cairncross, xxi–xxiv) that Jonson made those changes, and even that those changes constitute the "additions" found in the 1602 quarto edition. His role in that revision gains more likelihood given that he was in dealings with Henslowe on 5 January 1597, and we find Henslowe paying Jonson for additions to the play on 25 Sept. 1601 and 22 June 1602 (Foakes 238, 182, 203).

Dido and Aeneas

Wilson (1951 303) points to another reference in *Hamlet* to an Admiral's tragic property, saying "there can be little doubt that the [Hecuba] speech [Hamlet] quotes had some connection with the lost *Dido and Aeneas.*" Chambers disagrees: In his Arden *Hamlet* edition (1895), he devotes a long note (150–51) to the connection between the *Hamlet* speech and a different Dido/Aeneas play: Marlowe and Nashe's earlier and extant *Dido Queen of Carthage* (ca. 1591–93; printed 1594). He reprints the relevant Marlowe passage in Appendix E (197–98), and says the lines, "which [*Hamlet*] imitates," "were obviously meant to challenge comparison" with *Hamlet*'s Hecuba speech. He adds in *Elizabethan Stage* (1923, iii 427) that "There is nothing to connect [Marlowe and Nashe's *Dido Queen of Carthage*] with the Admiral's *Dido and Aeneas* of 1598."

Wilson, however (1971 184), accurately points out that "apart from one striking parallel [ll. 476–78]," the Hecuba speech "seems to owe nothing at all" to the Marlowe/Nashe version. That parallel (2.2.476–77):

But with the whiff and wind of his fell sword
Th' unnerved father falls.

Compare Marlowe:

Which he disdaining whiskt his sword about,
And with the wind thereof the King fell downe:

However, even that one parallel is actually missing in the published text. The linchpin, "wind," is an editorial emendation. The quarto prints "wound."

The emendation originates in Collier (1831, III 226), who in one of the more amusing justifications I've read for an emendation, admits that he made it *because* it echoes *Hamlet:* "Here I have substituted *wind* for *wound* (as it stands in the old copy), in conformity, probably (i.e. certainly), with the author's meaning, and with the following corresponding lines in *Hamlet*." Chambers, Wilson, and even Bowers in his Marlowe edition (1973, I 23), where his textual collation reveals the emendation, inexplicably reproduce Collier's fancy.

So aside from the general subject, the *Hamlet* Hecuba speech shows no relationship to Marlowe's mighty lines. (It's worth noting by contrast, Shakespeare's similar usage, penned in the same years as *Hamlet* and in similar Trojan setting, in *Troilus and Cressida*: "the fanne and winde of your faire sword" [5.3.41], along with *Hamlet's* "fanned and winnowed opinions." [5.2.153]) The chronology supports this non-connection: The Marlowe/Nashe play doesn't rear its head in extant records following its 1594 publication. *Dido and Aeneas* was played by the Admiral's Men in January 1598 (Foakes, 86).

Chambers (1923, iii 374), noting that Jonson received £1 (Foakes 73, 85) from Henslowe on Dec. 3, 1597 "upon a boocke wch he showed the plotte unto the company which he promysed to dd unto the company at crysmas next," says it's "possible that this was *Dido and Aeneas*, produced by the Admiral's on 8 Jan. 1598"—though he thinks it "more likely that *Dido and Aeneas* was taken over from Pembroke's repertory." I would only add that both could be true; Jonson was paid to revise the old Pembroke property for revival.

If the Hecuba speech is playing on any actual play, the most likely candidate is (Jonson's revision of?) *Dido and Aeneas*, and possibly Jonson's acting therein.

Richard III

Wilson (1971 204, following Simpson 658) also points out that Hamlet's line to the Lucianus player—"come, 'the croaking raven doth bellow for revenge'" (3.2.241–42; internal quotes here are the Oxford editors' additions)—is an obvious riff on a line from the anonymous old *True Tragedy of Richard III*: "The screeking Raven sits croking for revenge." It's worth printing that whole passage, as it rather epitomizes the class of old-fashioned tragedy that *Hamlet* is responding to throughout. "Revenge" is repeated sixteen times in seventeen lines (Brazil 1880–96).

Meethinkes their ghoasts comes gaping for revenge,
Whom I have slaine in reaching for a Crowne.
Clarence complaines, and crieth for revenge.
My Nephues bloods, Revenge, revenge, doth crie,

The headlesse Peeres comes preasing for revenge,
And every one cries, let the tyrant die.
The Sunne, by day shines hotely for revenge.
The Moone by night eclipseth for revenge.
The stars are turnd to Comets for revenge,
The Planets change their coursies for revenge.
The birds sign not, but sorrow for revenge.
The silly lambs sit bleating for revenge.
The screeking Raven sits croking for revenge.
Whole heads of beasts come bellowing for revenge.
And all, yea all the world I thinke,
Cries for revenge, and nothing but revenge.
But to conclude, I have deserved revenge.

It's not surprising to find this play—about revenge against a younger brother
who supplanted and murdered his nephew to usurp the crown—rearing its
head in *Hamlet*. Further evidence that the play might have been in Shakespeare's mind is the similarity between Claudius's contrition speech (3.3.36–72)
and Richard's in *True Tragedy* (Brazil 1402–23):

The goale is got, and golden Crowne is wonne,
And well deservest thou to weare the fame,
That ventured hast thy bodie and thy soule,
But what bootes Richard, now the Diademe
Or kingdome got, by murther of his friends,
My fearefull shadow that still followes me,
Hath sommond me before the severe judge,
My conscience witnesse of the blood I spilt,
Accuseth me as guiltie of the fact,
The fact, a damned judgement craves,
Whereas impartiall justice hath codemned.
Meethinkes the Crowne which I before did weare,
Inchast with Pearle and costly Diamonds,
Is turned now into a fatall wreathe,
Of fiery flames, and ever burning starres,
And raging fiends hath past their ugly shapes,
In studient lakes, adrest to tend on me,
If it be thus, what wilt thou do in this extremetie?
Nay what canst thou do to purge thee of they guilt?
Even repent, crave mercie for thy damned fact,
Appeale for mercy to thy righteous God,
Ha repent, not I, crave mercy they that list.
My God is none of mine.

As in *Hamlet*, the speech depicts a murderous usurper agonizing about
being judged in heaven, then giving up on his repentance. The strict verbal

parallels between the speeches lie in rather predictable usages, given the subject matter—kingdom, murder, judge/justice/judgment, blood, guilt, crown, repent, and mercy. But the stolen diadem appears in Hamlet's "A cutpurse of the empire and the rule, That from a shelf the precious diadem stole" (3.4.89–90), and a pearl ("union") in a crown—a quite singular trope—figures rather prominently in *Hamlet*'s final scene.

True Tragedie (composed sometime between 1585 and 1592) was entered in the stationer's register 19 June 1594, and printed the same year. There's no further explicit sign of it prior to *Hamlet*. But on 22 June, 1602, we find Henslowe paying (already noted re: *The Spanish Tragedy*): "unto Bengemy Johnsone . . . in earneste of a boocke called Richard Crockbacke & for new adicyons for Jeronymo the some of x[ll]" (Foakes, 203). This leads Wilson (1951 303) to think that *True Tragedy* "may have belonged to the repertory of the Admiral's Men," and that *Crookback* was a revision of that play. This would help explain why Shakespeare brought such an old play to mind (in two separate passages), seven years after its publication. Since Jonson had already received two pounds for *ST* additions the preceding 25 Sep, 1601, and with ten pounds (a reasonable-to-good paycheck for a whole new play) being paid out for those additions plus *Crookback*, both Chambers (1923, ii 179) and Wilson (1951, 302) believe that *Crookback* was largely complete by July of 1602.

Jonson was widely (self-)reputed to be a slow writer, as evidenced in *Parnassus, Satiro-mastix,* both the induction and the Apologetical Dialogue to *Poetaster,* and at least two postumous elegies, among others. So it's possible that he already had *True Tragedie* in hand in the fall of 1601—when Shakespeare was turning to his revision of *Hamlet.* (This group of playwrights at least sometimes knew what their competitor-compatriots were working on. A close-at-hand example is Jonson and Dekker's mutual awareness of, and proleptic responses to, their rivals' *Poetaster* and *Satiro-mastix* in that spring, summer, and fall of 1601.)

Among Our Best for Tragedy

Jonson was involved in other revenge tragedies for the Admiral's in these years as well; Henslowe paid him for work on *Page of Plymouth* (with Dekker, August/September, 1599; Foakes, 123) and *King Robert II of Scotland* (with Chettle, Dekker, "& other Jentellman," [Chambers, *E. S.* iii 428, presumes Marston], Sept. 1599; Foakes 124). Schleiner (34), also associates the "plotte" that Henslowe paid Jonson 20s for on 3 Dec 1597 (Foakes 73, 85) with the "playe boocke & ij ectes of a tragedie of Bengemenes plotte" for which Chapman received three pounds on 23 October 1598 (Foakes 100). (*Pace* Chambers 1923 167, 169.) In any case, there was *some* tragic plot by Jonson prior to October 1598, suggesting more than just rewrite work.

Given all this tragic work by Jonson over the period, two things stand out as odd—both in relation to that work, and in relation to each other: In Meres' 1598 *Palladis Tamia*, Jonson is included along with Shakespeare as one of "our best for Tragedie." But we know of no single-author tragedies by Jonson before *Sejanus* in 1603. None were included in his 1616 *Workes,* which he curated so carefully.

There seem to be two possible explanations: Either Meres is referring to rewrite work by Jonson, which seems unlikely, or Jonson authored or coauthored early tragedies like those discussed above, which were never mentioned or published, or have not survived, with his name attached. This suggests that Jonson was not proud of those early tragic efforts—either the script-doctor work or the presumed plays. Says Robert Evans (97–98), "perhaps Jonson, dissatisfied with the work [*Richard Crookback*], withdrew it from posterity's judgment. . . . Despite his early reputation as a competent writer of tragedies, and despite surviving records of his other works in this genre, *Sejanus* and *Catiline* are the only two tragedies he chose to print."

Many of Jonson's own statements support this. In his posthumously published *Discoveries*, for instance, he refers to "the *Tamerlanes*, and *Tamerchams* of the late Age, which had nothing in them but the *scenicall* strutting, and furious vociferation, to warrant them to the ignorante gapers." (Herford and Simpson VIII 587). Stern (107–10) provides a nice catalog of disdainful references in Jonson's plays to public theaters' "heavens" and "hells" and their associated spectacle, especially in tragedies. We find the elderly Jonson conveniently failing to acknowledge the tragic transgressions of his own blown youth. Given Jonson's famously thin skin and the dramatic culture of raillery here at the height of the *poetomachia*, this makes Jonson's tragic work an especially apt target for Shakespeare's allusions.

In *Hamlet,* we see a parody of all the bombastic tragedy Jonson had been (abashedly) involved in over preceding years, as both actor and author, and for which he had been satirized in *Satiro-mastix*, by the Chamberlain's Men, on the Globe stage, only months before.

Com'st Thou to Beard Me in Denmark?

Given Jonson's tragic history and his role in the poetomachia, and *pace* Wilson—who imagines the first player figured as Alleyn—it may be more reasonable to imagine the first player (in part) figured as Jonson. Jonson had been figured quite explicitly on London stages in at least half dozen plays over preceding years, including multiple times by the Chamberlain's (notably in *Satiro-mastix*), and including multiple instances in Jonson's own plays: as Asper in *Every Man Out* (1599, Chamberlain's), Criticus/Crites (Q/F) in

Cynthia's Revels (1600, Children of the Chapel), and Horace in *Poetaster* (1601, Children of the Chapel). It would have been extremely easy and in keeping with the theatrical times for the Shakespeare and the Chamberlain's to continue and expand on that apparently profitable tradition. Even a simple costume accoutrement might have served to make the identification obvious. And the means were to hand: *some* Chamberlain's actor had played Horace-cum-Jonson in *Satiromastix* in the months immediately preceding.

Figuring Jonson as a travelling player repeats and continues the image of Jonson/Horace from *Satiro-mastix*, ambling "(in leather pilch) by a play-wagon, in the high way." Now consider Hamlet's opening welcome to the players (2.2.425–27):

> Welcome, good friends.—O, my old
> friend! Thy face is valanced[12] since I saw thee last.
> Com'st thou to beard me in Denmark?

Compare this "bearding" to Tucca's sharper jibes at Jonson's skimpy beard in *Satiro-mastix*:

"thou thin-bearded Hermaphrodite", "thou has such a terrible mouth, that thy beard's afraide to peepe out" (I.ii.289)

"heere's the sweet visage of Horace; looke perboylde-face, looke; *Horace* had a trim long-beard, and a reasonable good face for a Poet." (V.ii.250–54)

We find another probable reference to Jonson's scanty beard in *Mucedorus*—c. 1590, with an edition "newly set forth" in 1598 and another in 1606. (It is extant in at least seventeen editions up to 1700, more than any other Elizabethan play.) "Envy" tells "Comedie":

> This scrambling Raven, with his needie Beard
> Will I whet on to write a Comedie

D. H. Craig (1990, 101) says "The writer must be referring to Jonson . . . and to Jonson's early satirical plays." The passage, which goes on to refer to the writer's troubles with "Magistrates"—presumably referencing *Isle of Dogs,* the Apologetical Dialogue to *Poetaster,* and/or *Eastward Ho!*—does not appear until the 1610 edition, but its composition date is uncertain.

Jonson himself seems to have been amused enough by a "companion's" proleptic epitaph to have recited it to Drummond (36):

> Here lies honest Ben,
> That had not a beard on his chen

All our portraits of Jonson show him with an acceptable beard, but portraits were often embellished, and they're all of an older Jonson. It's worth noting that the Chapel boys who Jonson wrote for used fake beards, often to comedic effect (Southern, 2009)—notably in Marston's *Antonia and Mellida* (1599) and *Antonia's Revenge* (1600), both of which have myriad parallels to *Hamlet* (the directions of influence are uncertain).

If the first player figures Jonson, we have here Burbage as Hamlet bearding Jonson for growing a beard since we "saw him last" (in *Satiro-mastix*), and asking, "have you come to beard me in *our own play*?" (*i.e., not* in a play picked up from Paul's Boys; rather "in a play by our own playwright"). The joke would be even richer if in addition to playing "the Ghost in his own Hamlet" (Rowe, 1709, for what that attestation is worth), Shakespeare also doubled the part of the first player. (Oldys' 1832 report of an account from Shakespeare's brother—that he saw Shakespeare playing old Adam in *As You Like It*—supports the possibility that Shakespeare played older men's parts.) We'd see a bearded player/Shakespeare *qua* Jonson being bearded by Hamlet/Burbage about his scanty beard. Metatheatricality, indeed.

To put him to his purgation

Hamlet strikes a distinctly "humourous" and Jonsonian note after the mousetrap—and glances at Jonson's purge of Marston/Crispinus' choler in *Poetaster*—when Guildenstern informs him that the king is "marvelous distemp'rd . . . with choler." (3.2.286–94)

> GUILDENSTERN The King, sir—
> HAMLET Ay, sir, what of him?
> GUILDENSTERN Is in his retirement marvellous distempered.
> HAMLET With drink, sir?
> GUILDENSTERN No, my lord, rather with choler.
> HAMLET Your wisdom should show itself more richer to
> signify this to his doctor, for for me to put him to his
> purgation would perhaps plunge him into far more
> choler.

The irony, if this suggestion is correct, is that Shakespeare in this whole players section is delivering exactly that purge. With Jonson figured as the player playing the king, we can find here Hamlet "mistaking" which king Guildenstern is referring to, just as he "mistakes" the cause of the king's distemper. To paraphrase: "for me to put the choleric Jonson to his purgation—to parody him further—would just make him more choleric."

Tucca egged Jonson on to further choler in exactly such manner in his *Satiro-mastix* epilogue to the audience (Penniman 394–95) written specifically for the Globe after the play's first playings by the Paul's Boys:[13] "if you set your hands and seals to this [clap for this play], Horace will write against it, and you may have more sport." Jonson did indeed plunge into more choler, provide more sport (which *Parnassus* later makes sport of), and "beray his credit" by replying in his Apologetical Dialogue to *Poetaster* (Roth 2002b).

We can find a few other jokes emerging if the first player is seen as (in part) a sendup of Jonson:

When Hamlet is giving his extended advice on acting, received with such admirable restraint by the first player, the player replies, "I hope we have reform'd that indifferently with us, sir." Here we have Jonson acknowledging that he's reformed his old-fashioned tragedizing . . . but only "indifferently."

If Jonson was involved in rewriting the Admiral's *Dido and Aeneas*, and Shakespeare did draw on that play for the Hecuba speech, we have an old-fashioned twist on Jonson's own words from that apprentice rewrite, coming from his own personified mouth.

It's tempting to suggest that Jonson had a hand in an Alphonsus rewrite as well, and influenced *Hamlet*'s "full thirtie times" speech, as it serves to explain Hamlet's "Wormwood, wormwood" comment in the midst of that speech—an interjection that goes unexplained by almost every editor,[14] In *Satiro-mastix* (II.ii.76–77) Horace/Jonson prophesies to himself, "Horace thy Poesie worm-wood wreathes shall weare." Hamlet's tossed-off line nicely fulfills that prophecy.

Likewise, Hamlet's "Pox, leave thy damnable faces and begin" (3.2.240–41) is doubly ironic in reference to a practice Jonson the actor was apparently known for, as revealed in two *Satiro-Mastix* passages: Tucca's "heere's thee coppy of thy countenance, by this will I learn to make a number of villanous faces" (v.ii.293–95), and the oath Horace is required to take: "you shall not sit in a Gallery, when your Comedies and Enterludes haue entred their Actions, and there make vile and bad faces at euerie lyne" (v.ii.340–42). Hamlet accuses the player (Jonson) of this, even as Hamlet is himself doing that exact thing, catcalling as his own "dozen or sixteen lines" (2.2.543) are being played. (This "damnable faces" line immediately precedes Hamlet's "croaking raven" line playing on *True Tragedie of Richard III*.)

This humorous treatment of Jonson by Shakespeare and the Chamberlain's Men makes sense in light of Jonson's relationship to that company. In 1598 he moved from Henslowe's factory to write *Every Man in His Humour* for the Chamberlain's Men (with Shakespeare in the cast), and *Every Man Out* in 1599. So the Chamberlain's were the vehicle for his first "breakout," single-author plays, which he chose to include in his *Workes*. Starting in 1600, though, pursuing his ambition for more genteel audiences, he abandoned them for the Children of the Chapel at Blackfriars. He used that venue to rail at his former cohorts, notably in *Poetaster*. As Jonson *qua* "Author" admits in the

Apologetical Dialogue, "Now for the Players, it is true, I tax'd 'hem." (Penniman 167.)

Parnassus Without the Prince?

There is one telling fact arguing against the conclusion that *Parnassus*'s purge happens in *Hamlet*. I find in *Parnassus* not a single allusion to *Hamlet*.[15] Nor, in their notes, do Smeaton, Arber, or Leishman, the play's primary editors—despite their magisterial cataloguing of allusions, antecedents, and parallels. Given *Hamlet*'s irresistible appeal to commenters going back at least to Nashe's 1589 reference, one would expect to find some scent or scintilla of *Hamlet* in *Parnassus*.

But we don't find any reference to *Troilus and Cressida* therein, either. (*Troilus* being the other most likely site for *Parnassus*'s purge.) In fact I can't find any reference, in the text or the editors' notes, to any then-unpublished play. The *Parnassus* author's knowledge of drama from the public stages seems to have been limited purely to dramatic literature, in fact largely to poetic miscellanies and commonplace books, and to gossip. Most of *Parnassus*'s second scene is devoted to two wits' gossiping about the recently published (1601) miscellany *Belvedere*, quoting snippets and snatches from that miscellany, and commenting on those snatches' authors.

The contempt expressed for public plays and players by characters throughout *Parnassus* may well reflect the *Parnassus* author's own Cantabrigian disdain. There are suggestions that he might have seen *Poetaster* and/or *Satiro-mastix* when they were played "privately" by the Chapel and Paul's boys, e.g., Kempe's "lusty humorous poets, you must untrusse" (1799), which Leishman says is "almost certainly an allusion" to *Satiro-Mastix*, not printed until 1602.[16] But I can find no indication that he had ever attended public plays. The adulation Gullio expresses for Shakespeare in *Returne I* (perhaps by a different author than *II Return*) names the sonnets, *Venus and Adonis* and *Rape of Lucrece*, plus *Romeo and Juliet* and *Richard III*. All of those works (excepting the sonnets, which were circulating in manuscript and were widely spoken of) had been in print for years when the *Returnes* were written, and were part of the general impression we find of Shakespeare among literateurs during the 1590s, as a "honey-tongued" and even frivolous writer of love poetry.

The *Parnassus* author appears to be quite similar to his characters Gullio and Amoretto—exquisitely sensitive to the literary fashions, rumors, and received opinions of the day, and an avid consumer of commonplace books like *Belvedere*, but largely ignorant of public plays. The university wits' preference for page over stage is embodied by Philomusus in his interchange with

Kempe (1796–97): "Indeed M. *Kempe* you are very famous, but that's as well for works in print as your parts in que."

The *Parnassus* author could easily have heard of the "purge" from others; we need have no expectation that he actually saw it being administered—that he ever saw *Hamlet,* or *Troilus and Cressida* for that matter.

Jonson's Response to the "Purge"

The chronology described here positions *Hamlet* as the culminating and concluding play in the *poetomachia.* No further plays entered that fray in ensuing months or years. Nevertheless, Jonson was not content to let matters lie. He composed the Apologetical Dialogue to *Poetaster*, presented it himself on stage as personified "Author," and suffered the legal consequences thereof (Roth 2002b).

Hamlet prophesies, upon hearing of the players' arrival, that "the King shall be welcome; his majesty shall have tribute of me. . . . the Humorous Man shall end his part in peace." (2.2.321–25). But Jonson doesn't seem to have taken the references to his tragical work as tribute, judging by the passage in the Apologetical Dialogue that many commenters have seen as referring to Shakespeare:[17]

> Onely amongst them, I am sorry for
> Some better natures, by the rest so drawne,
> To run in that vile line.

(137–39)

Jonson apparently viewed all that bearding as more of a purge. And the *Parnassus* author thought likewise—or at least represented William Kempe as thinking likewise. As "Author" (and speaker) of the Apologetical Dialogue's choleric response, Jonson does, in Kempe's words, "beray his [own] credit." Whether Jonson is responding to a "purge" in *Hamlet, Troilus*, both, another, or none at all, the humorous man does not end his part in peace.

Notes

1. References to *Parnassus* are to the Leishman edition. Shakespeare quotations and line references are to the 1986 modernized Oxford text, from the 2005 *Complete Works* (Wells et al.). *Poetaster* and *Satiro-mastix* references are to Penniman (1913). For all other quotations I have sought to use texts that are available online, except when it is necessary to reference a particular printed edition with no online reproduction. For secondary sources of evidence and analysis, credit for findings is attributed

to the originators wherever possible; later theorizations are not cited unless they contribute additional findings.

2. For detailed discussions of the poetomachian chronology, see Bednarz 9, and the thorough and cogent discussion in his Chronological Appendix, 265–76. Also Roth 2002b.

3. Examples include: Chambers, *E.S.* 4:40; P. Honan, *Shakespeare: A Life*, Oxford: Oxford University Press, 1998, p. 278; F. E. Shelling, *The complete plays of Ben Jonson*, London: J.M. Dent: 1910, p. 6 (available online at bibliomania. com/0/6/238/1090/13807/6/frameset.html).

4. Regarding Q1, MacDonald P. Jackson has examined "the scattered passages that are textually almost identical with their counterparts in Q2 and read like mature Shakespearean verse." (91 lines: ll. 2.110–25, 2.155–64 + 166–69, 4.15–32, 5.8b–18, 5.41–53, 7.31–51, and 7.340–48 in the modernized Thompson/Taylor Arden 3 Q1 text.) Multiple stylistic analyses convincingly support the dating of those passages' composition to the turn of the century.

5. Gregory Semenza sees *The Spanish Tragedy* as seminal in this development: "it establishes a dramatic mode consistent with the increasing epistemological indeterminacy of post-Reformation European thought and, in the process, establishes its most basic tool—theatrical self-awareness and/or self-scrutiny—as the basis of the early modern, and perhaps the modern, theatrical experience."

6. This play's depiction of a woman who'd murdered her husband confessing in response to a dramatic portrayal of her act—in a play that contains three dumb shows—may have been the proximate impetus for the mousetrap in *Hamlet*, though other similar accounts were in circulation, both contemporary and ancient.

7. This passage might serve as an example of the parodic view emerging earlier; some editors believe on rather tenuous grounds that it was composed as early as 1588–90. But we know from the title page of its 1599 edition (stationers' register: 17 Nov, 1599) that it had been "lately diuerse times acted by the right Honorable, the Lord Chamberlaine his Seruantes." The induction's ridicule of old-fashioned staginess rather undercuts the primary evidence for an earlier composition date: the play's use of old-fashioned "structure of the blank verse, the introduction of allegorical personages, the chorus and elaborate dumb-show before each act." (Hopkinson 1893, xiv) It is one of those allegorical personages, in fact ("Comedy"), who delivers the tirade against such musty stuff.

8. Marchette Chute (227) expresses a similar view.

9. Thorndike (1902) provides an admirably complete catalog of *Hamlet*'s relationships to earlier Elizabethan revenge tragedies.

10. Tom Rutter's *Shakespeare and the Admirals Men: Reading across Repertories on the London Stage, 1594–1600* offers many examples of the complex and multidirectional awareness and cross-influences between Shakespeare and Admirals Men dramatists in the years preceding the first playings of *Hamlet* as we know it. The book does not include a section on tragedies, however, and *Hamlet* is only mentioned a few times in passing.

11. Aubrey is typically amusing here in his handling of facts. Here's the full (and unlike Bowers', accurate) quotation from *Brief Lives*: "Then he came over into England, and acted and wrote at *The Green curtaine* but both ill, a kind of nursery or obscure Play house, somewhere in the Suburbes (I thinke towards Shoreditch, or Clarkenwell)." To quote Miles' *Life* of Jonson (p. 27): "The only theatre adjacent to Clerkenwell was the Red Bull, famous for its horrible 'tear-throat' style of acting, while the Curtain is in Shoreditch." (The Red Bull did not open until about 1605, long after Jonson switched from acting to playwriting.) Aubrey changes the color and conflates them into the "Green curtaine."

12. F1 prints val-/anct, Q2 valiant, Q1 vallanced. Every modern edition prints "valenced" with the interpretation of draped hence bearded. This is addressed to Hamlet's "old friend" the first player, not to the boy who plays women's parts. (Hamlet turns to him next with "what my young Lady . . . your Ladyship is nearer to heauen than when I saw you last.")

13. Tucca's "gentle-folkes (that walke I'the galleries)," "two pence a piece," and "two penny tenants" all tell us that we're hearing an epilogue presented at the Globe. His "when once (in an assembly of friers) I railde . . . " tells us that the Paul's Boys performance of *Satiro-mastix* happened prior. This in turn tells us that the published text came from the Globe, and that it was revised—at least by adding this epilogue—after it was played by the boys.

14. "Wormwood, Wormwood" is the F1 reading. The only gloss in the hamlet-works.org variorum explaining this line's import is Andrews' (1993) somewhat satisfying paraphrase: "that's the bitter truth." No other cited editor has offered an explanation. (Two most diligent annotators—Furness and Jenkins—don't even foot-note it.) The line (with the speech prefix: "*Ham.* That's wormwood") is printed marginally in Q2, adjacent to Baptista's "None wed the second, but who kild the first"—the only such instance of a marginally printed speech in that edition (or any press variants of that edition). It may be insignificant. Collier, in his 1843 edition, suggests that "The object might be to save room in the printing." But that surmise is deleted in his 1858 edition. No other editor cited in the *Hamletworks* commentary or textual notes, or that I'm aware of, has essayed an opinion on the meaning or import of this marginality.

15. One possible exception: the Recorder in *Parnassus* says that a commoner-turned-gentleman's "mawe must be Capon crambd each day" (1173), which is remin-sicent of Q1 *Hamlet*'s "the chameleon's dish, not capon-crammed" (1950). But it's not really so singular; "capon" turns up with variants of "cram" fairly frequently around this period in searches of Early English Books Online.

16. *Troilus*'s two 1609 quarto verions make it impossible to know where the *Parnassus* author might have seen the play. The "Quarto a" title page claims publication "As it was acted by the Kings Maiesties seruants at the Globe." That claim is absent on the title page of the amended Quarto b, which includes an additional leaf containing a preface, "A never writer, to an ever reader," which proclaims, "you have here a new play, never stal'd with the Stage, never clapper-clawed with the palmes of the vulgar." Peter Alexander (1928) examines the publication details, and suggests the play was (first) performed at, or even comissioned by, one of the inns of court. That theory is supported by Elton and Arlidge, both 2000.

17. Bednarz (236–38) demonstrates that only two of the Chamberlain's Men go untaxed in *Poetaster*: Shakespeare and William Sly.

Works Cited

Alexander, Peter. 1928. "Troilus and Cressida, 1609." *Library*, Vol.9 (3). 267.

Arlidge, Anthony. 2000. *Shakespeare and the Prince of Love*. Londong, Giles de la Mar. 108.

Armstrong, William A. 1954. "Shakespeare and the Acting of Edward Alleyn." *Shakespeare Survey* 7. 82–89.

Bradley, A. C. 1904. *Shakespearean Tragedy*. London. MacMillan and Co.

Brazil, Robert, ed. *The True Tragedy of Richard III*. 2005. elizabethanauthors.org/truetragedy02.htm

Bowers, Fredson. 1937. "Ben Jonson the Actor." *Studies in Philology*. 34, 3. July 1937. 392–406.

———— 1973. *The Complete Works of Christopher Marlowe.* Two volumes. Cambridge. Cambridge University Press.

Brooke, Tucker. 1911. *The Tudor Drama: A History of English National Drama to the Retirement of Shakespeare.* Boston. Houghton Mifflin. books.google.com/books?id=nfTQAAAAMAAJ

Cairncross, Andrew S. Ed. 1967. *The First Part of Hieronimo and The Spanish Tragedy.* Lincoln. University of Nebraska Press.

Chambers, E. K. 1895. Ed. *The Tragedy of Hamlet, Prince of Denmark.* Boston. D. C. Heath.

———— 1923. *The Elizabethan Stage.* Four volumes. Oxford. Clarendon Press.

Chute, Marchette, 1949. *Shakespeare of London.* New York. Dutton.

Clark, Andrew, 1989. Ed. Andrew Clark. *'Brief Lives,' chiefly of Contemporaries, set down by John Aubreay, between the Years 1669 & 1696.* Oxford. Clarendon Press.

Collier, John Payne. 1831. *History of English dramatic poetry to the time of Shakespeare.* London. John Murray.

Craig, D. H. Ed. *Ben Jonson: The Critical Heritage 1599–1798.* London: Routledge, 1990.

Drummond, William. 1842. *Notes of Ben Jonson's Conversations William Drummond Of Hawthornden January M DC XIX.* London: The Shakespeare Society. books.google.com/books?id=ubHPBcMk2OMC

Duncan-Jone, Katherine. 2001. *Ungentle Shakespeare.* London. The Arden Shakespeare/Thomson Learning.

Dyce, Alexander. 1831. Ed. *The Dramatic Works of Robert Green.* Vol II. London, William Pickering. books.google.com/books?id=0mtMAAAAcAAJ

Elton, W.R. 2000. *Shakespeare's Troilus and Cressida and the Inns of Court Revels.* Ashgate (Routlege 2016).

Erne, Lucas. 2003. *Shakespeare as Literary Dramatist.* Cambridge. Cambridge University Press.

Evans, Robert C. 1990. "More's 'Richard III' and Jonson's 'Richard Crookback' and Sejanus.'" *Comparative Drama*, 24, no. 2 (Summer 1990): 97–132. jstor.org/stable/41153453

Farmer, J.S. 1912. ed. *A Warning for Fair Women.* Computer transcription at archive.org/details/warningforfairwo00unknuoft.

Foakes, R. A. 2002. *Henslowe's Diary.* 2d Ed. Cambridge. Cambridge University Press.

Greg, W. W. 1926. *Alphonsus King of Aragon.* ed. for the Malone Society. Oxford. Oxford University Press.

Gurr, Andrew. 1963. "Who Strutted and Bellowed?" *Shakespeare Survey* 16. 95–102.

Herford, Charles Harold, and Percy Simpson. 1925. *Ben Jonson: The Man and his Work.* Vol. 4, corrected 1986 edition. Oxford. Clarendon Press.

Hopkinson, A. F.. 1893. A. F. Hopkinson, ed. *A Warning for Fair Women.* London. M. E. Sims.

Jackson, MacDonald P. 2018. "Vocabulary, Chronology, and the First Quarto (1603) of *Hamlet.*" *Medieval and Renaissance Drama in England*, vol. 31, pp. 17+.

Kirschbaum, Leo. 1937. "The Date of Shakespeare's Hamlet." *Studies in Philology* 34, no. 2 (Apr., 1937).

Knutson, Roslyn. 1995. "Falconer to the Little Eyases: A New Date and Commercial Agenda for the 'Little Eyases' Passage in Hamlet," *Shakespeare Quarterly* 46 (Spring, 1995): 1–31.

Leishman, J. B. 1949. ed. *The Three Parnassus Plays.* London. Ivor Nicholson & Watson.

Lodge, Thomas. 1596. *Wits Miserie and the Worlds Madnesse.* London. Adam Islip. In: *The Complete Works of Thomas Lodge.* Vol. 4. Hunterian Club. 1883.

McKerrow, Ronald B. 1905. ed. *The Works of Thomas Nashe.* London, A.H. Bullen.

Oldys, William. 1862. *A Literary Antiquary.* archive.org/stream/literaryantiquar00 oldyiala

Penniman, Josiah H. 1897. *The War of the Theatres.* Boston. Ginn & Company.

———— 1913. *Poetaster By Ben Jonson and Satiro-mastix By Thomas Dekker.* Boston. D. C. Heath.

Potts, Abbie Fidlay. 1954. "Cynthia's Revels, Poetaster, and Troilus and Cressida." *Shakespeare Quarterly,* 5, no. 3 (Summer 1954): 297–302.

REED. Records of Early English Drama. reed.library.utoronto.ca/content/ earl-pembrokes-players

Roth, Steve. 2002a "Hamlet as The Christmas Prince: Certain Speculations on *Hamlet,* the Calendar, Revels, and Misrule." *Early Modern Literary Studies* 7, no. 3 (January 2002): 5.1–89 shu.ac.uk/emls/07-3/2RothHam.htm.

———— 2002b "How Ben Jonson Berayed His Credit: Parnassus, Shakespeare's 'Purge,' and The War of the Theatres". *Ben Jonson Journal,* Fall 2002, 249. Ungated version available at princehamlet.com/jonson beray.html.

———— 2004. "Who Knows Who Knows Who's There? An Epistemology of *Hamlet* (Or, What Happens in the Mousetrap)". *Early Modern Literary Studies* 10, no. 2 (September 2004): 3.1–27. purl.oclc.org/emls/10-2/rothepis.htm.

Rutter, Tom. 2017. *Shakespeare and the Admirals Men: Reading across Repertories on the London Stage, 1594–1600.* Cambridge. Cambridge University Press.

Schleiner, Louise. "Latinized Greek Drama in Shakespeare's Writing of *Hamlet.*" *Shakespeare Quarterly,* 41, no. 1 (Spring, 1990): 29–48

Semenza, Gregory M. Colón. "The Spanish Tragedy and metatheatre." In *The Cambridge Companion to English Renaissance Tragedy,* ed. Emma Smith and Garrett A Sullivan. Cambridge: Cambridge University Press, 2010.

Simpson, Richard. "An Allusion in 'Hamlet'" *The Academy,* 19 Dec 1874. https:// babel.hathitrust.org/cgi/pt?id=mdp.39015018430937;view=1up;seq=802

Smeaton, Oliphant. 1905 ed. *The Return from Parnassus or The Scourge of Simony.* J.M. Dent and Co. Aldine House, London. play.google.com/books/reader?printsec= frontcover&output=reader&id=9VkqAAAAMAAJ&pg=GBS.PR5.

Smith, Emma. 2010. *The Cambridge Companion to English Renaissance Tragedy.* Cambridge. Cambridge University Press.

Southern, Antonia. 2009. "Beards" (letter). *The Times Literary Supplement.* 23 October 2009, 6.

Steevens, George, and Samuel Johnson, 1793. *The plays of William Shakespeare.* Fifteen volumes. London. T. Longman, etc.

Stern, Tiffany. 2010. "The Globe theatre and the open-air ampitheatres" in *Ben Jonson in Context,* Julie Sanders, ed. Cambridge. Cambridge University Press.

Thompson, Ann and Taylor, Neil. 2006, eds. *Hamlet.* Vol. 1. London. Arden Shakespeare/ Thomson Learning.

Thorndike, Ashley H. "The Relations of *Hamlet* to Contemporary Revenge Plays." PMLA,Vol. 17, no. 2 (1902): 125–220

Wallace, Charles William. 1908. *The Children of the Chapel at Blackfriars, 1597–1603.* The University Of Nebraska In University Studies And Reprinted Therefrom For The Author. books.google.com/books?id=lrwUAQAAIAAJ

Wells, Stanley, et al. 2005. *The Oxford Shakespeare: The Complete Works.* Oxford, Oxford University Press.

Wilson, J. D. 1951. *What Happens in Hamlet.* 3rd ed. Cambridge. Cambridge University Press.

———— 1971. Ed. *The Tragedy of Hamlet, Prince of Denmark.* 2nd ed. (first edition 1934; second edition first printed 1936; revised 1954; first paperback edition 1968). Cambridge, Cambridge University Press.

Articles

Heywood's *Ages* and *The Tempest*

Douglas Arrell

Thomas Heywood's five *Ages* plays, *The Golden Age*, *The Silver Age*, *The Brazen Age*, and the two-part *Iron Age*, were the blockbuster action films of their time. Featuring Jupiter and Hercules as superheroes in the first three plays of the cycle, they portray innumerable scenes of violence, including battles, group brawls, and one-on-one fights, with and without weapons. They also contain some of the most blatantly erotic scenes in early modern drama, notably in the seduction/rapes of Calisto and Danae. There is a great deal of spectacle, including various forms of flying and much use of fire and fireworks. There are huge casts, many requiring exotic costumes as gods and goddesses, centaurs, rivers, Amazons, babies, devils, Fates, and the Moon. Based primarily on William Caxton's *The Recuyell of the Historyes of Troye* and Ovid's *Metamorphoses*, they constitute the most ambitious theatrical undertaking of their time.[1]

The first three *Ages* were written and produced at about the same time as *The Tempest*. According to Heywood's preface to *The Golden Age* (SR 14 October 1611), by the time it was written the first three *Ages* had all "adventured the Stage" (A2r). *The Tempest* was produced at Court on 1 November 1611, and most scholars think it was relatively new at that time (Kermode xxi–xxii). The later *Ages* were apparently jointly produced by Heywood's company, The Queen's Men (or Queen Anne's Men), and Shakespeare's company, The King's Men. The evidence for this collaboration lies in two quotations. According to the Revels Accounts, on January 12–13, 1612, the "Queens players and the Kings men" played before the Queen and the Prince at Greenwich "the Siluer Aiedg: and ye next night following Lucr<e>c" (Streitberger 49).[2] In his preface to the two *Iron Age* plays, published in 1632 but probably referring to productions of about 1612, Heywood says: "these were the Playes often (and not with the least applause,) Publickely Acted by two Companies, uppon one Stage at once, and have at sundry times thronged three seuerall Theaters" (A4v). Since the King's and Queen's companies jointly presented *The Silver Age* at Court, one could guess that they were the two companies that produced the *Iron Age* plays; presumably the three theaters were the Globe, the Red Bull, and Blackfriars. It thus seems that at least some of the *Ages* plays were done as joint productions of the two companies.[3] The huge casts and production demands of the plays make this co-production arrangement seem likely. While the full extent and nature of this collaboration are unclear, it is worth exploring what the involvement of his company in this mammoth enterprise might have meant for Shakespeare while he was writing *The Tempest*.

In *Shakespeare and Ovid* Jonathan Bate points out a number of similarities between *The Tempest* and *The Silver* and *Brazen Ages* (253–54, 260–63). He leaves it open as to who might have influenced whom. Following earlier scholars, I have argued elsewhere that these plays of Heywood's are adaptations of *1* and *2 Hercules*, first presented by the Admirals Men in 1595 ("Heywood"); the features Bate cites would all have been in these earlier plays as I reconstruct them.[4] If my hypothesis is correct, then, there is no doubt that the influence is from Heywood to Shakespeare. But several features of the two works seem to make it clear that Shakespeare was the imitator. The most obvious similarity between *The Silver Age* and *The Tempest* is the presence in both plays of the three goddesses, Juno, Iris, and Ceres. As Bate points out, Ceres' long speech and song in the masque scene in *Tempest* resemble Ceres' long speech in *Silver Age*, although there are no close verbal parallels; in both cases Ceres' appearance is associated with a chorus of swains and their female partners, but in *The Silver Age* they sing while in *The Tempest* they dance. The three goddesses are central figures in the action of *The Silver Age*; they are minor figures in *The Tempest*, in a section of the play that could have been added late in the play's creation. Is it really likely that Heywood conceived the entire plot of his play in response to Shakespeare's brief scene? In fact, we know he did not, since the play continues a story begun in *The Golden Age* and mirrors one he had already portrayed in his poem *Troia Britanica*, published in 1609. For most part the *Ages* follow this work; the scenes of Proserpine's rape and Ceres' attempt to rescue her, for example, are closely anticipated in it (P1v–Q1v). Only the lingering effects of bardolatry, which assumes that the "minor playwrights" of the period could never have influenced the sublime Shakespeare, can have led Bate to question whether Heywood was the originator in this case.

Presumably, the costumes of the three goddesses were created for the earlier work and through to the cooperative arrangement between the two companies were reused for Shakespeare's play. Juno and Iris are very suitable figures to appear in a betrothal masque such as that in *The Tempest*. They have key roles in Ben Jonson's wedding masque *Hymenaei* (1606), which may have influenced the form the masque takes in this play (see Gurr "Another"). Juno is the goddess of marriage and Iris her invariable assistant. Ceres, however, is a bit less appropriate. It has often been suggested that she represents the future fertility of the happy couple (e.g., Allen 183–84), but her purview as a goddess is very much that of agricultural, not human, fertility. Metaphorically it may be reasonable for her to wish on this aristocratic, soon-to-be-urban couple "Earths increase, foyzon plenty, / Barnes and Garners, never empty" (*Norton Facsimile First Folio* ll. 1771–72), but a similar blessing is much more appropriately bestowed in *The Silver Age* upon a group of swains—that is, farm workers. The availability of Ceres' costume could certainly have played a role in Shakespeare's choice of this goddess for his masque. The mythological costumes in masques could be extremely expensive. The costumes for the 15 Olympian Knights in *The Masque of the Inner Temple and Gray's Inn*, presented in 1613 in honor of the wedding of Princess Elizabeth and the Elector Palatine (when *The Tempest* was also presented) were said to cost "above a hundred marks" each (about £67, for a total of £1005) (Edwards 128); of the outrageous total cost of *Oberon* (1611) of £2100, £1100 was for costumes (Hosley 48). While it is true that a theater company could not spend such sums on costumes, in these plays clearly destined for Court performance the costumes could not be too obviously cheap. Henslowe's *Diary* provides plenty of evidence that even ordinary theater costumes were very expensive (see Gurr *Shakespearean* 194). These single-use, one-of-a-kind dresses in the masque style must have been particularly so. Saving on a costume would be a far from insignificant reason for Shakespeare to choose to include Ceres in his masque.

The fact that both companies required the same three costumes for plays produced at about the same time is supporting evidence that they were engaged in a cooperative enterprise. Given the high cost of costumes, it is not believable that two companies would simultaneously pay for their own set of these very specialized dresses, in particular that the King's Men would have them constructed for one short scene. Alternative explanations do not seem likely, such as that each company was unaware that the other company was coincidentally using the same costumes, or that the two companies were competing to impress audiences with the best Juno, Iris, and Ceres outfits. By far the most likely explanation is that they were sharing these resources.

There is just a possibility that they also shared another highly specialized costume, and that this collaboration might help explain a small puzzle about Shakespeare' play. Caliban somewhat resembled a fish. This assertion has been questioned by some critics, who would rather see him as entirely human; they suggest that his fishiness consisted solely in his smell (see Vaughan and Vaughan 33). Although in his first scene Caliban's fishy smell is emphasized, he is still said to have fins: "Leg'd like a man; and his Finnes like Armes" (ll. 1072–73). In the later references to his fishiness there is no suggestion of smell. Trinculo says: "why, thou debosh'd Fish thou, was there ever man a Coward, that hath drunk so much Sacke as I to day? wilt thou tell a monstrous lie, being but halfe a Fish, and halfe a Monster?" (ll. 1376–79); later Antonio says: "one of them / Is a plaine Fish, and no doubt marketable" (ll. 2260–61).

But why should he resemble a fish? He shows no particular affinity to water. As a child of a witch and perhaps the devil, one would certainly expect him to be a monster, but the fish element seems inexplicable. In *The Brazen Age*, Hercules confronts a sea monster who is about to devour Hesione. Although he gives a graphic description of it as it approaches, all there is when it arrives is the laconic stage direction: *"Hercules kils the Sea-Monster"* (F1v). The most likely way that this event was staged was that an actor entered dressed as half a monster and half a fish and was killed by Hercules. We do not know for certain that the fight was done in this way, of course, but if there was a sea monster costume used in *The Brazen Age*, we would expect, given that it was highly specialized and no doubt expensive, it would be used for the monster in *The Tempest*. If so (and I admit this is a major "if"), it seems that this is another case, like that of Ceres, in which Shakespeare allowed the availability of the costume to influence his writing of the play, in this case in giving fish-like characteristics to Caliban.

In writing his masque Shakespeare may have taken advantage of the audience's likely familiarity with the previously produced *Silver* and *Brazen Ages*. Using the same costumes for the same goddesses would mean that many audience members would recognize them from the earlier play and this familiarity would help make the sudden appearance of these exotically dressed figures in *The Tempest* less jarring. Ceres' reference to "The meanes, that duskie *Dis,* my daughter got" (l. 1748) would not be lost on audiences who had just seen Pluto's abduction of Proserpine in *The Silver Age*; they may have known who "Marses hot Minion" (l. 1758) was from the Mars/Venus scene in *The Brazen Age*.

In a recent note in *Notes and Queries*, I proposed that the King's Men borrowed the eagle used to fly Jupiter in *Cymbeline* from the Queen's Men's production of *The Golden Age* ("Jupiter"). It seems likely that Shakespeare and his company also borrowed the flying technology of the Queen's Men for *The Tempest*. In the masque scene Juno is said to "descend" some 30 lines before she speaks. It has been suggested, most recently by David Mann, that this stage direction merely indicates that Juno comes down stairs; these might be portable stairs brought on stage for the purpose or tiring-house stairs if this is merely a promptbook warning to the actor. Mann points to Ceres' line "I know her by her gate [gait]" (l. 1763) to prove that Juno walks in (197). But "gate" is a rhyming word and therefore a weak one on which to base a theory; poets often stretch a point to find a rhyme. In any case, "gate" could refer to Juno's walk from her car to join the other two goddesses or merely to her general bearing as she enters (see Jowett 117–18). The facts that Iris refers to Juno just as she begins her descent and that she says "here Peacocks flye amaine" (l. 1732), as if pointing to peacocks portrayed on Juno's vehicle, suggest that Juno is visible from that point. The time to speak 30 lines would necessitate a very slow walk indeed down stairs, but it would not be too long for a gradual descent from the heavens; she might in any case remain hovering for a time in mid-air, as John Jowett suggests (117).

In *The Silver Age* Juno and Iris "*descend from the heavens*" on their first entrance (F1r). It is surprising that Mann, in his discussion of flying in *The Silver Age*, does not mention this scene, which is hard to envision other than as a lowering of the boy actors on a chariot-like car. It is true, as he says, that flying is surprisingly rare in the stage directions of the extant plays of the period, but he tries too hard to explain away the very clear instances of it in the first three *Ages* plays, created as he admits by a playwright/actor who was fully aware of what was practical in the three theaters in which they may have been performed, as well as at Court. We do not know exactly how the flying was managed, but discussion of the topic seems often to underestimate the resourcefulness of theater workers. As C. Walter Hodges says in his common-sense discussion of early modern stage effects, "a nation of skilled timber-framers and shipwrights" would be equal to the task of devising an apparatus to lower an actor relatively noiselessly from roof to stage (126). Given the flying expertise demonstrated by the Queen's Men throughout the first three *Ages*, often at climactic moments that seem designed to dazzle with spectacle, one cannot doubt that Juno on her dramatic first entrance really did fly here. In this co-production arrangement, *The Silver Age* Juno could have been portrayed by the same actor who subsequently played Juno in *The Tempest*; no doubt the same peacock-emblazoned car was used. The fact that the King's Men were in a position to borrow the flying technology of the Queen's company when Shakespeare wrote *The Tempest* supports the belief that Juno does fly in this play.[5]

The fact of the companies' joint involvement in the production of *The Silver Age* also helps answer another question about *The Tempest*. Does Ariel fly when appearing as a harpy? The stage direction reads: "*Thunder and Lightning. Enter Ariell (like a Harpey) claps his wings upon the Table, and with a quient deuice the Banquet vanishes*" (ll. 1583–85). While the description may not appear to suggest that he flies in, one must bear in mind that this stage direction was probably formulated by the scribe Ralph Crane at the time of the publication of the First Folio and may reflect the way the scene was staged at that time (Jowett 107–15).[6] Why would Shakespeare make Ariel's disguise that of a winged creature if he was merely to walk on stage? As Jowett points out, Ariel's reference to "this lower world" (l. 1587) suggests that he comes from the heavens (119). J. C. Adams contends forcefully that Ariel must have flown in this scene. He presents a number of arguments that admittedly rely heavily on Crane's directions; for example, he suggests that his exit ("*He vanishes in Thunder*" [l. 1616]) implies that he either sank through a trap door or flew up out of sight, and that the latter was more likely given Ariel's airy nature (410–14). He also relies on the basic argument that a flying harpy would simply be more effective; he imagines that:

after casting his spell upon the sword-arms of his enemies he scornfully flapped his wings and rose a few feet to a more elevated position in mid-air. There, dominating the stage, and with all eyes focused upon him, he could most effectively deliver Prospero's message. (413)

The Silver Age has a similar scene in which a winged character, probably played by a boy actor, flies. Responding to Ceres' call to "speake from the clouds," Mercury, according to the stage direction, *"flies from above"* (H1r). As Ariel-as-harpy may have done, he flies in, addresses one speech to those below, and then (presumably) flies out again. The technology of flying a single winged actor is quite different from that of lowering someone on a cloud or a car. It would have to involve some kind of harness like that used in modern stage flying. This technique seems to have existed at the time since there was a "flying Boye" in an entertainment at Salisbury House in 1608 (see Mann 195; Orgel and Strong 1.123). The fact that this technology was used in *The Silver Age,* and through the cooperative arrangement of the two companies was available to Shakespeare, strengthens the case that Ariel did fly in this scene in *The Tempest.*

Shakespeare apparently did not have a written source for *The Tempest.* If he was inventing his play while his company was rehearsing or performing the first three *Ages*, it is likely he picked up a few of their features. For example, Heywood's description in *The Golden Age* of Danae being set adrift in a "mastless" boat with the infant Perseus (K1v) surely is the source of this motif in *The Tempest.*[7] The fact that her father, Acrisius, has his kingship usurped by his brother, and is later restored to his throne by Perseus, might also have played into Shakespeare's thinking. In addition to borrowing Mercury's flying, Shakespeare may also have been influenced by his personality in *The Silver Age*. Although he appears only briefly, in his reply to Ceres Mercury describes how "as swift as lightning/I search't the regions of the upper world,/And every place above the firmament" (H1r). He goes on to describe the many parts of the cosmos that he visited in search of the abducted Proserpine, in a manner that reminds one of Ariel's boasting of his industriousness, all performed in an instant.[8]

But the most interesting possible borrowing is in the epilogue to *The Tempest*. Here are the last lines of *The Silver Age*, after the climactic scene in Hades, spoken by Homer, who is the chorus figure in the play:

> Our full Sceane's wane, the Moones arraignment ends,
> Jove and his mount, Pluto and his descends.
> Poore HOMER's left blinde, and hath lost his way,
> And knowes not if he wander or go right,
> Unlesse your favours their cleare beames display.
> But if you daine to guide me through this night,
> The acts of Hercules I shall pursue,

And bring him to the thrice-raz'd wals of Troy :
His labors and his death Il'e shew to you.
But if what's past your riper judgements cloy,
Here I have done : if ill, too much : if well,
Pray with your hands guide HOMER out of hell.

(L1v)

Although it is not labelled as such, clearly this is an epilogue. Its resemblance to the epilogue of *The Tempest* is obvious:

Now my Charmes are all ore-throwne,
And what strength I have's mine owne.
Which is most faint : now 'tis true
I must be heere confinde by you,
Or sent to Naples, *Let me not*
Since I have my Dukedome got,
And pardon'd the deceiver, dwell
In this bare Island, by your Spell,
But release me from my bands
With the helpe of your good hands :
Gentle breath of yours my Sailes
Must fill, or else my project failes,
which was to please : Now I want
Spirits to enforce : Art to inchant,
And my ending is despaire,
Unlesse I be reliev'd by praier
Which pierces so, that it assaults
Mercy it selfe, and frees all faults.
As you from crimes would pardon'd be,
Let your Indulgence set me free.

(ll. 2322–41)

A search of the last lines of all the extant plays usually dated to the decade previous to 1611 (not too difficult a task thanks to *Literature Online*) did not uncover another case in which the speaker asks the audience to free him from the milieu of the play with its applause. The motif works particularly well in the case of Heywood's play since the last scene occurs in a highly undesirable place, Hades, and as Homer is blind, his request that the audience guide him with its clapping is appropriate.[9] The motif works somewhat less well in the epilogue to *The Tempest*. At the end of the play Prospero announces that all will be sailing to Naples, and so there is no question of his being confined on the island, as the phrase "or sent to Naples" rather lamely acknowledges. He has promised that Ariel will provide "auspicious gales" and so the audience's help does not seem to be needed. These cavils do not, of course, obviate the poetic and thematic importance that many critics have attached to the epilogue, whether in the earlier view that it is Shakespeare's "farewell to the theatre" or in the more recent one that it is a revelation of his religious beliefs.[10] Some critics have doubted that the epilogue is by Shakespeare. Tiffany Stern (110–12) notes that prologues and epilogues were generally viewed as separate from the play and were often not by the same author; E. E. Stoll (726) feels the language of the epilogue is unworthy of Shakespeare, a view that Kermode (134) strongly rejects. The fact that the epilogue reflects the unusual format of the epilogue to *The Silver Age*, a play that Shakespeare clearly was familiar with and had borrowed from elsewhere, could be taken as evidence (though certainly not proof) that he did indeed write it.[11]

Shakespeare apparently borrowed less from *The Brazen Age*. There is, however, one clear element of similarity, pointed out by Bate, which is the use in both plays of Medea's conjuring speech from Arthur Golding's translation of the *Metamorphoses* (Bate 253–54; *Tempest* ll. 1984–2008; *Brazen* G1v; Golding 142). I argue in the essay cited above that the Medea scenes in *The Brazen Age* were in *2 Hercules* in 1595 and so if there is influence here it would seem that it is from Heywood to Shakespeare, but there is little sign that Heywood's use of this material affected Shakespeare, who clearly consulted Golding directly. The most likely scenario to explain this relationship is that Shakespeare saw Heywood's play and the Medea scene gave him the idea to refer to Golding's text when he later wanted to portray Prospero's conjuring.

The Tempest is a very different work from the first three *Ages* plays. In fact, it is in many ways their opposite. The *Ages* are long sprawling plays, with many characters and incidents and with a number of completely independent episodes that Heywood may have added to the earlier Hercules plays. *The Tempest* is a compact, highly concentrated work that lacks even a true subplot. The first three *Ages* cover a vast timespan, from the birth of Jupiter to the death of his son Hercules, and many milieus, from heaven to hell and everywhere in the ancient world. *The Tempest* takes place over a few hours on one small island. The *Ages* are full of action, including battles, murders, rapes, and fights of every sort. *The Tempest* is rather static, with a few threatened actions that do not materialize. In spite of one or two spectacular moments, *The Tempest* is a modest play in which words are paramount. The *Ages* are plays of action and spectacle with scarcely a moment of poetry. From a generic and structural point of view, it is hard to imagine two more disparate works.

Even more striking than the aesthetic differences between the two works are the moral ones. Heywood's main source was Caxton's *Recuyell of the Historyes of Troye*, which tries to treat a mishmash of classical stories as if they were a medieval romance. It attempts to portray first Jupiter and then Hercules as ideal knights, even though their behavior is far from ideal; although the authors of the *Recuyell* try to hide this fact as best they can, the net result is to show these characters who should be models of courtly behavior performing acts that are highly immoral from a Christian perspective. And although medieval commentators tried to find moral meaning in Heywood's other main source, Ovid's *Metamorphoses*, part of the appeal of this work to Renaissance readers was probably its lack of a moralizing framework; Ovid's world is one governed by Fortuna rather than Providence, where innocents can be victimized at random by capricious gods. The result are plays that must have seemed shocking to many in the Jacobean audience. By contrast, *The Tempest* seems to me to stand out among Shakespeare's plays for its rather strict Christian moral framework.

Most Renaissance literature conforms to the providential pattern, whereby in the end the good are rewarded and the evil punished; even tragedies at the very least show the evil characters definitely punished. But in the *Ages*, Jupiter rapes the innocent Calisto (and the less innocent Danae), Hercules kills the innocent Lychas, Medea tears apart her innocent brother Absyrtus and casts his limbs into the sea to divert the pursuing Oetes, all without any clear righting of the moral balance. Some of the randomness of the *Metamorphoses* is felt in the chance meetings of Jupiter with Calisto or Pluto with Proserpine, with disastrous consequences for both of them, or in Perseus' accidental killing of his father. While the theme of prophesies being fulfilled in spite of human attempts to evade them recurs several times, there is no sense that Jupiter's usurping the throne of Saturn or Acrisius being killed by Perseus are the result of the workings of a power for good, but rather of the Fates, who are indifferent to human values.

By contrast, the providential element is emphasized in *The Tempest* more than in any other of Shakespeare's plays. Prospero answers Miranda's question about how they got to the island by stating that it was "by providence divine" (l.267) and Ferdinand says Miranda is his "by immortall providence" (l. 2167). Even when Prospero refers in a more secular fashion to "bountiful fortune" (l. 289), or "a most auspitious starre" (l. 293), or Ariel-as-harpy to "destiny" (l. 1586), there is a feeling of a divine force for good working in the play. This thread reaches a climax in Gonzalo's prayer at the end:

> Looke downe you gods
> And on this couple drop a blessed crowne ;
> For it is you, that have chalk'd forth the way
> Which brought us hither.

(ll. 2182–85)

The characters who have sinned (or had the intent to sin) are clearly punished, although they are eventually forgiven by Prospero. In his appearance as a harpy, Ariel addresses Alonso, Antonio, and Sebastian as "three men of sinne" (l. 1586) and pronounces on them "lingering perdition" (l. 1610) if they do not repent. This language certainly suggests divine judgment.

Some recent interpretations of the play, of course, present very negative portrayals of Prospero and his motives (summarized in Vaughan and Vaughan 98–110). There is considerable force in the argument that Prospero exemplifies a racist or colonialist mentality, but it is very unlikely that Jacobean audiences viewed him in this way. Until the mid-twentieth century Prospero was universally viewed, both by critics and performers of the role, as a benevolent, if at times overbearing and irascible, figure. Even when increasing sympathy began to be felt for Caliban in the nineteenth century, Prospero as the embodiment of civilization (and often of Shakespeare himself) remained a fundamentally positive figure.[12] It is very unlikely that Jacobean audiences viewed him differently. To those who had just witnessed the randomness of fate in the first three *Ages*, the workings of Providence must have seemed reassuringly affirmed in Shakespeare's play, with Prospero with his magic powers its semi-divine agent.

Particularly striking is the contrast in the ways sexuality and marriage are portrayed in the two works. Jupiter is the hero of *The Golden Age* and his sexual behavior, including his rapes of Calisto and Danae and the list of his other conquests (*Golden Age* I3v-I4r), certainly does not reflect Christian values. Immediately after taking Juno as his wife, he announces that he will "woe and win" many other women, "Nor shall the name of wife be curbe to us/Or snaffle in our pleasures" (G4r). The same indifference to conventional morality is evident in Hercules, who forsakes his wife Deianeira for Omphale and whose other affairs, including his feat of impregnating the fifty daughters of Thespeius in one night, are mentioned (*Brazen Age* C1v, K3r). Women in the plays are often shown enjoying sex outside marriage, including Danae (who only pretends to resist Jupiter's advances), Semele, and Omphale. The adultery of Mars and Venus is played for laughs, with Venus's husband Vulcan the butt of the joke; the episode's cynical moral is: "None search too farre th' offences of their wives" (I3v), since it is better not to know of their affairs than to be scorned as a cuckold. The plays' distinctly risqué portrayal of sexuality contrasts with the idealized depiction of the relationship of Ferdinand and Miranda, discovered innocently playing chess.

Note the pointed contrast in the portrayal of Juno in the two plays. In *The Silver Age* she descends with Iris having at last seen through Jupiter's disguise as Amphitrio in his adulterous seduction of Alcmena. She comes "Roab'd all in wrath and clad in scarlet fury" to destroy the entirely innocent Alcmena and her unborn babies. Her description of her frantic spying and dogging of Jupiter's every move, and her threat to follow him to Heaven or to Hell with her "clamours," cause the awakening Socia to say: "Hey-ho, now I am dream'd of a scold" (F1v). Shakespeare, in portraying his Juno also making her entrance descending from the heavens, seems to present a deliberately contrasting image of the goddess; she is very much an idealized queen coming graciously to bestow her blessing on the chaste betrothed couple. The two Junos were identically dressed, riding in the same vehicle and perhaps played by the same actor. While both are presented as goddesses of marriage, the images they present of that institution are opposite; Heywood's Juno represents one of adulterous husbands and harridan wives, Shakespeare's one of "Honor, riches . . . Hourely joyes" (ll. 1767–69) experienced by the happy couple. The first audiences of *The Tempest* who had previously seen the Juno of *The Silver Age* must have been very struck by the contrast

Violence is the main method of settling disagreements in the *Ages*. Much of it is retributive, motivated by a desire to avenge a previous wrong. In a particularly notable chain of tit-for-tat violence, Hercules kills the Centaurs after Antimachus' attempt to ravish Hippodamia, Nessus seeks revenge by abducting Deianeira, Hercules kills Nessus with an arrow, the dying Nessus gives Deianeira the poisoned shirt that will kill Hercules. The most shocking example of the revenge ethic is Hercules' killing of Laomedon and razing of the entire city of Troy because he is not given the two horses promised for saving Hesione. The play conveys no sense that he has done anything wrong. The cycle of vengeance does not stop there. Hesione, who is given to Telemon as a concubine, "divines" that this action will result in another act of retaliation, Paris's abduction of Helen, which will, in turn, give rise to the ultimate revenge story, the Trojan War (*Brazen Age* H1v–H2r). It is reasonable to say, I think, that the *Ages* glorify vengeance.

By contrast, forgiveness is a dominant motif in *The Tempest*. In what many have seen as the turning point in the play (e.g., Wilson *Essential* 143; Boughner 8–9), Prospero renounces vengeance in favor of forgiveness:

> Thogh with their high wrongs I am strook to th'quick,
> Yet, with my nobler reason, gainst my furie
> Doe I take part: the rarer Action is
> In vertue, then in vengeance : they, being penitent,
> The sole drift of my purpose doth extend
> Not a frowne further.
>
> (ll. 1974–80)

Of course, several of Shakespeare's comedies end with forgiveness, but normally it is given in response to a repentant character who begs it, as when Bertram cries "O Pardon!" to Helena at the end of *All's Well*. In *The Tempest* forgiveness is given freely, without its being asked for and with no real evidence of repentance in the persons being forgiven; Prospero seems to acknowledge that his brother has not changed when he says "I do forgive thee,/Unnaturall though thou art" (l. 1034–35) and Antonio never shows any sign of remorse. Andrew Solmon calls this sort of forgiveness of one's enemy "Christ-like" (232). It is certainly the antithesis of the revenge ethic that Prospero specifically repudiates here.

Recognition of this apparently systematic opposition between the *Ages* and *The Tempest* might lead to answers to a few questions about Shakespeare's play. Critics have wondered why Shakespeare, having eschewed the classical unities in all his plays since *The Comedy of Errors*, and having just written a play, *The Winter's Tale*, that broke the rules in a particularly flagrant way, should have suddenly returned to this critical orthodoxy in *The Tempest* (see Kermode lxxi–lxxvi). Perhaps this choice was made in deliberate opposition to the first three *Ages*, which carry the rejection of classical precepts to the ultimate degree. Similarly, critics have often seen something significant in Prospero's reiterated injunctions to Ferdinand and Miranda that they must remain chaste before their marriage. His apparent obsession with the topic, which is also a central theme in the masque, has been variously viewed. John Dover Wilson thought it reflected Shakespeare's guilt for his own pre-marital sex with Anne Hathaway (*Meaning* 11). More recent commentators have seen Prospero's moralistic emphasis as a manifestation of his patriarchal desire to control Miranda's sexuality (Thompson 408), his aristocratic concern about the purity of his dynastic line (Aughterson 236–37), or his paternal suspicion of a man who is the son of his enemy and an admitted womanizer (Hapgood 425). While any or all of these theories could have a grain of truth, perhaps the desire to oppose the particularly unchristian portrayal of sexuality and marriage in the *Ages* was an additional motivating factor.

There is little in Shakespeare's other works, or in what we know of his biography, to suggest that he was strongly preoccupied with religion, and even less to suggest that he would be upset by the unclassical structure of the *Ages*, since his own usual practice was highly unclassical. One wonders, then, what could have been behind the implied critique of the *Ages* that *The Tempest* embodies. We get a tiny hint of the relationship of Heywood and Shakespeare, at just the time the *Ages* and *The Tempest* were being performed, in Heywood's endnote to *An Apology for Actors*, published in 1612 (without entry in the Stationers' Register). In it Heywood attacks his former publisher, William Jaggard, for the mess he had made of publishing his long poem *Troia Britanica* in 1609. He also points out that Jaggard included extensive passages from that work in the 1612 edition of *England's Parnassus*, a collection of poems published as "by W. Shakespere." He says he is particularly concerned that readers may think that he had pirated them in *Troia Britanica*, and that Shakespeare was asserting his authorship of them by publishing them under his own name. In the most significant passage, he says:

> But as I must acknowledge my lines not worthy his patronage, under whom he hath published them, so I know the Author Much offended with Mr Jaggard (that altogether unknown to him) presumed to make so bold with his name. (G4r–G4v)

Note the nuance here in the cause-and-effect suggested by the "as . . . so" construction. We could paraphrase the passage as follows: "because I admit that my poems are not good enough to be ascribed to him, Shakespeare was very angry with Jaggard for publishing them under his name." This phrasing seems subtly to give away the fact that Shakespeare felt the poems attributed to him were of inferior quality and that he communicated this view to Heywood, who humbly agreed. Although Heywood pretends to be merely reporting Shakespeare's anger with Jaggard, the somewhat hurt and placatory tone of the endnote suggests that he himself may also have been the object of Shakespeare's ire.

Shakespeare's negative assessment of Heywood's poetry occurred just at the time that the King's Men were involved in a massive co-production of four of Heywood's five *Ages* plays, plays that apparently proved popular.[13] It involved the King's Men playing a subsidiary role to a company that had distinctly less prestige, although the Red Bull had not yet developed the image of a popular lower-class venue that later characterized it (Griffith 14–16). The contrary nature of *The Tempest* could reflect Shakespeare's dissatisfaction with this collaboration and perhaps unhappiness at the success of the *Ages*, which he may have viewed as "not worthy" of the company of which he had long been the chief dramatist. In her biography *Ungentle Shakespeare*, Katherine Duncan-Jones suggests that Shakespeare's state of mind became increasingly dark in 1612, that he was "deteriorating into a bitter, wary 'ungentle' man" (245). While her evidence for this statement seems a bit meager, if it is true, one could say that Shakespeare's experience with his company's involvement in the collaboration on the *Ages* might have contributed to this negative outlook.

Although it is a plausible reading of the facts, I do not propose the theory that Shakespeare wrote *The Tempest* because he was depressed or angry at his company's involvement in the production of the *Ages* as an addition to the already shaky edifice of Shakespearian biography. We cannot know for sure what his motives were. But it is a definite fact that, although he made use of the costumes and technology of the *Ages* productions and even borrowed from the plays, Shakespeare wrote a work that was morally and aesthetically in many respects their opposite. This contrariness seems to me to be too pointed to be accidental and must have been evident to contemporary audiences who saw the works juxtaposed. Whatever Shakespeare's motivation, his decision to write against (as it were) Heywood's plays was the source of some of the unique qualities of *The Tempest*, causing him by reaction to return to a structure he had long rejected and to adopt a Christian moral perspective less visible in his earlier work. The result is a play that is not only very different from the *Ages* but also in a number of respects very different from the rest of Shakespeare's oeuvre.

Notes

1. The text of the *Recuyell* is a free translation by Caxton published in 1475 of a French text with a complicated history. I follow scholarly convention in citing him as its author.

2. Presumably the author of the accounts was mistaken and Heywood's very popular play *The Rape of Lucrece* was presented by the Queen's Men alone, since they had been performing it since at least 1607. But it is possible that this was a special joint production of the play.

3. The title page of *The Golden Age* attributes the play solely to the Queen's Men, and so it does not seem to have been part of a co-production. However, if my suggestion is correct, that the King's Men used the eagle that flies Jupiter at the end of *The Golden Age* for Jupiter's appearance in *Cymbeline*, the two companies were already sharing resources prior to *The Silver Age* ("Jupiter"). The published versions of the later *Ages* do not specify a producing company.

4. My recent note in *Notes and Queries* contains a strong conformation of this theory; see "Hercules."

5. The flying scene in *The Silver Age* also has a bearing on another objection of those who question whether Juno arrives by air in *The Tempest*. Irwin Smith suggests that if she flew in and then left her vehicle to join the other goddesses, the car would either have to remain on stage, where it would be in the way of the dancers, or be hauled up empty, a contrivance "which is unexampled in the stagecraft of the period" (416). But at the end of the scene of Juno's entrance in *The Silver Age*, Juno and Iris, having reached earth, leave on foot in order for Juno to put on the habit of a "beldame"; their car presumably was drawn up empty.

6. Ralph Crane was also almost certainly responsible for the "*Names of the Actors*" section at the end of the Folio text (Vaughan and Vaughn, 127). His description of Caliban as "*a salvage and deformed slave*" may reflect his costume in a later staging of the play, since it seems to differ from the "half a fish and half a monster" portrayed in the text. The original costume was no doubt cumbersome and fragile; dressing Caliban as a "savage" was much easier and most subsequent Calibans adopted this image, even though the text contradicts it.

7. One might have thought that this was a common motif, but editors of *The Tempest* do not seem to have found this to be the case, although Kermode says vaguely that the motif was "not uncommon in the legends of saints" (146). More to the point is the scene in Greene's *Pandosto* in which Bellaria's baby is set adrift in "a little cock boat"; we know Shakespeare read this since it is the primary source of *The Winter's Tale* (see Fitcher, ed., 415–16). But the setting adrift of a parent and child in *The Golden Age* is the closest parallel to the motif in *The Tempest*. Heywood's treatment of the scene follows that in Caxton's *Recuyell* (1.167–69).

8. This similarity was also noted by Ernest Shanzer (23). Of course, he assumed that Heywood was imitating Shakespeare.

9. The fact that he refers only to Hercules' acts in describing the next play, and not to the non-Hercules material that Heywood probably added to *2 Hercules* to create *The Brazen Age*, suggests that this speech was part of the earlier play. In fact, in *The Brazen Age* Heywood omitted all portrayals of Hercules' labors.

10. The former view is much cited by Stoll, who opposes it. For the religious significance of the epilogue, see Beauregard.

11. According to Tiffany Stern (88), the epilogue format of *The Tempest* was reused "in much the same words" in later plays. She cites Thomas Neale's 1637 amateur play, *The Warde*. She does not mention the use of it in *The Silver Age*.

12. See especially Christine Dymkowski's comprehensive history of performances of the role (13–34).

13. The evidence for the popularity of the *Ages* plays lies in the facts that *The Silver Age* was produced at Court, that the companies chose to continue the series to five plays, all very expensive to produce, and that the tone of Heywood's prefaces conveys self-satisfaction. *The Golden Age*, he says, has "past the approbation of Auditors" (A2r). He hopes the change from gold to silver in the second play will not "bee any weakening of his worth, in general opinion" (A2r). As we have seen, he claims the *Iron Age* plays were much applauded and played to thronged audiences.

References

Adams, J. C. "The Staging of *The Tempest*, III. Iii." *Review of English Studies* 14 (1938): 404–19.

Allen, Don Cameron. "*The Tempest*." *The Tempest: Critical Essays*. Ed. Patrick M. Murphy. New York: Routledge, 2001. 173–89.

Arrell, Douglas. "Hercules' Pillars: A New Identification of Properties in Henslowe's Inventory." *Notes and Queries* 66 (2019): 519–21.

———. "Heywood, Henslowe, and Hercules: Tracking *1* and *2 Hercules* in Heywood's *Silver* and *Brazen Ages*." *Early Modern Literary Studies* 17, no. 1 (2014): 1–21.

———. "Jupiter's Descent in *Cymbeline*: A Suggestion." *Notes and Queries* 65 (2018): 543–46.

Aughterson, Kate. *Shakespeare: The Late Plays*. Basingstoke: Palgrave Macmillan, 2013.

Bate, Jonathan. *Shakespeare and Ovid*. Oxford: Clarendon, 1993.

Beauregard, David N. "New Light on Shakespeare's Catholicism: Prospero's Epilogue in *The Tempest*." *Renascence: Essays on Values in Literature* 49, no. 3 (Spring 1997): 158–74.

Boughner, Daniel C. "Jonsonian Structure in *The Tempest*." *Shakespeare Quarterly* 21 (1970): 3–10.

Caxton, William, trans. *The Recuyell of the Historyes of Troye*, by Raoul Lefèvre. Ed. H. Oskar Sommer. 2 vols. London: David Nutt, 1894.

Dymkowski, Christine, ed. *The Tempest*. Shakespeare in Production. Cambridge: Cambridge University Press, 2000.

Edwards, Philip, ed. "*The Masque of the Inner Temple and Gray's Inn*," by Francis Beaumont. *A Book of Masques in Honour of Allardyce Nicoll*. Cambridge: Cambridge University Press, 1967; rpt. 1970. 127–77.

Fitcher, John, ed. *The Winter's Tale*, by William Shakespeare. The Arden Shakespeare, 3rd series. London: Bloomsbury, 2010.

Golding, Arthur. *Shakespeare's Ovid, Being Arthur Golding's Translation of the Metamorphoses*. Ed. W. H. D. Rouse. London: De La More Press, 1904.

Griffith, Eva. *A Jacobean Company and its Playhouse: The Queen's Servants at the Red Bull Theatre (c. 1605–1619)*. Cambridge: Cambridge University Press, 2013.

Gurr, Andrew. "Another Jonson Critic." *The Ben Jonson Journal* 18, no. 1 (2011): 27–44.

———. *The Shakespearean Stage*. 3rd ed. Cambridge: Cambridge University Press, 1992.

Hapgood, Robert. "Listening for the Playwright's Voice: *The Tempest*, 4.1.139–5.1.132." *The Tempest: Critical Essays*. Ed. Patrick M. Murphy. New York: Routledge, 2001. 419–37.

Hosley, Richard, ed. *"Oberon, The Fairy Prince,"* by Ben Jonson. *A Book of Masques in Honour of Allardyce Nicoll.* Cambridge: Cambridge University Press, 1967; rpt. 1970. 45–93.

Heywood, Thomas. *An Apology for Actors.* London: Nicholas Okes, 1612.

———. *The Brazen Age.* London: Nicholas Okes for Samuel Rand, 1613.

———. *The Golden Age.* London: William Barrenger, 1611.

———. *The Iron Age.* London: Nicholas Okes, 1632.

———. *The Silver Age.* London: Nicholas Okes for Benjamin Lightfoote, 1613.

———. *Troia Britanica, or Great Britaines Troy.* London: W. Jaggard, 1609.

Hodges, C. Walter. *Enter the Whole Army: A Pictorial Study of Shakespearean Staging 1576–1616.* Cambridge: Cambridge University Press, 1999.

Jowett, John. "New Created Creatures: Ralph Crane and the Stage Directions in '*The Tempest.*'" *Shakespeare Studies* 36 (1983): 107–20.

Kermode, Frank, ed. *The Tempest,* by William Shakespeare. The Arden Shakespeare, 2nd series. New York: Methuen 1954. Rpt. Walton-on-Thames: Thomas Nelson and Sons, 1997.

Mann, David. "Heywood's *Silver Age*: A Flight Too Far?" *Medieval and Renaissance Drama in England.* 26 (2013): 184–203.

Orgel, Stephen, and Roy Strong. *Inigo Jones: The Theatre of the Stuart Court.* 2 vols. Berkeley: University of California Press, 1973.

Schanzer, Ernest. "Heywood's *Ages* and Shakespeare." *Review of English Studies,* New Series 11 (1960): 18–28.

Shakespeare, William. *The Tempest. The First Folio of Shakespeare.* The Norton Facsimile. Ed. Charlton Hinman. New York: W. W. Norton, 1996.

Smith, Irwin. *Shakespeare's Blackfriars Playhouse: Its History and its Design.* New York: New York University Press, 1964.

Solomon, Andrew. "A Reading of *The Tempest.*" *Shakespeare's Late Plays: Essays in Honour of Charles Crow.* Ed. Richard C. Tobias and Paul G. Zolbrod. Athens, OH: Ohio University Press, 1974. 213–24.

Stern, Tiffany. *Documents of Performance in Early Modern England.* Cambridge: Cambridge University Press, 2009.

Stoll, Elmer Edgar. "The Tempest." *PMLA* 27 (1932): 699–726.

Streitberger, W. R., ed. *Jacobean and Caroline Revels Accounts, 1603–1642.* Malone Society Collections XIII. Oxford: Malone Society, 1986.

Thompson, Anne. "'Miranda, Where's Your Sister?': Reading Shakespeare's *The Tempest.*" *William Shakespeare The Tempest: A Case Study in Critical Controversy.* 2nd ed. Ed. Gerald Graff and James Phelan. Boston: Bedford/St. Martin's, 2009. 402–12.

Vaughan, Virginia Mason, and Alden T. Vaughan, eds. *The Tempest,* by William Shakespeare. The Arden Shakespeare, 3rd Series. Walton-on-Thames: Thomas Nelson and Sons, 1999.

Wilson, John Dover. *The Essential Shakespeare: A Biographical Adventure.* Cambridge: Cambridge University Press, 1932.

———. *The Meaning of* The Tempest. The Literary and Philosophical Society of Newcastle-upon-Tyne, 1936.

"Subject to a tyrant, sorcerer": A Hyper-Intuitive Reading of *The Tempest*

Peter Krause

Contemporary literary criticism is often so determined to investigate allegedly previously unexplored nuance, depth, and minutiae in a text that it perhaps forgets about the value of what is obvious. While the intertwined significance of race, language, and colonial power dynamics in Shakespeare's *The Tempest* has been studied thoroughly, the role of magic in relation to this trio of potent themes remains curiously unexplored, especially in the last two decades of scholarship. From Prospero's preoccupation with studying spells that enables Antonio to usurp his throne, to the sorcerer's control over Caliban and the already cursed, twice-enslaved Ariel, magic pervades the play and defines its major relationships and key scenes. Prospero's "art" is mentioned explicitly in the text 13 times, meaning that it is not only a device visible from the altitude of the reader, but also a topic of frequent discussion within the world of the play itself. Yet magic is not a democratic force in *The Tempest*. Sorcery is selectively distributed among characters in a way that replicates the hierarchy of race and colonial subjugation familiar in sixteenth- and seventeenth-century texts. In short: only white characters, and the racially ambiguous spirits who serve them, wield magic successfully, or potentially have access to it. Expressly non-white, subaltern characters are denied magical powers, resulting in a story that is more authoritarian than much recent scholarship will admit.[1] This analysis proposes that studying the possession or lack thereof of magic as an indication of literacy, knowledge, and overall political power offers a unique perspective on the already exhaustively examined topics of racial difference and power dynamics in *The Tempest*. At the risk of making overly simple connections, we might say that understanding magic as power and power as coloniality illuminates the divide between those who have: Prospero, Ariel, and their lesser spirits, and those who lack: namely Sycorax and Caliban. Especially when considering how best to teach the play to undergraduates and non-majors, I submit that there is elegance in such simplicity and value in pursuing a straightforward reading of a text that often invites dizzyingly complicated analyses and improbable rhetorical contortions.

Before commencing with a reading of the intertwined roles of magic, race, and agency in *The Tempest*, let us first consider what has been written previously about these themes. What follows is by no means exhaustive, but rather is meant as a general overview of select important contributions in recent decades. I am grateful for and indebted to all of those who have penned compelling pieces, both simple and complex, about *The Tempest* in years past. Philip Mason's *Prospero's Magic*, published in 1962, exemplifies the mid-twentieth century trend of reading the play against the historical backdrop of sixteenth- and seventeenth-century colonialism.[2] Of Mason's six chapters, four are devoted to political and sociological commentary on the state of the world in the wake of widespread decolonization in the nineteenth and twentieth centuries. Mason employs Prospero and the concepts of magic and paternalism not literally, but rather metaphorically as a lens through which to understand British domination of its colonies and, subsequently, its loss of those satellites after World War II. The essays, originally delivered as a series of lectures at the University College of the West Indies, resonate more in the register of postcolonial studies than in literary studies, as only two of his chapters include close readings of any of Shakespeare's plays at all (*The Tempest*, *Othello*, and *King Lear*).[3] However, Mason's discussion of Prospero's reliance on spells speaks to the synonymous nature of magic and power: "Prospero is not just a scholar, a recluse or a hermit . . . His study is magic. This means that he wants power; what else is magic but power?"[4] This salient comparison of magic and power shall serve as a through-line that this essay tracks through the decades of scholarship that followed Mason.

Throughout the 1970s and 80s commentary on *The Tempest* and the relationship between Prospero and his subjects (Caliban, Ariel, and, arguably, Ferdinand) adheres more to the text, drawing conclusions about the play itself rather than its significance as a touchstone in postcolonial studies. Julia Briggs and Alden Vaughan, respectively addressing the theater as a space in which seventeenth-century geopolitical anxieties are acted out and treating Caliban as an indigenous American character, both view Prospero's singular, privileged status as the sole commander of magic as ancillary to aspects of race and metatheatricality.[5] Briggs does make the familiar and valuable claim that Prospero functions as a theatrical director of all action that takes place on the island "stage," but does not go further than highlighting the Neoplatonism of the duke doing his best to shape the reduced world around him.[6] Similarly, John S. Mebane, writing in 1989, interprets Prospero's impious use of magic (in the Faustian sense of overreaching) as a comment on the sometimes desperate lengths to which both individuals and their works of art should go to achieve restoration and resolution, as is the tradition in early modern romance.[7] While Mebane's analysis is apt, we should distinguish between the orderly, Utopian society that Prospero genuinely believes he orchestrates and the restrictive regime he actually installs. Indeed, while Mebane claims that in the wake of scholarship on *The Tempest* in the 1980s "it no longer seems tenable to view Prospero and his magic as essentially evil, but the arguments in favor of the ambiguity of Shakespeare's magician and his art are formidable," we should recall that Prospero's use of magic is tantamount to colonial subjugation and, thus, thoroughly ethically reprehensible.[8] However, the tendency to forgive Prospero that Mebane espouses ("ambiguity" over "evil") encapsulates exactly the kind of thinking that this analysis seeks to deconstruct.

Regarding coloniality and the nature of political power in the play, Barbara Fuchs, writing in 1994, proposes that elements of English interest in Ireland, the Americas, and the Mediterranean are all likely inspiration for the play and, as such, are all equally useful without mutually excluding one another.[9] While Fuchs's analysis considers Caliban as an Irish subject and Prospero as his British conqueror, her article has more to do ultimately with expanding the scope of interpretive possibilities than with scrutinizing power distribution. Fuchs's argument, like that of Mebane, Briggs, and Vaughan, does not adequately account for the essential role that magic plays in the text. Similarly limited, though certainly insightful in numerous other ways, Peggy Simonds offers a reading of *The Tempest* as an endorsement of "reform during an Age of Reformation" in which Prospero, failed duke forced to play sovereign in a smaller arena, embodies all of the qualities that a political leader should jettison in the name of reform.[10] This is an especially compelling interpretation because it acknowledges the tyranny at the heart of Prospero's rule. In Simonds's reading, Prospero appears as the antithesis of Machiavelli's eponymous character in *The Prince:* a negative example of all that a ruler should embody. While Simonds's argument about Shakespeare's intentional juxtaposition of a dictatorial Prospero with the classical ideal of the just ruler, Orpheus, is cogent, her suggestion that Prospero is negligent in tending to his family is less convincing. Despite his authoritarian attitude toward his subjects, Prospero is able to provide far more care than any other parent in the play, especially Sycorax, who is denied all presence in the play and, consequently, can do nothing to alleviate her son's servitude. As a sovereign and mage, Prospero may be magisterial, but as a father he is arguably devoted and accommodating.

A product of the 1980s and 90s turn towards New Historicism, Paul Brown's work proposes that *The Tempest* is understood best as a play that engages in nuanced discourse with English colonialism, particularly with respect to Ireland.[11] Brown informs close readings of key scenes with historical context about both the play's alleged inspiration (a story of a shipwreck near Bermuda) and the milieu of sixteenth- and seventeenth-century colonialism to produce an interpretation of Prospero as a shrewd sovereign who uses magic, language, and music to outmaneuver others vying for control of the island. This analysis owes much to Brown's insights. Brown's article is thorough in its exploration of Prospero's command of magic, but it does not address *lack* of magic as an indication for a *lack* of power among the other characters, namely Caliban. It is this imbalance between Prospero and Miranda (father endowed with magical powers who tends to his daughter and could presumably teach her how to wield magic herself) and Sycorax and Caliban (deceased and inaccessible mother and impotent, subjected servant) that this analysis wishes to explicate. When Brown discusses "Prospero's investment in the power of narrative to maintain social control," he means the ruler's use of sorcery.[12] Yet, Brown overlooks Prospero as a magician and instead reads the displaced duke as a mighty storyteller, a playwright within a play whose power is theatrical and directorial rather than political and supernatural. "Prospero's narrative can be seen, then, to operate as a reality principle, ordering and correcting the inhabitants of the island, subordinating their discourse to his own," writes Brown.[13] This view of Prospero as the master of both narrative and language in the play is fruitful, but we should expand this reading. Brown identifies correctly the overt theatricality of Prospero's rule, but perhaps under-interprets the literal magic that is the grounds on which such drama rests.

More recently, the topics of magic, race, and power in *The Tempest* have been addressed from a variety of useful angles, though I maintain that none of them takes up Mason's strikingly simplistic assertion that magic constitutes total power in the play. Nor does contemporary scholarship further Brown's argument about Prospero's use of magic to control the island by examining those characters who lack magic and, consequently, do not determine their own individual narratives. Writing in 2016, Tom Lindsay complicates traditional readings of Caliban as Prospero's slave by suggesting that Prospero, with a repertoire of spells, books, and music at his disposal, functions more as a teacher and patron than as a dictator, which transforms Caliban from a spiteful subject into a disgruntled but receptive student.[14] However, like Brown, Lindsay emphasizes what *is* at the expense of considering what *is not*. Specifically, his work leaves gaps containing the possible, the hypothetical, and the unexplored that all warrant exploration. While much scholarship on *The Tempest* and wronged minority figures focuses understandably on Caliban, Kelsey Ridge suggests that Ariel is actually the rightful owner of the island and, as such, is victimized more than contemporary scholarship generally acknowledges.[15] Ridge's article is refreshing because it shifts the focal lens away from Prospero and Caliban to consider a character about whom less has been written, but she also perhaps imports many popular assumptions about race, magic, and power without questioning them.

Offering an uncommon interpretation that this analysis leans on heavily, Debapriya Sarkar close reads portions of the text that describe what happened *before* the story begins in order to better understand otherwise inaccessible characters like Sycorax and past events like the usurpation of Prospero's power by Antonio.[16] Treating the play as a meditation on storytelling and the making of narrative possibilities, Sarkar scrutinizes potentiality, ambiguity, and inconclusiveness in the play. This enables readers to read *The Tempest* as an unstable field of questions rather than an entrenched canonical work the major themes of which have been exhaustively unpacked. Likewise, by interpreting "monstrosity" as something internal yet contagious that individuals choose to enact in language, Kristen Wright adds a novel interpretation to an ancient concept, and one that was very potent in the early modern period.[17] This essay is less indebted to Wright's reading than to Sarkar's, though I do import her suggestion that Caliban is hardly the only "monstrous" character in the play and extend it to Prospero, the once righteous duke deformed by excessive power.

Having sketched a rough outline of relevant scholarship about race and magic in *The Tempest,* let us now consider briefly how best to examine in 2022 a text that has been the object of continuous study for over 400 years and about which seemingly every interpretative angle has been explored. Given that this essay advocates for an unorthodox, if also obvious, reading of *The Tempest* it is fitting that we might consult an atypical source for insight on how to achieve a unique reading of the play that capitalizes on interpretive simplicity: Pierre Bourdieu's notion of "habitus."[18] Bourdieu defines habitus as:

> systems of durable, transposable dispositions, structured structures predisposed to function as structuring structures, that is, as principles which generate and organize practices and representations that can be objectively adapted to their outcomes without presupposing a conscious aiming at ends or an express mastery of the operations necessary in order to attain them. (53)

In essence, habitus describes the intangible superstructures that pervade and govern environments, but are so complete and seamless that they may appear invisible. Creating "a world of already realized ends—procedures to follow, paths to take—", it is akin to ether, air, or, as David Foster Wallace outlines in *This is Water: Some Thoughts, Delivered on a Significant Occasion, about Living a Compassionate Life,* water.[19] On using critical thinking skills to identify and pierce our most fundamental assumptions about social reality, Wallace diagnoses habitus in his own terms, positing, "the most obvious, ubiquitous, or important realities are often the ones that are the hardest to see and talk about."[20] Habitus is a description of both the substance and governing dynamics that pervade daily life to such a degree that it is difficult to identify and discuss. It is an invisible social force, always in play but often unconsidered, like Freud's unconscious and Marx's socioeconomic class.

The relevance of habitus to *The Tempest* is clear if we understand magic to be the most significant force within the play, so obvious and permeating that it is easy to overlook. In Bourdieu's view, human societies are always enveloped in habitus, whether they know it or not. In Wallace's anecdote, fish are so immersed in water that they ask incredulously: "What the hell is water?"[21] In *The Tempest* systems of meaning are so omnipresent that, from the inside, they appear to constitute reality itself. I submit that this is how magic functions in *The Tempest*. Prospero's spells and sorcery pervade the play like an unseen ether in which all of the characters enact their subplots. Brown identifies language and theatricality as the water in which the characters are immersed, but in fact it is Prospero's magic. Yet, as I have attempted to illustrate, magic has been deemed too obvious and too simplistic to merit substantial examination in much relatively recent scholarship about *The Tempest*. Incorporating Bourdieu and Wallace allows for the possibility that what seems to be flat and self-evident can actually reveal startlingly clear, simple explanations.[22] Occam's razor is rarely the favored tool of the literary critic, and countless compelling readings of texts have been identified by abandoning simplicity in favor of complex, even masterful, logical and rhetorical contortions. However, in this case let us consider the equally elegant possibility of the stunningly simple: In *The Tempest* magic equals power, and power explains the play.

If the reader will permit the deployment of a neologism, this ultra-intuitive reading of the play (as opposed to the popular critical pursuit of counterintuitive readings) relies heavily on assumptions established by Mason and Brown, both of whom submit that Prospero's magic is integral to his authoritarian governance of the island.[23] As alluded to earlier, Sarkar too has discussed the realm of possibility, potentiality, and the potent question of "what if?" in the play, especially regarding the unstaged lives of Sycorax, Caliban, Ariel, and Miranda.[24] Thus, this analysis will draw upon such past scholarship in order to put pressure on the significance of magic in the play through questions like the following: How would the power dynamic on the island be different if Sycorax, Prospero's magical counterpart and presumed enemy, were still alive? Why does Prospero not teach Miranda how to command spirits? If Sycorax were alive, would she similarly instruct Caliban how to practice magic? In a 2019 article for *The Washington Post*, two former students of Harold Bloom, Palmer Rampell and Jordan Brower, recall Bloom's fondness for querying a play's unstaged possibilities: "What was Lear like before the start of the play?"[25] While I acknowledge the limitations, as well as the indulgence, of posing hypothetical speculations that exceed the text, I also note the unique usefulness of contextualizing the story in the flow of time. What happens before act 1 and after act 5 is relevant to a complete interpretation of the text. Similarly, querying "what if?" allows us to juxtapose what Shakespeare provides in the play with other alternative or parallel possibilities.

As such, this essay examines not only presences in the play, but also significant absences. Absent, unstaged events that are worth considering include the reign of Sycorax and Caliban over the island, the death of Sycorax, Prospero's self-education in magic, and Prospero's banishment. Thus, before the curtain lifts a kind of symmetry appears between the two magical parents, Prospero and Sycorax, and their children, Miranda and Caliban. Yet, this symmetry is foreclosed even before the play begins, as Sycorax dies prior to the shipwreck that brings the cast of disparate characters together on Prospero's island. Consequently, the possibility of equality appears and then vanishes, establishing a foundation of inequity on which the rest of the story is built. Understood along these lines, the conceit of the play takes on an antebellum or antepeccatum quality. Read this way, what the audience witnesses is mere aftermath. Just as the unstaged backstory of *Romeo and Juliet* establishes the grounds for a play about two lovers from feuding families, so too does what happens before act 1, scene 1 in *The Tempest* lay the crucial groundwork for a play about the triumph of asymmetry and inequity over balance.

Many of Shakespeare's most artfully constructed plays entail conflict between two opposing yet symmetrical forces, but we must question whether this applies to *The Tempest* as well. On the subject of proportionality in the play, Mebane writes, "The distinctive character of *The Tempest* derives in large part from its calm—one is tempted to say serene—sense of balance."[26] Mebane is only partially right. Balance does figure in *The Tempest,* but only after the establishment of enormously disproportionate power dynamics between the haves and the have nots. Balance is rendered more interesting due to the legacy of its upset. In contrast, *Romeo and Juliet* is a play in which opposing forces are described as balanced and proportional from the first line: "Two households, both alike in dignity."[27] Similarly, *The Life of King Henry the Fifth* pits sovereign against sovereign: "My duty to you both, on equal love, / Great Kings of France and England," proclaims Burgundy.[28] Even *Antony and Cleopatra* is a story of king versus queen and empire against empire: "Equality of two domestic powers / Breeds scrupulous faction," claims Antony himself.[29]

Conversely, *The Tempest* is structured by an imbalance of power epitomized by the magical governing the non-magical. Mebane, arguing for balance and symmetry in the play, asserts that the text "permits us to entertain the possibility that humankind possesses an unknown, perhaps indeterminate, creative potential, and yet the heart of the work is its insistence that we cannot fulfill ourselves until we discover our proper relationship with our fellow human beings."[30] Yet, one of the most important visible relationships in the play is between Prospero and Caliban and Ariel, over both of whom the sorcerer wields enormous power. Indeed, the "creative potential" that Mebane mentions is not so universal, as only Prospero, as artist, teacher, sovereign, and director, is able to contrive situations that serve his own interests. Regarding "humankind" and the "fellow human beings" that Mebane mentions, we must recall that Caliban is fundamentally denied status as a human being for most of the play, which frustrates claims that the play affirms human universality. Indeed, Prospero refers to Caliban as a "tortoise"[31] when he first appears onstage, and later Stephano and Trinculo call him "devil,"[32] "monster,"[33] "cat,"[34] and "moon-calf,"[35] among other dehumanizing monikers. Similarly, Ariel, neither human nor monster, is situated outside of the realm of humanity as a natural spirit, as Prospero refers to them[36] as "malignant thing"[37] and "my slave"[38] when first appearing onstage. So, we must conclude that Mebane's reading, while thorough and compelling, understandably overlooks indicators of power imbalance that are so large and glaring that they paradoxically recede and become background. *The Tempest*, from the very first act, does not establish itself as a play in which noble houses vie for greatness or well-matched empires go to war. Rather, the play is essentially a story of powermongering, subjugation, and the uncontested rule of one magically endowed sovereign.

In order to understand fully the function of magic as dictatorial tool in the play, let us examine the ways in which it is discussed in the text. Recounting the items that he was able to smuggle out of Milan when he was ousted, Prospero tellingly describes his books of spells as "volumes that/I prize above my dukedom."[39] This statement can be read two ways: as a lament that he devoted too much attention to the study of magic while serving as duke, but also as an unapologetic assertion of his priorities as scholar (or, indeed, mage) first and sovereign second. Either way, the tomes of spells are framed as essential objects in the play without which Prospero would be just another marooned castaway. The play's second scene establishes unambiguously that Prospero's primary advantage over others is due to his ability to cast spells, as Caliban relays:

> I must obey. His art is of such pow'r
> It would control my dam's god, Setebos,
> And make a vassal of him.[40]

In this passage Caliban responds to Prospero and Miranda's insults by issuing the language of a spell that is rendered impotent by the fact that he has no magical abilities. As Brown highlights, Caliban's only escape from and recourse to Prospero's magic is through dreaming, a far less potent form of escaping nature's laws and creating fictions.[41] Whether or not Sycorax's "earthy and abhorred commands" were learned like Prospero's abilities or simply an intrinsic part of her character as an exotic, ostensibly evil African witch is unclear, but what is clear is Caliban's frustrated desire for such powers. After all, he is the only other character in the play besides Miranda whose parent possesses supernatural abilities.

Bearing in mind Sarkar's astute advice that readers should consider "other play-worlds, where characters could adopt another role or inhabit another state," it is prudent to trace the lineages and circles of influence of Prospero and Sycorax and consider how the narrative might have unfolded differently.[42] It is reasonable to assume that Prospero might have taught Miranda (and, eventually, perhaps Ferdinand) how to cast spells, just as it is reasonable to consider that Sycorax might have done the same for Caliban if given the opportunity. By attempting to invoke the "southwest" wind Caliban calls on wind from the southeast (i.e. moving southeast to southwest), implying that such a wind would carry with it the spirits, vexations, and intoxicants of the east, the Orient, or Africa, his late mother's homeland.[43] It is important to note that Caliban's curses are not simply slurs or epithets, but carry the connotation of being attempts at sorcery—retaliation against Prospero's curses that beset Caliban with "cramps" and "aches."[44] Indeed, in the same scene Caliban, lashing out at Prospero and Miranda, announces, "All the charms / of Sycorax—toads, beetles, bats, light on you!"[45] Thus, Shakespeare complicates the asymmetrical relationship between tyrannical wizard and his resentful servant by suggesting that, in another narrative, Caliban might respond with spells of his own taught to him by his mother, which would upset the fundamental power dynamics that structure the reality of the play.

Caliban's impotent spells are attempts at performative utterances in the sense that J. L. Austin describes them in *How To Do Things With Words*, namely as speech acts that *do* something in the world .[46] We can understand the matrimonial "I do," the legalistic "I sentence you . . . " and the christening "I hereby name this ship . . . " as all being convergences between speech and act, where one is indistinguishable from the other. The same can be said for sorcery that is based in speech and text. While the dialogue of Caliban and the majority of the other characters may strive for results, whatever they may be, only Prospero's words are guaranteed to enact actual change. As such, in the controlled sphere of the island his words are—literally—law, both legalistic and gravitational. This is why on the island only he can author his own triumph or undoing, as his famous pronouncement in act 5 illustrates:

> I'll break my staff,
> Bury it certain fathoms in the earth,
> And deeper than did ever plummet sound
> I'll drown my book.[47]

Only with three assertions of direct personal action ("I'll break," [I'll] "bury," and "I'll drown") can Prospero alter the course of the play, as he alone governs it with his spells. Caliban curses, Ariel protests, and Ferdinand, Stephano, Miranda, etc. chatter, but only Prospero commands. What more absolute power is there? It is only after he has surrendered all power that the actions and, tellingly, the action *verbs* of others finally influence his fate, as his monologue to the audience in the play's final lines remind us: "As you from crimes would pardoned be, let your indulgence set me free."[48] Having surrendered his god-like powers to govern life on the island, Prospero allows the cast of characters, members of the audience, and readers forever after to enunciate their own performative "utterances" in the form of dialogue, applause, and commentary.

Of course, it is crucial to consider not only the play's most famous scenes and its fourth-wall-breaking ending, but also its alternate universe, if you will. If we follow Sarkar's example and further consider the unstaged possibilities and foreclosed potentialities of the play, the "missing scene[s]"[49] and events "forever at the brink of appearing,"[50] then it is reasonable to consider how the story might be radically different if Sycorax survived and was present to contest Prospero's domination of the island. Doing so is a useful thought experiment because it actualizes one of the play's many implied but denied possibilities. Early in the play, Prospero tells Miranda and Ariel of Sycorax:

> This blue-eyed hag [who] was hither brought with child
> And here was left by th' sailors. Thou, my slave [Ariel],
> As thou report'st thyself, wast then her servant;
> And, for thou wast a spirit too delicate
> To act her earthly and abhorred commands,
> Refusing her grand hests, she did confine thee,
> By help of her more potent ministers,
> And in her most unmitigable rage,
> Into a cloven pine; within which rift
> Imprisoned thou didn't painfully remain
> A dozen years.[51]

The parallels between Sycorax's arrival on the island and Prospero's are undeniable. Sycorax and her child Caliban are marooned on the island against their will, just as Prospero and Miranda are set adrift by Prospero's usurping brother, Antonio. Upon encountering Ariel, the island's original inhabitant, Sycorax attempted to press the spirit into her service and, when he refused, imprisoned him in a tree. This use of sorcery as a tool of bondage evokes Prospero's authoritarian treatment of both Ariel and Caliban, who presumably only obey the mage because of the magical power with which he threatens them. "Earthly and abhorred commands" and "unmitigable rage" are descriptions that could just as easily describe Prospero given his behavior in the story. The circumstances of Sycorax's death are unclear, though the fact that she is described as being "with age and envy / Was grown into a hoop" implies that she succumbed to illness or old age.[52] In short: it is only by chance that Prospero's previous reign over the island is uncontested, which validates the notion of considering other "chances" or possibilities that haunt the play and hover at its peripheries. In other pages and across other stages Prospero and Sycorax, equally matched, might hurl spells at each other, which would fundamentally alter the power dynamics, and likely the narrative outcome, of the play. Hamlet so memorably proclaims in the eponymous play: "There are more things in heaven and earth, Horatio, than are dreamt of in your philosophy."[53] Yet, in *The Tempest*, it is clear that, until the play's final scenes, Prospero works hard to foreclose the possibility of any "things" dreamt of in anyone else's philosophy.

We must ask: what is the ability to dictate events and manipulate others in a closed space but power? Sarkar reminds us that the "the ability to create a theatrical plot by organizing events chronologically is inextricable from the power to control the space of the stage", and it is vital to note that it is only chronology that separates Prospero the mage (connoted positively) from Sycorax the witch (connoted negatively), and the presumably equally matched duel that such a chronological merging would have precipitated (One can imagine an alternate opening line, "Two magical households, both alike in exile . . .").[54] "While all of Shakespeare's plays contain multiple narrative threads," continues Sarkar, "*The Tempest* . . . turns to events that will never occur in order to put distinct pressure on the fantasy of unity of plot."[55] This is a striking, unique way to examine an early modern play: as a weaving together of various subplots, some of which are staged and some of which exist only hypothetically, in the offstage realm of implication or possibility. It is, as Sarkar says, all "fantasy," and one fantasy is just as valid as another. Such notions, combined with a commitment to recognizing the large, obvious element of magic in *The Tempest* rather than looking beyond it in favor of obscure or unlikely readings, results in a wider field of interpretative possibilities for the text. Regarding inter-genre transformations that occur in the play itself, Mebane posits that Prospero's sorcery moves the story "from discord to harmony, tragedy to comedy."[56] Yet, what I suggest we read closely is the fact that for the duration of the plot the play is comedy for Prospero and tragedy for Caliban, Ariel, and even Ferdinand. What gratifies Prospero subjugates the others. What is harmonious in the mage's scheming is discordant for those at his mercy.

Contrasting the supposedly magnanimous magic of Prospero with the malignant magic of Sycorax, Mebane suggests, "false conceptions of human nobility and freedom are associated with *goetia*, such as the evil magic of Sycorax, a travesty of Prospero's benevolent art."[57] We can take issue with Mebane's diagnosis of Sycorax's magic as "evil" for two reasons. First, the character is foreclosed before the play even begins, so audience members have no access to Sycorax at all, which makes it impossible to truly know her character. We only receive enormously subjective impressions through Prospero. Second, the pronouncement of Sycorax's magic as "evil" assumes that Prospero's magic is "good" or "benevolent," which is, as this analysis has attempted to establish, debatable to say the least. Yet, again it is useful to attach language meant to describe others to Prospero, as "false conceptions of human nobility and freedom" describes accurately how he orchestrates events around him, tantalizing Ariel and Caliban with promises of freedom and framing his tyranny as benevolence. Recounting Sycorax's powers, Prospero describes them as "mischiefs manifold, and sorceries terrible," which is also arguably an accurate depiction of his own magical meddling, given the powerless positions that others must assume around him.[58] "Prospero," writes Brown, "utilizes the previous regime of Sycorax as an evil other. Her black, female magic ostensibly contrasts with that of Prospero in that it is remembered as viciously coercive, yet beneath the apparent voluntarism of the white, male regime lies the threat of precisely this coercion."[59] Thus, we see the articulation of the collapse of difference between Prospero and Sycorax. Like many dictators installed by revolution, Prospero sees his reign as a positive improvement on the villainous governance of the past ruler without realizing that his methods are, at best, not so dissimilar and, at worst, a descent into tyranny. Also like all dictators, Prospero is paranoid about "the possibility of an event (a successful coup) that never occurs," which speaks to the nature of all colonial rule, always threatened by the prospect of uprising by "restless natives" and of the presence of "barbarians at the gates."[60] Prospero continually articulates his reign by casting spells because he must: to discontinue sorcery is to surrender all control and all agency.

However, as suggested earlier, this tyranny is easily read as simply the antics of a strict teacher. Prospero's role as a schoolmaster, discussed in depth and from various angles by Lindsay, is both fascinating and perplexing. "As much as *The Tempest* explores colonialist discourse and humanist values," writes Lindsay, "it is also, in a more basic way, a drama about the workings of Prospero's household and schoolroom, his 'cell.'"[61] Prospero's "cell" functions as a household and a classroom in which he dictates for the rest of the cast of characters movements, interactions, and distribution of knowledge. His two primary students, Miranda and Caliban, benefit from his presence since he is, for most of their time on the island, the only adult present. Prospero instructs Miranda in the humanistic tradition. He even teaches Caliban language, the use-value of which the grudging pupil declares is knowing how to curse (which further emphasizes the centrality of magic in the play, if we read "curse" as "cast spells"). However, Prospero's role as instructor is inconsistent since his greatest intellectual achievement, and the one to which he previously devoted an obsessive amount of time and energy, is the mastering of magic. Despite Sarkar's suggestion that we envision alternate plots, we must admit that Prospero never exhibits any desire to teach Miranda or anyone else his sorcery in the plot that Shakespeare offers. It is possible that he does not wish to burden his daughter with the same Faustian obsession that led him to be so easily overthrown by his brother. Yet, he also defends his own status as a teacher who is capable of magic, even suggesting that other teachers (presumably not learned in spells) would be less effective: "Have I, thy schoolmaster, made thee more profit/Than other princes can, that have more time/For vainer hours, and tutors not so careful.[62] Consequently, we see Prospero occupy the paradoxical, perhaps even hypocritical, position of advocating for the benefit of magical instruction for Miranda without ever imparting his own knowledge to her. His is a cruel, imperial, and exclusive sorcery. As readers, we can only wonder whether Sycorax or other parental characters in the play would have been as severe with their powers, or if they might have been more pedagogical.

By way of arriving at a conclusion, let us consider one final excerpt from Brown's essay that describes the range of Prospero's influence:

> In his powerful narrative, Prospero interpolates the various listeners—calls to them, as it were, and invites them to recognize themselves as subjects of his discourse, as beneficiaries of his civil largesse. Thus for Miranda he is a strong father who educates and protects her; for Ariel he is a rescuer and taskmaster; for Caliban he is a colonizer whose refused offer of civilization forces him to strict discipline; for the shipwrecked he is a surrogate providence who corrects errant aristocrats and punishes plebeian revolt. Each of these subject positions confirms Prospero as master.[63]

Brown's description of Prospero's command of all other characters in his orbit is accurate, but we should scrutinize the nature of that command, which is wholly magical. Prospero is only able to protect and educate Miranda due to his supernatural abilities, and he is only able to furnish her with a potential husband due to his ability to conjure the storm. Similarly, he was only able to free Ariel from Sycorax's entrapment using his spells, and his continued control of the spirit is contingent upon those spells. Regarding the shipwrecked Italians, Prospero must rely on his powers not only to sink their ship and guide them to the island, but also to do so without inflicting undue harm, which presumably requires more finesse than someone without magic would be able to accomplish:

> I have with such provision in mine art
> So safely ordered that there is no soul—
> No, not so much perdition as a hair
> Betid to any creature in the vessel.[64]

All of the verbs used to describe Prospero's manipulation of others around him in the two excerpts above ("interpolates," "calls," "invites," "educates," "protects," rescue[s]," "offers," "forces," "corrects," "punishes," "positions," and "ordered") are related to his magical abilities. Indeed, they approximate to "bewitch," "enchant," or "hex." Each verb examined above could be followed by the phrase "with magic" and the phrases would still ring true. Indeed, Prospero's name itself is built around the verb "to prosper," and this is exactly what he does with his supernatural abilities: manipulates things and people around him for his own gain. As is evident above, in Prospero's mouth the language of the play and the language of sorcery collapse into one another to reveal the classic description of colonial subjugation of a powerful outsider over native inhabitants.

The claim that *The Tempest* is a story about colonialism is an established argument, but factoring in the supernatural nature of the power that underwrites such domination allows for novel interpretations. Imbued with magical abilities, Prospero's abilities far exceed that of a mere sovereign. Indeed, such powers deify him and degrade all others to such a degree that they must exist in a separate category all together. "Much of *The Tempest*," writes Mebane, "is a dramatic debate over the question of whether humanity is bestial or godlike, Caliban or Ariel; the implied answer is that we are both and that our lower faculties must be guided and disciplined by the mind and spirit."[65] Yet, this juxtaposition between bestiality and godliness can be read in a way that only underlines Prospero's authoritarian rule, since he himself is the closest approximation of god in the play, as his magic enables him to control everything from the weather to the destinies of others. Thus, Prospero proclaims himself to be godlike and, whether implicitly or explicitly, decrees that Caliban is an antithetical beast. Even if we accept Mebane's argument, does not that make Prospero even more of a tyrannical puppetmaster, presuming to orchestrate all of the relationships in the play, despite the obvious reluctance or outright resentment of some? Taking such a simple, straightforward position accomplishes what is arguably necessary in studies of *The Tempest*: an uncomplicated understanding of the immoral power that Prospero enjoys at the expense of others. All other readings of the play, whether they seek simplicity or complexity, must acknowledge this fact, and it is worth letting simplicity color our interpretation rather than dismissing it.

Notes

*I would like to extend special appreciation to Corey McEleney at Fordham University for his rigorous editorial expectations, as well as Larry Lockridge at New York University and Jeff Myers, previously at Goucher College, both of whom provided invaluable background on Shakespeare and Early Modernism.

1. As Ridge discusses, most characters in the play, including Prospero and Caliban, are never described as being white or black. However, the consensus in the scholarship as well as in trends in casting and depictions of these two in performances is that Prospero is white and Caliban is non-white, whether African, Native American, or another race. For a thorough investigation of race in *The Tempest* see: Kelsey Ridge, "'This Island's Mine': Ownership of the Island in *The Tempest. Studies*" in *Ethnicity and Nationalism,* vol. 16, no. 2, (2016): 231–45, Paul Brown, "'This thing of darkness I acknowledge mine': *The Tempest* and the discourse of colonialism" in *Political*

Shakespeare: Essays in cultural materialism, Jonathan Dollimore and Alan Sinfield, eds., 2nd ed. (Ithaca: Cornell University Press, 1994), 48–70, and Alden T. Vaughan, "The Americanization of Caliban" in *Shakespeare Quarterly*, 39, no. 2, (Summer 1988): 137–53.

2. Phillip Mason, "Prospero, King Lear, and the Colonial Father" in *Prospero's Magic: Some Thoughts on Class and Race*, (London: Oxford University Press, 1962), 75–97.

3. Ibid, vii.

4. Ibid, 86.

5. Julia Briggs, "The Court and its Arts" in *This Stage-Play World: English Literature and its Background 1580–1625*, (Oxford: Oxford University Press, 1983): 119–59 and Alden T. Vaughan, "The Americanization of Caliban" in *Shakespeare Quarterly*, 39, no. 2, (Summer 1988): 137–53.

6. Julia Briggs, "The Court and its Arts" in *This Stage-Play World: English Literature and its Background 1580–1625*, (Oxford: Oxford University Press, 1983): 129.

7. John S. Mebane, *Renaissance Magic and the Return of the Golden Age: The Occult Tradition and Marlowe, Jonson, and Shakespeare,* (Lincoln: University of Nebraska Press, 1989), 179.

8. Ibid.

9. Barbara Fuchs, "Conquering Islands: Contextualizing *The Tempest*" in *Shakespeare Quarterly,* 48, no. 1, (Spring 1997): 45–62.

10. Peggy Muñoz Simonds, "'Sweet power of music': The Political Magic of 'the Miraculous Harp' in Shakespeare's *The Tempest*" in *Comparative Drama* 29, no. 1 (Spring 1995): 61–62.

11. Paul Brown, "'This thing of darkness I acknowledge mine': *The Tempest* and the discourse of colonialism" in *Political Shakespeare: Essays in cultural materialism,* Jonathan Dollimore and Alan Sinfield, eds., 2nd ed. (Ithaca: Cornell University Press, 1994), 48–70.

12. Ibid, 63.

13. Ibid, 66.

14. Tom Lindsay, "'Which first was mine own king': Caliban and the Politics of Service and Education in *The Tempest*" in *Studies in Philology* 113, no. 2 (Spring 2016): 397–423.

15. Kelsey Ridge, "'This Island's Mine': Ownership of the Island in *The Tempest. Studies*" in *Ethnicity and Nationalism* 16, no. 2 (2016): 231–45.

16. Debapriya Sarkar, "The Tempest's Other Plots" in *Shakespeare Studies* 45, (2017): 203–31.

17. Kristen D. Wright, "'This thing of darkness I acknowledge mine': Man's Monstrous Potential in *The Tempest* and *Titus Andronicus*" in *Disgust and Desire: The Paradox of the Monster,* (Leiden: Brill, 2018), 171–96.

18. Pierre Bourdieu, *The Logic of Practice* (Palo Alto: Stanford University Press, 1992).

19. David Foster Wallace, This is Water: Some Thoughts, Delivered on a Significant Occasion, about Living a Compassionate Life (New York: Little, Brown, 2009).

20. Ibid, 8.

21. Ibid, 4.

22. Ibid, 15.

23. See Phillip Mason, "Prospero, King Lear, and the Colonial Father" in *Prospero's Magic: Some Thoughts on Class and Race* (London: Oxford University Press, 1962), 75–97 and Paul Brown, "'This thing of darkness I acknowledge mine': 48–70.

24. Sarkar, "The Tempest's Other Plots," 203–31.

25. Palmer Rampell and Jordan Brower, "How Harold Bloom misunderstood the fall of the humanities" in *The Washington Post.* October 24, 2019.

26. Mebane, *Renaissance Magic and the Return of the Golden Age* 198.

27. Stephen Orgel and A.R. Braunmuller, eds. "Romeo and Juliet" in *The Complete Pelican Shakespeare* (New York: Penguin, 2002), I.i.1.

28. Stephen Orgel and A.R. Braunmuller, eds. "The Life of King Henry the Fifth" in *The Complete Pelican Shakespeare* (New York: Penguin, 2002), V.ii.23–24.

29. Orgel and Braunmuller, eds. "Antony and Cleopatra." *The Complete Pelican Shakespeare.* New York: Penguin, 2002. I.iii.47–48.

30. Mebane, *Renaissance Magic and the Return of the Golden Age* 198.

31. Orgel and Braunmuller, eds. "The Tempest" in *The Complete Pelican Shakespeare* (New York: Penguin, 2002), I.ii.316.

32. Ibid, II.ii.56.

33. Ibid, II.ii.64.

34. Ibid, II.ii.82.

35. Ibid, II.ii.109.

36. "Them" is more accurate than "him" or "her" as Ariel's gender is somewhat ambiguous, as the character is often staged as either feminine, masculine, or androgynous.

37. Orgel and Braunmuller, eds. "The Tempest" I.ii..257.

38. Ibid, II.ii..270.

39. Orgel and Braunmuller, Ibid., I.ii.167–168.

40. Ibid, I.ii.373–75.

41. Paul Brown, "This thing of darkness I acknowledge mine," 66.

42. Sarkar, "The Tempest's Other Plots," 210.

43. For a discussion of "Orientalism" in Western literature, see Edward Said, *Orientalism* (New York: Vintage, 1979). For examinations of Orientalism in Shakespeare's work in particular, see Jyotsna Signh, "Shakespeare and the Civilizing Mission" in *Colonial Narratives/Cultural Dialogues: "Discoveries" of India in the Language of Colonialism,* (London: Routledge, 1996), 101–28 and Debra Johanyak and Walter S.H. Lim, eds., *The English Renaissance, Orientalism, and the Idea of Asia,* (New York: Palgrave, 2009).

44. Ibid, I.ii.369–70.

45. Ibid, I.ii.339–40.

46. J. L. Austin, *How To Do Things With Words* (Cambridge, Harvard University Press, 1975), 23.

47. Orgel and Braunmuller, eds. "The Tempest," V.i.54–57.

48. Ibid, Epilogue, 19–20.

49. Sarkar, "The Tempest's Other Plots," 216.

50. Ibid, 206.

51. Orgel and Braunmuller, eds. "The Tempest," I.ii.269–79.

52. Ibid, I.ii.258–59.

53. Orgel and Braunmuller, eds. Hamlet" in *The Complete Pelican Shakespeare* (New York: Penguin, 2002), V.i,169–70.

54. Sarkar, "The Tempest's Other Plots," 215.

55. Ibid, 224.

56. Mebane, *Renaissance Magic and the Return of the Golden Age,* 184.

57. "Goetia" is medieval Latin for the ability to summon demons. See Mebane, *Renaissance Magic and the Return of the Golden Age,* 194.

58. Orgel and Braunmuller, eds. "The Tempest," I.ii. 264.

59. Brown, "This thing of darkness I acknowledge mine," 61.
60. Sarkar, "The Tempest's Other Plots," 223.
61. Lindsay, "Which first was mine own king," 400.
62. Orgel and Braunmuller, eds. "The Tempest," I.ii.172–74.
63. Brown, "This thing of darkness I acknowledge mine," 59.
64. Orgel and Braunmuller, eds. "The Tempest," I.ii.28–31.
65. Mebane, *Renaissance Magic and the Return of the Golden Age*, 186.

Works Cited

Austin, J. L. *How To Do Things With Words.* Cambridge, Harvard UP, 1975.
Brown, Paul. "'This thing of darkness I acknowledge mine': *The Tempest* and the discourse of colonialism" in *Political Shakespeare: Essays in cultural materialism,* Jonathan Dollimore and Alan Sinfield, eds., 2nd ed. Ithaca, NY and London: Cornell Univ. Press, 1994. 48–70.
Briggs, Julia. "The Court and its Arts" in *This Stage-Play World: English Literature and its Background 1580–1625*, Oxford: Oxford Univ. Press, 1983, 119–159.
Fuchs, Barbara. "Conquering Islands: Contextualizing *The Tempest*" in *Shakespeare Quarterly,* vol. 48, no. 1, Spring 1997, 45–62.
Johanyak, Debra, and Walter S.H. Lim, eds., *The English Renaissance, Orientalism, and the Idea of Asia.* New York: Palgrave, 2009.
Lindsay, Tom. "'Which first was mine own king': Caliban and the Politics of Service and Education in *The Tempest*" in *Studies in Philology*, vol. 113, no. 2, Spring, 2016, 397–423.
Mason, Phillip. "Prospero, King Lear, and the Colonial Father" in *Prospero's Magic: Some Thoughts on Class and Race*, London: Oxford Univ. Press, 1962, 75–97.
Mebane, John S. *Renaissance Magic and the Return of the Golden Age: The Occult Tradition and Marlowe, Jonson, and Shakespeare.* Lincoln and London: Univ. of Nebraska Press, 1989. 174–199.
Orgel, Stephen, and A.R. Braunmuller, eds. "The Tempest" in *The Complete Pelican Shakespeare.* New York: Penguin, 2002. 736–761.
———. "The Life of King Henry the Fifth" in *The Complete Pelican Shakespeare.* New York: Penguin, 2002. 1128–1164.
———. "Romeo and Juliet" in *The Complete Pelican Shakespeare.* New York: Penguin, 2002. 1251–94.
———. "The Tragical History of Hamlet Prince of Denmark" in *The Complete Pelican Shakespeare.* New York: Penguin, 2002. 1347–91.
———. "Antony and Cleopatra" in *The Complete Pelican Shakespeare.* New York: Penguin, 2002. 1651–1700.
Rampell, Palmer, and Jordan Brower. "How Harold Bloom misunderstood the fall of the humanities." *The Washington Post.* October 24, 2019.
Ridge, Kelsey. "'This Island's Mine': Ownership of the Island in *The Tempest. Studies*" in *Ethnicity and Nationalism,* vol. 16, no. 2, 2016, 231–245.
Said, Edward. *Orientalism.* New York: Vintage, 1979.
Sarkar, Debapriya. "The Tempest's Other Plots" in *Shakespeare Studies* 45 (2017): 203–31.
Signh, Jyotsna. "Shakespeare and the Civilizing Mission" in *Colonial Narratives/Cultural Dialogues: "Discoveries" of India in the Language of Colonialism,* London: Routledge, 1996, 101–28.

Simonds, Peggy Muñoz. "'Sweet power of music': The Political Magic of 'the Miraculous Harp' in Shakespeare's *The Tempest*" in *Comparative Drama.* 29, no. 1 (Spring 1995): 61–90.

Vaughan, Alden T., "The Americanization of Caliban" in *Shakespeare Quarterly* 39, no. 2 (Summer 1988): 137–153.

Wright, Kristen D. "'This thing of darkness I acknowledge mine': Man's Monstrous Potential in *The Tempest* and *Titus Andronicus*" in *Disgust and Desire: The Paradox of the Monster,* Leiden: Brill, 2018, 171–96.

Timon of Athens, the Absent Mercer, and Nothing

Poet: "To th' dumbness of the gesture/ One might interpret." (1.1.33–34)

David M. Bergeron

The opening Folio stage direction of *Timon* seems quite straightforward: "*Enter Poet, Painter, Ieweller, Merchant, and Mercer, at seuerall doores.*" It soon becomes apparent that this Mercer does not speak in the scene or have any specified action. Thus, since Samuel Johnson in the eighteenth century, various editors have chosen to delete the Mercer from the play: he vanishes, a case of missing in action. To cite four editions just from the beginning of the twenty-first century, we find this range: the Oxford *Timon* (2004) retains the Mercer and offers a rationale for that decision; the RSC *Complete Shakespeare* (2007) lists the Mercer but places only this name in parenthesis, as if downgrading his pertinence; the Arden *Timon* (2008) completely removes this character from the play; so does the Norton edition (2016). What should the reader think of this? What about the classroom, cluttered with different editions that take irreconcilable opposite actions? What implications occur, if any, for the theater?

I ask two fundamental questions: what is the Mercer's textual and editorial status, and what does he signify for the play? I argue that Timon metaphorically becomes the Mercer, who can function as the synecdoche for Timon. Minor characters in Shakespeare, as we know, even speechless ones, may offer insight into major characters and the play's issues. The minor character the Scrivener, for example, in *Richard III*, unnamed, appears once and speaks only 14 lines, but in them he offers a trenchant moral analysis of the situation after Hastings' execution. Even a silent Mercer may have meaning and significance for Timon.

I explore the Mercer's textual presence in terms of *text*, *theater*, and *theme*, raising questions about the grounds on which an editor might remove this character, clearly called for in the Folio, the authoritative text. I wonder about what if any difference the deletion means in the theater. I also ask, how might

161

this Mercer contribute to the play's themes, suggesting that, like the Mercer, Timon becomes mute and reduced to nothing. The play's narrative trajectory moves from the "soul of bounty" to "nothing," foreshadowed by the Mercer. I find my sanction for this approach in the Poet's reaction to the Painter's creation in the opening scene. The Poet points out several features of the painting and justifies his comments thus: "To th' dumbness of the gesture / One might interpret" (1.1.33–34).[1] The Mercer may be "dumb," but we may freely interpret him. I therefore make a case for retaining the Mercer, who, like Violenta in 3.5 of *All's Well,* does not speak but resonates with meaning for Timon and *Timon.* We may also recall the "dumbness" of the reunion of Leontes and Perdita in 5.2 of *The Winter's Tale.* After many years of separation, they discover each other, but the audience does not get to hear them speak. The First Gentleman reports: "There was speech in their dumbness, language in their very gesture" (5.2.14–15).[2] The silent Mercer may nevertheless" speak" in a language of gesture and signification. Finally, in this analysis, I ponder whether the Mercer's presence in the text may offer further possibility for Thomas Middleton's involvement in the play.

Ordinarily when I have thought about missing elements in Shakespeare's plays, I have thought in terms of absent characters. For example: Claribel in *The Tempest.* She never appears; yet, she is the reason the traveling party has been in the Mediterranean. Indeed, the play pays considerable attention to her, revealing that her wedding in Tunis sent the Italian group to Africa. Her remoteness and Ferdinand's presumed death disrupt any plan of succession in the kingdom. Shakespeare dangles her above the play, absent but not forgotten. Similarly, we cannot overlook the absent presence of Apollo in *The Winter's Tale.* This powerful god looms over the play; but he speaks only through the oracle, which Cleomenes and Dion have experienced at Delphi. We witness the effects of Apollo's power and the fulfillment of his prophecy, but we never see him.

A classroom experience, however, changed my approach to Shakespeare's omissions or silence. Several years ago, when teaching *All's Well That Ends Well,* I asked the students to turn to Act 3, scene 5; and I called their attention to the opening stage direction, wanting to highlight the dominance of women in the scene. I read aloud the list of characters who enter the scene; this list includes Violenta. A student interrupted me and observed that his edition did not include Violenta. This surprised me. The student was correct, but this raised issues that I had not anticipated. I had no answer for Violenta's absence from the other edition, although I noted that she does not speak. My curiosity had been seriously piqued, and I set out on my quest for Violenta.[3] Haunted by this editorial problem, I have begun to pay more attention to stage directions.

Much Ado about Nothing can serve as a precursor to the Mercer editorial problem in the later *Timon.* I refer to the opening stage direction of *Ado,* which includes "Innogen," the stated wife of Leonato; she also appears at the beginning of 2.1. She fits the definition of a "ghost" character, one who does not speak, nor does anyone refer to her. Innogen, however, appears in both the authoritative Quarto of 1600 and in the Folio. But since Lewis Theobald in the eighteenth century (sounds familiar), she has usually been omitted in editions of the play. Claire McEachern, editor of the Arden edition, writes: "Editors since Theobald have concurred that despite her persistence in the entry SDs Shakespeare ultimately found her more powerful in her absence than her presence, and so she has been retired from the fray."[4] McEachern thus omits Innogen from the text. Here this editor seems to follow a well-established practice, sanctioned in part by Stanley Wells, who writes: "editors from Theobald onwards have understandably regarded it as part of their duty in tidying up the text to sweep her away."[5] Some resistance can be found in essays by Michael Friedman and David Baker, who argue for retaining Innogen for what she can signify in the play.[6] Friedman sees theatrical purposes for her, and Baker suggests that "Innogen instigates a rereading of other characters and their relationships" (233). Innogen can lead us to the Mercer. I find encouragement for my pursuit in Laurie Maguire's observation: "stage directions and speech prefixes invite renewed attention."[7]

How have editors of *Timon* dealt with the Mercer? My survey of 19 editions of *Timon*, ranging from 1905 to 2016, reveals that *twelve* of them omit the Mercer, *five* include him, and *two* muddy the waters by retaining the name but treating it differently from the other characters' names. All editors who remove the Mercer ultimately derive their authority (knowingly or not) from Samuel Johnson, as noted above. When they offer no explanation, we gain no insight into their decision making. My earliest example comes from K. Deighton's 1905 Arden edition, which omits the Mercer and provides no explanation. The two subsequent Arden editions also erase him, but H. J. Oliver (1963) writes that the Mercer "seems to refer to a character originally intended to appear in this scene but finally omitted."[8] Anthony Dawson and Gretchen Minton in the 3rd Arden (2008) provide an explanation for the omission.[9] They observe that the Folio "adds a *Mercer*" (p.159n); actually, the more accurate way of stating the issue would acknowledge that they have *removed* something. Along with other editors, Dawson and Minton think that the Mercer appears as a misinterpretation of the speech prefix of "*Mer*" for the Merchant in the early lines of the scene.

The Cambridge editions follow suit by omitting the Mercer, starting with the 1956 text, edited by J. C. Maxwell, who suggests that the Mercer may have been an "idea which Sh did not follow up."[10] John Dover Wilson in 1961 omits the Mercer but offers no explanation. In the New Cambridge edition, Karl Klein writes that the appearance of the Mercer may have been the misinterpretation of the speech prefix,[11] an idea that the latest Arden editors echo. G. R. Hibbard in the New Penguin *Timon* claims: "there is no part for this character, who looks like a false start on Shakespeare's part, and he has therefore been omitted from this edition."[12] Are editors therefore expected to remove all things that they regard as a "false start"? In making a case for *Timon*'s imperfections, presumably partially caused by an inferior manuscript, Charlton Hinman calls attention to the Mercer as a "ghost" character. He writes in the *Complete Pelican Shakespeare* (1969): "What we can infer is an original intention of having five speakers in the opening passage, then the failure to remove all trace of the mercer."[13] Hinman, nevertheless, retains the Mercer, as does the subsequent Pelican editor, Frances Dolan.[14]

In the fifth edition of his *Complete Shakespeare*, David Bevington omits the Mercer, but adds to the stage direction: "[The Poet and Painter form one group, the Jeweler and Merchant another]."[15] He offers no explanation for the disappearance of the Mercer. Since he adds material, space cannot have been the issue. G. Blakemore Evans in the *Riverside Shakespeare* deletes the Mercer and comments in a note: "perhaps Shakespeare intended a separate character in the Mercer, but he has no lines."[16] Evans equates spoken lines with "character": no lines = no character.

The editor of *Timon* in the second *Norton Shakespeare* also expands the opening direction: "Enter POET [at one door], PAINTER [carrying a picture at another door, followed by] JEWELLER, MERCHANT, and Mercer, at several doors."[17] One immediately notices that the Mercer, while included, has been downgraded typographically. What does that mean? Included but without conviction? A curious thing happens on the way to the third *Norton Shakespeare*, prompted by its abandoning the Oxford text. Eugene Giddens in the latest Norton omits the Mercer, offering an explanation only in the digital edition.[18] Giddens also strips the stage direction of its former excess, while dispensing with the Mercer.

In *A Textual Companion* to their Oxford complete edition of the plays, Stanley Wells and Gary Taylor in their textual notes indicate that "Some editors delete" the Mercer; they, instead retain him.[19] They even provide an exit for the Mercer in the opening scene "on the analogy of the Senators' passage over the stage; the Mercer exists to make a visual impression." Interestingly, editors and commentators do not get excited about or rush to delete the mute Senators who cross the stage in 1.1 and almost immediately exit, presumably. In *The New Oxford Shakespeare* (2016) Francis X. Connor, the editor of *Timon*, retains the Mercer but notes that "The Mercer does not speak in this scene. His presence may indicate that there are more people onstage than the speaking parts."[20]John Jowett in the single volume Oxford Shakespeare (2004) includes the Mercer and provides a rationale that I will tap into.[21] He also has the lengthy additions to the stage direction that we saw above in the 2nd Norton, but at least he does not diminish the Mercer typographically. The Mercer has stood his ground.

This brief survey of what editors have done regarding the appearance of the Mercer in the opening stage directions of *Timon* documents a widespread disregard of the Folio text, often offering no explanation or rationale for the tacit decision. Such editors *cause* the Mercer's absence. Of course, editors could take a relatively easy way out by looking at the Folio text, where at the end of *Timon* we find on a page by itself "The Actors Names"—most unusual in the Folio. Indeed, Margreta de Grazia and Peter Stallybrass note that "none of the quartos published in his [Shakespeare's] lifetime feature lists of characters; the Folio includes lists for only seven out of thirty-six plays, and in every case the list appears *after* rather than *before* the play."[22] This list in *Timon* does *not* include the Mercer, although it names the Poet, Painter, Jeweler, and Merchant. This same curious list also does not record any female characters, and it does not include the important Steward, sometimes referred to as Flavius. Because we cannot trust this cast list on the matter of the Steward or the women, we have little reason to trust it on the issue of the Mercer. This list has dubious authority, in terms of a possible link to the playwright.

Instead, editors generally have posited ideas of a mistake, a false start, a misinterpretation, a failure to revise, to sanction removing the Mercer.[23] Hinman blamed Shakespeare for failing to "erase" the trace of the Mercer, but that "problem" has been solved by many subsequent editors. Thereby, editors raise vexing questions about editorial practice. I suggest that the Mercer does not exist as a "textual" problem, as in the typical sense of a "crux" of some kind; rather, he creates for some an "editorial" problem.[24] On what grounds do editors ignore the Folio text? On what basis do they not explain the omission? What boundaries exist within which one can reliably make such decisions? What keeps this from being merely subjective? I think that we confront here the idea of "perfecting" the text, as memorably articulated by Stephen Orgel, who writes: "the basic assumption of most editorial practice is that behind the obscure and imperfect text is a clear and perfect one, and it is the editor's job not to be true to the text's obscurity and imperfection, but instead to produce some notional platonic ideal."[25] Although Orgel probably envisions larger problems than a mere stage direction, the point remains valid nevertheless. Clearly some editors have chosen to see the Mercer "as some kind of 'accidental substantive': [he's] substantive but apparently an accident that Shakespeare did not clean up."[26] Silent editors who silently remove the silent Mercer raise disturbing questions about editorial practice. These editors embrace a formula: mute character + no designated action= delete. The ease with which some editors discard the Mercer prompts a consideration of the prominence of "nothing" in the play.

Dawson and Minton, editors of the 2008 Arden, confront editorial problems and decisions that pertain to the two epitaphs in the play's closing scene.

Their comments offer an instructive perspective about the work and challenge that editors face. Dawson and Minton answer positively to the question: "might Shakespeare have changed his mind in the course of writing but neglected to cancel the rhymed lines he had first written, which then ended up being inadvertently printed?" (103). That is, Shakespeare intended eventually to decide between the two epitaphs and delete in whole or in part one. The editors admit that they seek a kind of "aesthetic consistency, all the while acknowledging that doing so can be subjective and even wrong-headed" (106). In other words, editors regularly make interpretive judgments in what here seems to be a tidying up of the text. These two editors also engage in an interpretive act when they omit the Mercer, for example. They seem to ignore their own statement that the play contains a "tension between speech and silence, presence and absence" (103). The Mercer exists in that tension. Then, why try to resolve it?

Part of the difficulty about the Mercer seems to be: does a character who does not speak even exist as a character? Since Aristotle's time, we know that a play consists of several parts, only one of which is the characters. Stephen Orgel has confronted this issue in his essay "What Is a Character?," the companion piece to his "What Is a Text?" He begins by asserting that characters are "not people, they are elements of a linguistic structure, lines in a drama . . . words on a page."[27] But, what if the "character" has no words? Such a position leads Orgel to assert that "the character is the script"; "what actors do, after all, is not perform actions but recite lines, and the character is the lines" (8). This judgment rules out all speechless characters, of which many appear in Shakespeare's plays. This understanding of what a character is informs the viewpoint and practice of the editors Hibbard and Evans, for example, who imply that to be a character, the person must speak. But, actors move on stage, make gestures, respond to what others say, and many other actions that do not require verbal expression. They may even indulge in "dumb gestures." I insist that the Mercer is, by any other name, a "character," requiring editors to accept him. He could appear speechless throughout the opening scene, moving about, showing the garments that he brings, engaging in unrecorded conversation with other characters, smiling, frowning. He thereby looks for all the world like a character.

Editors of *Timon* do not consistently follow the practice of omitting speechless characters. The Arden 3 edition offers a prime example of this inconsistent reaction. They readily delete the Mercer, as noted above, but they do nothing about the Senators who enter around 1.1.36 and say nothing. The Folio stage direction says simply: *Enter certaine Senators*. All modern editions indicate that the Senators depart almost immediately. In a commentary note, Dawson and Minton imagine all kinds of action for the Senators, even though they could not imagine such for the Mercer. The Arden editors write: "As the Senators arrive (either singly or in small groups), they greet each other and perhaps the Merchant and Jeweller as well" (163). They add: "it would be possible for a production to allow some of the Senators to remain on stage, in order to swell the number of *suitors* whom Timon greets *courteously* at 96.2" (164). In other words, many dumb gestures seem possible, but not for the Mercer.

How does the theater respond to this Mercer? Given editorial treatment, one can anticipate that productions typically do not include the Mercer. Why would they include a mute character who has no prescribed action? Why assign an actor to this part? If a production retains the Mercer, he might enter carrying rich cloths, such as silks and satins, a sign of his guild. He could, as suggested above, engage in unrecorded conversation with the others. The Mercer could also linger, as does the Merchant. An imaginative director could doubtless find various ways to utilize the non-verbal Mercer. The Senators who enter at line 38 in the opening scene do not speak either and apparently leave shortly—at least, that is what modern editions indicate. Being mute does not in itself demand removal from the play.

The Arden 3 editors provide an extensive survey of theater productions across several centuries (109–45). No review of these performances indicates the presence of the Mercer. My examination of 12 more recent productions, including ones by the RSC (2018–19), Stratford Festival Ontario (2017), the Folger Theatre (2017), and the Oregon Shakespeare Festival (2016), reveals no documented appearance of the Mercer. I have seen only one professional production of *Timon*, the one performed in London at Shakespeare's Globe Theatre in 2008. I confess that I was not on the lookout for the Mercer during this production, so I have resorted to a copy of the program of this somewhat bizarre dramatic rendition. Sure enough, the Mercer's name does not appear in the cast list. Without knowledge or recollection of the opening stage direction or the text in front of us, we would not think that anything had gone awry. This production thoroughly erased a trace of the Mercer. Well, not quite, at least not in the printed program. On page 3, a very small photograph of the Folio's opening page of *Timon* appears. If one squints and looks carefully, one sees the opening stage direction, which, of course, includes the Mercer. Doubtless unintentional, this theater has preserved a "trace" from the original text. Despite the efforts of editors and theater producers, the Mercer remains stubbornly in the Folio's opening stage directions, compelling a focus on why he should be in the play.

I suggest that the Mercer represents three qualities of the play: *material*, *moral*, and *narrative*. But first, exactly what or who is a Mercer? John Jowett in the Oxford *Timon* has the most extensive commentary on the Mercer of any edition, and it is brief. He observes that a Mercer is a "dealer in silks, velvets, etc. He might be denoted on stage by carrying cloths or garments" (169). Jowett adds: "The Mercer visually introduces the theme of consumption and debt." Curiously, in Jowett's Middleton edition of the play, he reduces the function to one who adds "to the substance and bustle of the gathering clients" (471). The Mercer seems imperiled again. John Bromley has noted: "Fine fabrics, damask, satin, silk, linen, hats and trinkets were originally among their [the Mercers'] stock-in-trade."[28] The emphasis on garments and dress calls attention to material qualities, a surface understanding that pervades *Timon*.

The Mercers in London date from the late twelfth century; as their purposes expanded, they became increasingly powerful. "By the sixteenth century the Mercers had been the premier company of the city of London for well over a century."[29] In fact, among the twelve principal guilds (or "livery companies") of London, "the Great Twelve," the Mercers ranked first in precedence and therefore prestige. Membership in one of the 12 conferred citizenship, and their ranks chose Aldermen and the Mayor of London. Interestingly, King James became a "citizen of London" only when in summer 1607 he accepted membership in the Clothworkers guild. A month later his son and heir apparent Prince Henry became a Merchant Taylor, and therefore a citizen. The writer Anthony Munday regularly referred to himself in his publications as "Citizen and Draper." Although a member of this guild, Munday did not actually practice this trade—a common situation.

In 1606, King Christian IV, King of Denmark came to London to visit his sister, Queen Anne. Henry Roberts reports on part of the king's experience: he "tooke his Coach with his companie, and passed on to the Exchange, viewing the beawtie of Cheapside, and the riches of the inhabitants, the Goldsmiths, Mercers, and other wealthy trades, all the way setting their commodities to sale."[30] In a word, the Mercers existed among the wealthy and powerful elite of London, including in their membership the first Earl of Pembroke, Sir Thomas Gresham, Sir Lionel Cranfield, the Earl of Bedford, and much more recently, Sir Winston Churchill. Such an understanding enhances the possibility of an appreciation of the Mercer in *Timon*.

Connections between the guilds and the theater world abound. The acting companies themselves bear a resemblance to the structure of the guilds: shareholders, major actors, minor actors, boy actors (who served a kind of apprenticeship), plus other functionaries. David Kathman, by focusing on the Grocers, Goldsmiths, and Drapers, lays out many of the interconnections between the guilds and theater.[31] He lists over 50 theater people who held membership in a guild. We may immediately think of Ben Jonson, who belonged to the Bricklayers. Kathman's list also includes: James Burbage (Joiners), Thomas Goodale (Mercers), Anthony Munday (Drapers), John Heminge (Grocers), John Lowin (Goldsmiths), John Shank (Weavers), Richard Tarlton (Haberdashers), John Webster (Merchant Taylors), and John Young (Mercers), among many others (47–49). It takes no leap of fantasy for a playwright to include a Mercer.

Dramatists would have been readily familiar with London's guilds, even if not themselves a member. Thus, we can think of several plays with guild members in them: for example, Yellowhammer, Goldsmith, in *A Chaste Maid in Cheapside;* Quomodo, Draper, and a Mercer who does not speak but is referred to, *Michaelmas Term;* the Grocer, *Knight of the Burning Pestle;* and Touchstone, Goldsmith, *Eastward Ho!.*

A Mercer appears in every act of Francis Beaumont's *The Woman-Hater* (1607), except the first. Although the dramatist sets the play in Italy, the Mercer clearly derives from the London environment. Beaumont describes him as a "City Gull in love with learning."[32] This would-be scholar gets linked up with the Pandar to no beneficial end. When the Mercer first enters in 2.2, the stage direction refers to him as "Mercer *a citizen*" (2.2.1 SD). He says: "taffaties, silke-grogerams, sattins and velvets are mine, they shalbe yours" (4–5), reflecting his trade. (I observe that the speech prefix for the Mercer in the quarto text of 1607 is "*Mer,*" rather diminishing the Arden editors' point that "*Mer*" can only stand for the *Merchant* in *Timon.*) The Pandar instructs the Mercer, who seeks not only learning but a wife: "your offers must be full of bounty, velvets to furnish a gowne, silks for petticoats and fore-parts" (4.2.29–30). In an expansive mood, the Mercer promises to establish a hospital for "all broken Poets, all Prose-men that are fallen from small sense, to mere letters" (66–67). And the Pandar commends him: "Sir ye are very good, and very charitable: ye are a true patterne for the Citie Sir" (71–72). Despite his thirst for knowledge and good works, the Mercer falls for a whore, named Francessina, and marries her in act 5. Certainly his presence in this play from the period of *Timon*'s composition shows how a Mercer, "full of bounty," might function in drama.

On two occasions in the Shakespearean era, the Lord Mayor of London came from the ranks of the Mercers: 1603 and 1607. Following tradition, the Mercers would have therefore been responsible for honoring the new mayor with a civic pageant on the day before his inauguration, 29 October.[33] By 1603, the practice of the Lord Mayor's civic pageant had been well established. But in this year, the virulent outbreak of the plague severely curtailed the pageant. Thus, Sir Thomas Bennet had to be content with a truncated event, as the company's records indicate: "for the avoiding of the gathering together of people for the sicknes there was nether trompet drome banner stremer nor Pageant."[34] In 1607, scant records reveal nothing about what might have taken place, and no text survives.

Thus, even a mute Mercer in *Timon* might represent, like Timon himself, bounty, excess, extravagance, and indulgence, the sort of qualities that abound in this play and underscore the *materialistic* world. Paradoxically, the Mercers' guild also gains renown as a group of benefactors of worthy causes, therefore embodying a *moral* function of good works. Perhaps Timon has such in mind when he says: "We are born to do benefits" (1.2.98). The guild, for example, established the Hospital of St. Tomas of Acon in the late twelfth century. As Sutton notes, "The company represented civic respectability and responsibility, with its several schools, almshouses and charities."[35]

Although no longer engaged in its original trade functions, the "Company administers great estates and numerous benefactions among which are St. Paul's School, Mercers' School, Gresham's Royal Exchange, and Gresham College"—all of these established in Shakespeare's time.[36] With this understanding, we can imagine the Mercer in *Timon* standing as a rebuke to Timon's "feast-won, fast-lost" friends, even to Timon himself. The play's Mercer, therefore, can simultaneously function as a contrast to the play's rampant materialism while seeming to embody it. The Mercers' armorial shield reinforces the guild's serious purpose: "Gules issuant from a bank of clouds a figure of the Virgin couped at the shoulders proper vested in a crimson robe adorned with gold, the neck encircled by a jeweled necklace."[37] The guild's motto, "*Honor Deo,*" joins the Virgin's image to solidify its claim to good works. Such a moral purpose highlights how far *Timon* fails to articulate such noble intent, with the exception of Flavius the faithful Steward and occasionally Alcibiades, as in 3.5 in which he defends a friend before the Senate and suffers banishment as a result of that good deed.

The Mercer, by mere presence, can represent the characters' overindulging, consuming practice, but also suggest a righteous one, manifested in good works, which remain, of course, in short supply in the play. Timon, of course, attempts at good works, but mainly to "buy" friendship. The play thus offers a satiric critique of amoral behavior. Given the play's binary opposition between charitable deeds and self-indulgence, it might seem a stretch to find in the Mercer also a *narrative* purpose. How can that work for a character who never speaks nor apparently engages in any prescribed action?

In answer to my second fundamental question I suggest that the Mercer not only highlights thematic qualities in the play, but he also points toward a narrative trajectory of moving to *nothingness*. He does not have a name, and he also remains mute, hence embodying *nothing*. Editors who remove him confirm the "nothing" of the Mercer, this person of "dumb gesture." That quality defines the direction of the play, as Timon becomes like the Mercer, nameless and mute, assuring the narrative path of "bounty" to "nothing." Obviously, Timon's fate does not depend on the Mercer, but he can serve as an analogue to Timon's development. Shakespeare uses the word *nothing* 27 times in *Timon*, making it second only to *King Lear* among the tragedies in its quantity. That word choice underscores the importance of this concept in the play. In this highly "allegorical" play, the Mercer can stand for "Nothing."[38] The Poet's dumb portrait of Fortune in the first scene (ll. 63–89) clearly exists as a harbinger of Timon's fate. Fortune's favor changes as she shifts her mood. In the opening scene, within a few lines we find markers of Timon's destiny in the Mercer and in Fortune. As Lear memorably tells the momentarily rather mute Cordelia, "Nothing will come of nothing" (1.1.90).[39] Timon seems to invert this idea by moving from great wealth and bounty (something) to being destitute in the woods outside of Athens, reduced to misanthropy and nothing—a diminution of identity. Shakespeare uses the word *bounty* 18 times in the play, more often than in any of his other plays, deliberately emphasizing the tension.[40] By play's end, Timon may recall the desperate Edgar, naked and bereft in *Lear,* when he cries: "Edgar I nothing am" (3.2.21). Likewise, Timon stands between identity ("I") and "nothing." To put the matter another way, part of Timon's epitaph says: "Seek not my name" (5.4.71); now he has become nameless and mute. Lucius says that Timon "is shrunk indeed" (3.2.61), and Flavius comments that Timon is "nothing but himself" (5.1.117).[41]

The first banquet scene (1.2), rich in its plenty, presided over by Timon, whom the Third Lord characterizes as "the very soul of bounty" (206) displays considerable opulence, which may recall the wealth of the Mercers' guild. One can imagine that the nameless women who represent the Amazons in their masque enter not only with lutes but with striking garments, silks and velvets, the stock in trade of the Mercers' guild, and manifesting the material world. Timon indeed thanks the women: "You have done our pleasures much grace, fair ladies, / Set a fair fashion on our entertainment" (142–43): costume display, alluring but transient and only superficial. The sumptuous nature of the banquet rivals the report of a banquet given by James Hay, one of the transplanted Scots who followed King James to England and there prospered, becoming Earl of Carlisle and in 1618 Earl of Doncaster. One account observes: "At one major feast one hundred cooks . . . worked for eight days preparing the food. A grand total of sixteen hundred dishes was not unknown, and the quality of the food matched the abundance."[42] No wonder that Hay enjoyed great reputation as the giver of magnificent banquets. Timon fits in that category. The opening stage direction indicates: "*A great banquet served in.*" Excess abounds. In an obvious effort to purchase friendship, Timon laments: "I have often wished myself poorer, that I might come nearer to you" (97–98). The play shows how quickly this situation can change, as Timon begins a descent into nothing.

As the Mercer may symbolize both the material and moral worlds, so may the two banquet scenes: the first full of abundance in substance and food, the second, ripe with Timon's moral judgment on his friends. Although several characters at the first banquet have names, in the second one (3.6) *only* Timon has a name; the friends are anonymous, no identity, which points toward nothing.[43] They have failed a test of friendship; they will become nothing to Timon. Servants bring in the covered dishes, and Timon welcomes the friends to the feast. He says to them: "Your diet shall be in all places alike; make not a City feast of it" (67–68). The "City feast" would refer to some great feast given in London's Guildhall, or at the Mercers' hall. Timon follows with what amounts to a perverse prayer, which builds to the conclusion: "For these my present friends, as they are to me *nothing*, so in *nothing* bless them, and to *nothing* are they welcome" (83–85, my emphasis). Timon's first explicit statement about the nothingness of this world leads to his invitation: "Uncover, dogs, and lap" (86). He has reached a nadir of his experience, as he stares into the abyss of nothing, stripped of wealth and status.

Such a bleak view becomes apparent in Timon's wrenching soliloquy spoken outside the Athenian walls (4.1). From such a city, Timon claims, "Nothing I'll bear from thee/But nakedness" (32–34). He desires that his hatred may grow to encompass all. This harsh, biting moral judgment accompanies him into the woods, the location of the rest of his experience, now bereft of the material world's garments, reduced to the thing itself, nothing remaining.

In the bleak woods outside of Athens Alcibiades arrives and asks Timon his name, he responds: "I am Misanthropos and hate mankind" (4.3.54). He, in effect, says to Alcibiades, "seek not my name." Discarding his name, Timon, like the Mercer, has become anonymous, nothing. He scorns the friendship that Alcibiades offers, saying, "I had rather be alone" (100). Timon engages in a word battle with Apemantus, whom Timon drives him away, saying: "I am sick of this false world, and will love naught" (373). Not only does Timon not love anyone, but also he also loves "nothing." The only potential alteration of that view comes in the appearance of Flavius (456ff). But even the Steward's faithfulness and love cannot redeem Timon.

Failing to understand and not having been present at the second banquet, the Painter and Poet enter in 5.1, echoing the play's opening but absent the Mercer and the others. When the Poet asks the Painter what he has brought for Timon, the Painter responds: "Nothing at this time, but my visitation. Only I will promise him an excellent piece" (18–19). Indeed, the two bring nothing to Timon, except a baseless promise. Their materialistic world comes up against Timon's moral, if extreme, judgment, as he drives them away. The Senators from Athens arrive, seeking Timon's help in warding off a possible invasion by Alcibiades. Flavius has warned them: "he is set so only to himself/That nothing but himself . . ./Is friendly to him" (116–18). Timon instead is a friend to nothing. The Senators claim to bring Athens's love; but Timon sees through that, stating, paradoxically, that "nothing brings me all things" (187). In truth, his "something" (bounty) has brought him nothing. Timon enigmatically says, "let four words go by and language end" (219).[44] Could it be that Timon anticipates four words that later appear in one version of his epitaph: "Seek not my name" (5.4.71)? His mysterious death, which we do not witness, unlike other tragic figures, underscores the "nothing" of his ending. The naked Timon stands in stark contrast not only to his original abundance but also to wealthy Mercer: one without clothes, the other with sumptuous garments.

I have explored the Mercer's thematic purpose and textual presence. But how did this Mercer come into the text? Jowett in the Oxford *Timon* suggests that "Middleton probably added the Mercer" (169), an idea that Dawson and Minton in the Arden edition immediately discount. Jowett does not provide "evidence" for this claim. Both the Oxford and Arden editions confront the question of Middleton's collaboration with Shakespeare on this play and accept the likelihood.[45] Recent scholarship makes a strong case for Middleton's notable presence in the play's final text. I think, with no concrete evidence, that Middleton may well have inserted the Mercer in the play. Perhaps in confronting Shakespeare's incomplete and vexing manuscript, Middleton thought that the scribbled "Mer" in the speech prefixes meant "Mercer," instead of "Merchant." After all, a Mercer is a merchant, but a merchant is not a Mercer: one is generic, the other, a specific guildsman.

In fact, we have no definitive way of knowing what happened to the play's text from the time of its composition until its publication in 1623 with almost two decades intervening between probable time of composition and publication. Editors have noted convincingly the many textual problems with the text in its published form. We can only imagine when or how Middleton collaborated with Shakespeare on this play: did he actively participate, or did he revise a more-or-less completed text? Perhaps he looked at the play's opening stage directions and decided that they needed an additional flourish with specific reference to an active London guild, given the play's emphasis on commerce and money.

In addition to Middleton's keen interest in London, manifested in his series of "city comedies," two of which include members of a guild, from 1613 onward he enjoyed an intimate involvement with London's guilds, writing eight civic pageants in honor of Grocers (3), Drapers (3), Skinners, etc. Middleton's last publication before his death was the Lord Mayor's Show for 1626, *The Triumphs of Health and Prosperity*.[46] In 1620, the City of London appointed Middleton as City Chronologer, a source of pride for the playwright who in the 1623 edition of Webster's *The Duchess of Malfi* contributed a commendatory verse and signed himself as "*Poeta & Chron. Londinensis*." Middleton wrote the Lord Mayor's Shows for 1621, 1622, and 1623. The 1623 Lord Mayor's Show bears the title *The Triumphs of Integrity*. Thus, in the immediate years leading up to the publication of the Folio, London and its guilds would have been much on his mind, which might have prompted the idea of a Mercer. Middleton's first Lord Mayor's pageant, the magnificent *The Triumphs of Truth*, honors the Grocers, a guild second only to the Mercers in precedence.

To complicate matters, Middleton, as suggested above, may have seen the manuscript's abbreviation of "Mer" in the opening lines and throughout the Merchant's appearance. The playwright would have known that "Mer" could just as readily stand for "Mercer," as it does in the Beaumont play. Nothing

distinctive stands out about a generic "merchant," whereas a "Mercer" comes
into the play with recognizable prestige and prominence, ranking first among
the 12 great companies in the City of London, therefore worthy of being an
analogue for Timon. The "Merchant" speaks little in the opening scene, and
nothing extraordinary. Apemantus asks him, "Art not thou *a* merchant" (my
emphasis,1.1.236), to which the character responds, "Ay, Apemantus" (237).
Apemantus manifestly did not ask him if he were "the" merchant. This would
be the only hint that "Mer" might stand for "Merchant." But, of course, a
Mercer is very much a merchant as well. If we substitute "Mercer" for every
instance of "Merchant," this replacement works just as well. Only modern
editors have decided to write out the character's name as "Merchant"; not
so in the Folio text, which consistently uses simply "*Mer.*" By so doing,
these editors shut down the possibility that Middleton really intended "Mer"
to be "Mercer." Could the inclusion of a Mercer in *Timon* be a bid for recognition and possible employment? Who knows? Middleton as possible
creator of the Mercer remains a tantalizing, if unprovable, idea. Shakespeare
does not refer specifically to London's guilds, which is not surprising; but
Middleton does often. In a play about wealth and consumption, just any old
merchant will not do. A Mercer, on the other hand, resonates with great
significance, as I have argued.

Given the Mercer's textual reality, theatrical possibility, and thematic resonance, I think that editors should retain the Mercer. His presence enriches
the play's thematic possibilities, underscoring the play's ideas of profligate
consumption, moral good works, and a narrative trajectory that moves inex-
orably toward nothing. The Mercer symbolizes and hints at what Timon
becomes. We remain to ponder his absent presence, recalling Flaminius'
memorable image: "nothing but an empty box" (3.1.15), a nameless Mercer
and a Timon, stripped of former identity: "seek not my name." Timon claims
that "nothing brings me all things" (5.1.187); but, in fact, it might be more
accurate to say that "all things bring him nothing." Shakespeare's "dumb
gesture" of the Mercer, which I have interpreted, may indeed present a fore-
taste of the play's development and themes. Editors who remove the Mercer
truly render him as "nothing." Editors delete the Mercer; Timon deletes himself. Shakespeare articulates the effect of "dumbness" this way in *The Winter's
Tale* in words of the First Gentleman: "There was speech in their dumbness,
language in their very gesture" (5.2.14–15). Those gestures of unspoken
actions may impact mood and understanding as powerfully as spoken words.
The Mercer, who is a character, deserves a chance.[47]

Notes

1. All quotations from the play will come from *Timon of Athens*, ed. Frances Dolan
(New York: Penguin, 2002).
2. *The Winter's Tale*, ed. Frances E. Dolan (New York: Penguin, 1999).

3. See my, "*All's Well That Ends Well*: Where is Violenta?" *Explorations in Renaissance Culture* 29, no. 2 (2003): 171–84.

4. *Much Ado about Nothing*, ed. Claire McEachern (London: Arden Shakespeare, 2006), 140.

5. Wells, "Editorial Treatment of Foul-Paper Texts: *Much Ado about Nothing* as Test Case," *RES* 31 (1980): 3; 1–16.

6. Michael D. Friedman, "'Hush'd on Purpose to Grace Harmony': Wives and Silence in *Much Ado about Nothing*," *Theatre Journal* 42, no. 3 (1990): 35–63. David Weil Baker, "'Surpris'd with all': Rereading Character in *Much Ado about Nothing*," in *Second Thoughts: A Focus on Rereading* (Detroit: Wayne State University Press, 1998), 228–48.

7. Laurie Maguire, "The Value of Stage Directions," in *Shakespeare in Our Time*, eds. Dympna Callaghan and Suzanne Gossett (London: Bloomsbury, 2016) 153; 149–53. For additional study of stage directions, see Alan C. Dessen, *Elizabethan Stage Conventions and Modern Interpreters* (Cambridge: Cambridge University Press, 1984); and Dessen and Leslie Thomson, *A Dictionary of Stage Directions in English Drama 1580–1642* (Cambridge: Cambridge University Press, 1999). None of these sources looks at the opening stage direction of *Timon*.

8. *Timon of Athens*, ed. H. J. Oliver (London: Methuen, 1963), 3.

9. *Timon of Athens*, ed. Anthony B. Dawson and Gretchen E. Minton (London: Bloomsbury, 2008).

10. *Timon of Athens*, ed. J. C. Maxwell (Cambridge: Cambridge University Press, 1956), 102.

11. *Timon of Athens*, ed. Karl Klein (Cambridge: Cambridge University Press, 2001), 70n.

12. *Timon of Athens*, ed. G. R. Hibbard (Harmondsworth: Penguin, 1970), p. 146, Commentary Notes.

13. *Timon*, ed. Charlton Hinman in *The Complete Pelican Shakespeare* (Baltimore: Penguin, 1969), 1137.

14. *Timon of Athens*, ed. Frances Dolan (New York: Penguin, 2002). Dolan notes that the Mercer does not speak.

15. *The Complete Works of Shakespeare*, ed. David Bevington (New York: Pearson, 2004), 1297.

16. *The Riverside Shakespeare*, ed. G. Blakemore Evans (Boston: Houghton Mifflin, 1997).

17. *The Norton Shakespeare*, *Timon*, ed. Katherine Eisaman Maus (text: Oxford) (New York: W W Norton, 2008), 2270.

18. *Timon*, ed. Eugene Giddens in *The Norton Shakespeare 3* (New York: W W Norton, 2016), 2580. In his "Textual Comment" on the opening stage direction, Giddens suggests that "'*and Mercer*' describes the occupation of the merchant (as a dealer in textiles)." But Giddens adds: "The Merchant does not say anything about his wares; instead, he serves as a foil for the Jeweler." This statement might seem to undermine the identification of Mercer with Merchant.

19. Stanley Wells and Gary Taylor, *A Textual Companion* (Oxford: Clarendon Press, 1987), 1502.

20. *The New Oxford Shakespeare*, general eds. Gary Taylor, John Jowett, Terri Bourus, Gabriel Egan (Oxford: Oxford University Press, 2016), 2439.

21. *Timon of Athens*, ed. John Jowett (Oxford: Oxford University Press, 2004), 169. Jowett takes the same approach in his edition of *Timon*, included in *Collected Works of Thomas Middleton*, gen. eds. Gary Taylor and John Lavagnino (Oxford: Clarendon, 2007).

22. "The Materiality of the Shakespearean Text," *Shakespeare Quarterly* 44, no. 3 (1993): 267. This important article appears, 255–83.

23. For an interesting discussion of "false starts," see E. A. J. Honingmann, "Shakespeare's Deletions and False Starts, Mark 2," in *Shakespeare's Book: Essays in Reading, Writing and Reception*, eds. Richard Meek, Jane Rickard, and Richard Wilson (Manchester: Manchester University Press, 2008), 165–83.

24. Similar issues appear in my "*All's Well That Ends Well*: Where Is Violenta?," cited above.

25. Stephen Orgel, "What Is an Editor?" in *The Authentic Shakespeare: And Other Problems of the Early Modern Stage* (New York: Routledge, 2002), 16.

26. Here I am more-or-less quoting from my essay on "Violenta," cited above, 181.

27. Orgel, "What Is a Character?," in *The Authentic Shakespeare*, 8. This essay originally appeared in 1996.

28. John Bromley, *The Armorial Bearings of the Guilds of London* (London: Frederick Warne, 1960), 168.

29. Anne F. Sutton, *The Mercery of London: Trade, Goods and People, 1130–1575* (Aldershot: Ashgate, 2005), 507. For a reliable guide to London's guilds, see George Unwin, *The Gilds and Companies of London* (rpt. London: Frank Cass, 1966). Ian Doolittle, *The Mercers' Company 1579–1959* (London: Mercers' Company, 1994) includes in Table 1 a list of the contributions of the Mercers in the Jacobean era to the Crown, the Virginia plantation, and the Palatinate, among others (62).

30. Henry Roberts, *Englands Farewell to Christian the Fourth* (London, 1606), sig. B2.

31. David Kathman, "Grocers, Goldsmiths, and Drapers: Freemen and Apprentices in the Elizabethan Theater," *Shakespeare Quarterly* 55, no. 1 (2004): 1–49.

32. Quotations come from the text edited by George Walton Williams in *The Dramatic Works in the Beaumont and Fletcher Canon*, gen. ed. Fredson Bowers (Cambridge: Cambridge University Press, 1966), 1: 156.

33. For a history of the Lord Mayor's Show, see my *English Civic Pageantry 1558–1642*, rev. edition (Tempe, AZ: Arizona State University Medieval and Renaissance Texts, 2003). See also, Tracey Hill, *Pageantry and Power: A Cultural History of the Early Modern Lord Mayor's Show, 1585–1639* (Manchester: Manchester University Press, 2010).

34. *Collections III: A Calendar of Dramatic Records in the Books of the Livery Companies of London 1485–1640*, ed. Jean Robertson and D. J. Gordon (Oxford: Malone Society, 1954), 61. I have slightly modernized the entry.

35. Anne Sutton, *The Mercery of London*, 507.

36. John Bromley, *Armorial Bearings*, 168.

37. Bromley, 168–69.

38. Critics have long commented on the play's allegory. See for example my "*Timon of Athens* and Morality Drama," *CLA Journal* 10 (1967): 181–88; Anne Lancashire, "*Timon of Athens*: Shakespeare's *Dr. Faustus*," *Shakespeare Quarterly* 21 (1970): 35–44.

39. *King Lear*, ed. Stephen Orgel (New York: Penguin, 1999). *Timon* and *Lear* share a number of features, such as ingratitude and nothing.

40. See Coppélia Kahn's "'Magic of Bounty': *Timon of Athens*, Jacobean Patronage, and Maternal Power," *Shakespeare Quarterly* 38, no. 1 (1987): 34–57.

41. For recent commentary on the issue of "nothing," see Caitlin West, "Performing nothing: The abject body in response to exaggerated speech and action in *King Lear* and *Timon of Athens*," *Shakespeare Institute Review* 4 (2019): 18–27. The author does not discuss the Mercer.

42. Roy E. Schreiber, *The First Earl of Carlisle: Sir James Hay* (Philadelphia: American Philosophical Society, 1984), 5.

43. Dawson and Minton in the Arden edition (2008) editorially intervene in the opening stage direction by giving names to the friends. The Folio text does not name them; this absence seems purposeful to me. The Arden editors, eager to remove the Mercer, now augment the text.   `

44. The latest Arden editors emend "four" to "sour," which does not seem an improvement to me and does not clarify the meaning.

45. For further discussion, see MacDonald P. Jackson, "Early Modern Authorship: Canons and Chronologies," in the *Textual Companion to the Collected Works* (Oxford: Oxford University Press, 2007), 80–97. Jowett offers a convenient summary of Middleton's contribution in the Oxford edition: 144–53. These arguments take us far from Charlton Hinman's claim in the 1969 *Complete Pelican Shakespeare:* "There is now pretty general agreement that *Timon of Athens* is not a collaborated work, partly by someone other than Shakespeare" (1138). The scholarly winds now blow in another direction.

46. See my "Thomas Middleton, Thomas Middleton in London 1613," *Medieval and Renaissance Drama in England* 27 (2014): 17–39.

47. I offer my thanks to Jonathan Lamb, and especially Jeremy Lopez, for their insights and help with this essay.

City Walls, Borders, Boundaries:
Coriolanus and Affective Political Engagement

Gregory W. Sargent

From inauspicious beginnings, the London city wall survived the threats of destruction and inattention until the reign of Edward IV, when the responsibility for upkeep and improvements fell to various city guilds.[1] By the time of the first performances of Shakespeare's *Coriolanus* in 1609, the city walls and borders manifested as focal points of civic authority (as in the Mayoral processions)[2] and as potent spatial repositories of political emotions. The historical participation in projects of improvement combines with the felt proximity of city walls in early modern drama to create a complex matrix of feelings of involvement. In *Coriolanus*, Shakespeare exploited rumblings of social unrest from the Midlands grain riots and unease with the transition to a Jacobean monarchy, transposing this assemblage of affects onto the walls of Rome, represented within the Blackfriars as the walls of London.[3] The staging of violation and deliberate incursions upon city walls and borders in his last tragedy allows Shakespeare to explore the relationship between the theatrical public and the formation of political feelings. By focusing on the way that the dramatic representation of walls shaped affective responses and by linking those responses to political realities, this article aims to expand upon the knowledge of how plays participated in the political world and how that participation shaped new iterations of the social construction of space.[4]

For the early modern dramatist and for the contemporary reader/viewer of the play, the staging of city walls carries a deliberate and meaningful consequence for the congruence of spatial production and theatrical semiotics.[5] I turn to Henri Lefebvre to provide the foundation for a theory of the production of space, notably the idea that while space can be used and consumed, it is also a means of production.[6] Similarly, as a material aspect of the staging of the play, city walls signify in ways that will allows us to gesture toward the complex matrix of meanings that make up what I call politic feelings. As these walls and borders became codified as elements of new conceptions of social space, their close association with the public theaters made them useful and productive as sites of contention and representation wherein drama can, as Jean Howard explains, "make cognitive and ideological sense of life in the city."[7]

I draw attention to the physical proximity of the city wall to the playhouses and to the historical events during the writing and performance of the drama to complicate an argument about the political readings of the play. I wish to re-position the play as an example that stages the violation of city walls not just for political exigency, but also as emotional or feeling gestures that converge around city walls as part of a matrix of emergent spatial practices. I want to trace the way in which the city wall works as an emotional tie for the spectator and to show how Shakespeare uses that emotional tie to make complex arguments about space, political power, and civic pride. Thus, violations of space are the impetus of the transaction that indicates an audience member's involvement and apprehension of the emotional valence of the text. The walls of the play on stage, whether they are visible or not, are the walls of Rome and London in *Coriolanus* simultaneously. In Shakespeare's text, the wall or borders violated are Corioles in the first act by Caius Martius, Tullus Aufidius's home in the fourth act by Caius Martius, and the Volscian camp in the fifth act by Volumnia, Virgilia, and Young Martius. Martius breeching the walls of Corioles neatly fits a definition of violation; when his mother, wife, and son come to the Volscian camp, the sense of violation maps less on to the denotation of the word, but the connotation makes clear how the incursion is entirely dependent on the kind of liminal, interdisciplinary space that a city wall represents and how this space provides for affective political engagement. In the brief moments of history that I trace, I show that there existed a connection between the citizen audience of the play and the London wall that cements the foundation for an emotional response to the symbolic walls of the play.

The terms "affective relationship" and "politic feelings" indicate a methodological understanding of similar things. These are not identical notions, though they share many congruencies. A great part of the difficulty is to avoid assigning anachronistic characteristics of feelings or emotions to the people that make up the early modern theatrical audience. For Shakespeare and the early modern audience, Galenic humoral theory maintained a strong influence upon the determination of emotional responses as consequences of bodily reactions. However, in *The Reformation of Emotions in the Age of Shakespeare*, Steven Mullaney argues against the validity of a Galenic theory as an etiology of emotion, remarking that humors influenced temperament, not emotion.[8] Mullaney understands emotions as mental states by reading feelings (or affective relations) as both social and material things. For him, the phenomenology of emotions in the sixteenth and seventeenth centuries points to the transactional and enacted nature of emotions: "The apprehension of involvement, the social element of an emotion, is also the moment of embodiment."[9] Further, Arab et al. write that the biological explanation of emotions cannot offer the only way to explain the impact of affect upon the social formation of an audience; they conclude, "Affect's generation and circulation through social networks suggest that it can be a shared or collective experience."[10] This is akin to the "assemblages" that Drew Daniel constructs to demonstrate the conception and transmission of melancholy. By drawing out the connection between bodies and semiotics, between the physical display and the utterance of emotion, Daniel affirms the necessary embodiment of a cultural phenomenon that generates physical effects while spreading outward through cultural participation.[11]

I share Mullaney's skepticism of the criticism that would allow one to subsume the emotions under the passions or temperaments to explicate and produce a reading of Galenic theory that accurately reflects the lived social experience of how an audience member might feel when watching a play. As an audience member, the words or actions of a play cause one to form an affective relationship with any number of theatrical semiotic signifiers, whether it is the character, the place or setting, the ideas, or the actual experience of being in the theater (and more likely some combination of these things). The nuance and subtlety of these things range far beyond the starkly defined humors and their relative heat and cold or wetness and dryness. As such, the plays create affective significance in an audience's experience through spatial violation, both real and fictional. This becomes the politic feelings that assemble the matrix of human emotion, politics, and social practice that result from the playgoing experience.

The act of reading, generally, and the viewing of drama, particularly, are types of interactions that rely on investments in time, attention, and feeling. Drama, whether read or seen, will reciprocate the investment with something akin to accrued interest. I posit this fiscal metaphor because it helps give a place to feelings and emotions within the whole of the literary/dramatic enterprise. As part of the (many) exchanges taking place in early modern theater, those of feelings or emotions become more palpable as a part of a transaction. This is what makes the idea of the social and material nature of emotions so apt for theater. A spectator will embody an emotional response while watching a play because she is inherently involved. The sociality of the theater combined with its transactional nature (both feelingly and economically) make drama a singularly valuable vehicle for the study of feelings or emotions. Herein, I fold this idea into the complex interdisciplinary space of the plays' city walls and borders, along with the violations of such spaces. Excitingly, the play suggests an emotional connection to space at key moments of violation through the language of Caius Martius, Volumnia, and Tullus Aufidius. This couples with the affective relationship that many in the audience had with the London city wall to suggest that the play unfolds a complex relationship between the politics that govern the city and the way in which the populace maintained an emotional connection with city walls, borders, and other emerging spaces as products of a proto-capitalist market economy.

Shakespeare's Roman tragedy was very likely written during or right after a peasant rebellion in the Midlands and explicitly references one of the popularly stated causes of this violence.[12] I draw attention to this fact to justify the notion of violation as a prism through which to read the play text. Necessarily, violation is a loose term; however, this play relies on the action of disruption from the norm that violence represents. One may argue that there would be no plot without dramatic upheaval or conflict, and certainly, violence is a kind of conflict that energizes drama. Nevertheless, violence, as I represent it, has a particular resonance with this play, especially considering the staging of city walls, borders, and boundaries. Violence can be overt or subtle, but the kinds of violence around city walls makes this play a cultural text that has something to say about the way a contemporary audience might think (or be led to think) about the use of space and how these spaces relate to the power structures within the city or the nation. Shakespeare's walls are no less the walls of London, even though they signify as the walls or Corioles or Rome. The playwright demands of the viewer or reader that we think about the space of the walls, their use, and what that kind of border or demarcation means to a society that travels within and without these spaces. That we might continue to associate violence with walls indicating borders between nations makes the study of the violations of the space of walls in these plays especially meaningful, reinforcing the vitality of these old texts as social signifiers.

It must have been a tense atmosphere for the opening scene of Shakespeare's *Coriolanus* inside the roofed theater of Blackfriars in 1609. The scene is an armed company of "mutinous Citizens" (1.1.0 sd)[13] clamoring for cheap corn. The First Citizen says, "You are all resolved rather to die than to famish?" (1.1.4–5). A tenor of threat is in the air from the opening lines. The recent rioting in the Midlands and the years of dearth that were part of the cause of the civil unrest cannot have escaped the minds of the spectators viewing the play for the first time. I wonder (and speculate that they also might have asked) if any of those present would have felt safer knowing they were inside the city walls. Though the London city wall would not have been visible from inside the theater, patrons surely sensed its proximity to the west end performance space. Alone, the city wall or the anti-enclosure violence may not suggest much significance for scholars of drama. However, under the aegis of the play *Coriolanus*, these two things take on a mantle heavily laden with meaning and social import. The political valence for which the play is justly celebrated bleeds into an ongoing debate about the emerging notions of the cultural use of space.[14]

When the violation of space induces an affective significance for the audience, a kind of blended feeling emerges that cannot be entirely distinguished from the political context of the play. A wealth of criticism aiming to understand the political contexts of Shakespeare and his main source author, Plutarch, supports this interest in the affective political engagement inspired

by the text. In the case of the parallels that the play draws between Martius
and King James, Shannon Miller avers that Shakespeare's drama is "a textual
negotiation of the political tensions of the period" and further, "Such parallels
between noted traits of James and the actions of Shakespeare's Coriolanus
are achieved through alterations to the Plutarchan source."[15] Drawing a connection between Martius and James sets in relief the national sentiment regarding the unifying of England and Scotland. Alex Garganigo contends that James
is central to understanding *Coriolanus* and Menenius's fable of the belly
because: "James made his body the centerpiece of his argument for Union."[16]
That Garganigo understands the fable of the belly to come not from Plutarch,
but from John Russell's 1604 *Treatise of the Happie and Blissed Union Betuixt
the Tua Ancienne Realmes of Scotland and Ingland*, shows that Shakespeare
amended his source to maximize the affective impact that a retelling of the
belly fable would have upon an audience aware of James's political actions.
Further, the critical view that Shakespeare's knowledge of Machiavelli's texts
The Prince, *The Discourses*, and *The Art of War* influenced his treatment of
Plutarch gives nuance to the ways in which Shakespeare effected a sway upon
audiences' emotional reactions. Patrick Ashby surmises, "I take the view that
Shakespeare's interest in 'Machiavellian' ideas prompted him to misrepresent
his Plutarchan source in order to examine the paradoxical effects of idealistic
inflexibility, and to indicate the moral challenges posed by conceptual indeterminacy."[17] These examples underscore the important connection between
politics and affect and they lend credence to the idea that Shakespeare created
a drama that manipulated the Plutarchan story to limn affective political
engagement for his audience.[18]

More subtly, *Coriolanus* deals with the root of First Citizen's complaint,
that laws are made to support high interest rates in moneylending, by showing
from whence the problem stems. The whole tirade against a negligent government essentializes the problems of famine, usury, and legal support as
creations of a greedy ruling class. For Leah Marcus, this play becomes the
power struggle of the civic inhabitants of Rome with their Patrician ruling
class, a mirror of London localities struggling with an expanding monarchical
reach. The danger (or excitement) is in the way in which it reflects London
in the early years of Stuart rule. She writes, "It is the Rome of the early
republican period, a Rome which is, like early Jacobean London, expanding
out to incorporate the suburban areas around it . . . dominated by fierce civic
pride and clamor for the preservation of local autonomy."[19] Like Marcus, I
recognize the way in which this drama strains the relationship of the citizens
and the patricians and uses the space of the city to do so. However, unlike
Marcus's astute reading of the play, I wish to complicate the political resonance of the affective dynamics of the drama. Her reading shows the politics
of the city played out on the stage with the result being "the enactment of
tragedy—the self-imposed fall of a noble general—[which] does not so much

flout the laws and customs of the city as display their increasing power."[20] I do not see the play reflecting the increased power of the customs and laws of a city; rather, I understand the play to cultivate and experiment with different affective relationships to certain geographic or chorographic markers that then externalize the civic attachment to the city. In effect, the citizens feel certain ways about the city because of how they act when confronting the city walls or borders and how they understand those walls and borders to be social constructions with a particular use value. I suspect that Shakespeare would not have wanted to align a character in his play so obviously close to the monarch or to a city that was litigating abuses of local authority. In this distance between Rome and London, *Coriolanus* must give life to other ways of examining the city and its citizens.

It is this sense of perspective between Rome and London that gives the play its affective dynamics, which I read through their political and martial contexts. By creating distance through dramatic semiotic signifiers like the city walls and the less tangible walls of the Volscian camp, the characters and the audience must view the actions of the play as exchanges across space and ideology. I want to show the "inherently transactional"[21] nature of emotions by pointing to a connection between ancient Rome and London that will illustrate the strength of the affective perspective carried by actors and audience. As part of a continuation of the Humanist reformation of educational goals, Roger Ascham's *The Schoolmaster* (1570) seeks to trade in on the kind of exchange that characterizes the paragon of culture in ancient times. He posits, "When Italy and Rome have been, to the great good of us that now live, the best breeders and bringers-up of the worthiest men, not only for wise speaking, but also for well-doing, in all civil affairs."[22] Wise speaking and well-doing were the marks of that great civilization and Ascham would teach young sixteenth-century English children to do those same things. Helpfully, he builds up what Cathy Shrank designates as "The intellectual and emotional connection between ancient Rome and early modern England ("us that now live"); he also demonstrates the necessary relationship between linguistic competence ("wise speaking") and participation in civil affairs."[23] Though she does not term it so, Shrank uncovers one way that the affective exchange can function, and does function, in this play.[24] The emotional connection between Rome and London happens as one of those moments when the audience intuits their involvement and the social transaction of emotion embodies that feeling within them.[25] I would like to underscore the importance of the myth of Britain's founding by Brutus and the way that this presents a part of the affective connection that the play draws upon in order to create its own emotional exchanges. To put it concretely, the walls of Rome and the walls of London represent the emotional perspectives whose transaction, or movement between the characters trade upon and transmit to the audience to create emotional affiliation.

What follows is my explication of three moments when a violation of city walls or boundaries happens at affectively generative points in the play. Briefly, they are in the first act when Martius attacks and enters Corioles alone, in the fourth act when Martius sneaks into Aufidius's house in Antium, and in the fifth act when Volumnia, Virgilia, and Young Martius enter the Volscian camp to plead for Rome. All three are instances of the violation of walls or boundaries that carry political valence. Though the incursion upon Aufidius's house is not quite the same as a city wall, Martius's action is no less political, his violation of the space, in a sense, being more upon the city (that bears the dwellings of his enemies), than on the house or domestic space. The violence in the language in each case beckons the audience to consider the ways in which they are connected to the walls and borders being transgressed. This is the foundation for the affective connection that participates in a political dynamic, giving a stage presence to politic feelings.

With characteristic quick pace, Shakespeare writes the battle scene at the wall of Corioles in such manner as to incite the audience to emote, perhaps even to feel a swell of excitement at seeing the action from the Romans' point of view. The First Senator from Corioles sets up the ground to explicitly invoke the walls of the city. He cries out from the balcony to Martius and the Romans below,

> Hark! our drums
> Are bringing forth our youth. We'll break our walls
> Rather than they shall pound us up. Our gates,
> Which yet seem shut, we have but pinned with rushes;
> They'll open of themselves.
> *Alarum afar off.*   Hark you, far off!
> There is Aufidius. List what work he makes
> Amongst your cloven army.

(1.4.15–21)

The battle is set to begin. The walls that the Romans would storm (Lartius calls for "Ladders, ho!" [22]), are the central focus here, thanks to First Senator. They house the gates that will soon pour the youth of Corioles forth. In the Senator's construction, those gates that would seem to hold the Romans back actually have another function, that of keeping the Corioleans within. It is a typical martial taunting for him to say that his enemies are safer outside of the walls because they hold back the army within. Yet, the gates are weakly fastened, only with rushes are they made closed. This is the site of contention over a wall that would seem to be permeable, except this is not, for the moment, characterized as a weakness. This speech primes Shakespeare's audience for an affective political engagement with walls because the First Senator does two things: first, as stated above, he remarks that the walls shall not contain the army of Corioles; second, he reminds Martius that Aufidius is making short work of the other part of the Roman army. First Senator tries to capitalize on the notion that he has outthought the Roman general. He speaks as though to confirm that the government of Corioles has done a better job leading the people, that they have been the better politicians. His words underscore this when he claims that Corioles would "break our walls / Rather than they shall pound us up." The wall means less to the First Senator because it can be so permeable. The danger to the Romans is both within and without the wall, therefore, for the First Senator, the wall is not an important site of contest; instead, it will only be the site of Martius's defeat. The political body of Corioles need not be tied to the wall and the possible defenses it might provide because they are the better political leaders, having prepared for the battle in a way that Martius did not expect. From the audience's perspective, the wall of Corioles, at this moment, is not an important signifier of place; it serves more to show a kind of unity of political ability within the city. This is an important counterpoint to the walls of Rome and will be a key detail in the explication to follow when Martius storms Corioles alone. However, in the present moment of the play, the result of the political affect associated with the wall in question is that the audience feels the devaluing of the significance of the wall and an alignment to the kind of government that can govern, as it were, without walls. This is an important distinction to bring up early, for the play will complicate the idea of walls and borders, what they mean, and how they are used. Critics have struggled with this as a way to read the play; Lisa Hopkins infers, "The walls of Rome are certainly important in *Coriolanus*, but perhaps not in the ways we would expect, for *Coriolanus* is an oddity. It is a Roman play, but has no obvious political agenda."[26] I would concur with Hopkins—were this the only example of how the characters in the play talk about walls—that I did not expect a wall to, of necessity, be invisible or easily permeable when the politicians are doing an adequate job. I would not characterize the play as an oddity; more precisely, it is a play much in keeping with Shakespeare's career-long interest in the machinations of the Roman republic. On an entirely surface level, this alone posits the political agenda of this play, though we would be well advised to debate the deeper meanings of this agenda. I believe that *Coriolanus* offers a way of thinking about the beginning of a republican government while maintaining a necessary artistic distance from actual events or people (specifically the monarch) to allow the drama to signify as a text that trades on producing political affect. As I have shown, city walls are a key to transmitting this kind of affect to an audience.

Caius Martius brings to bear the clinching locus of affect and politics upon the city wall when he makes use of the rhetorical mode of amphiboly. Ranked by George Puttenham in *The Arte of English Poesie* as "the worst abuse or vice in rhetoric,"[27] amphiboly (in the Greek) or ambiguitas (in the Latin) shows itself to be immensely helpful when considering emotional currents that we might not know about with any certainty. Our modern usage keeps the term ambiguity in a similar sense, but there is more at stake here for the dramatic use of this rhetorical device, so I will use the less familiar term of amphiboly to describe the shifting and slippery language that Shakespeare sometimes uses to elicit and express emotional valence. It is far more than the dramatist being ambiguous; there is too much "maybe" left in that term, leaving a feeling of either/or instead. Rather, from a logical disposition, amphiboly delivers with a "both/and" kind of conjunction. The term expresses the weight of the interpretation that the text demands of its audience. Similarly, its relative unfamiliarity will help distinguish the term's importance. Martius's full skill of oration is on display as he tries to inflame his troops,

> They fear us not, but issue forth their city.
> Now put your shields before your hearts, and fight
> With hearts more proof than shields. Advance, brave Titus.
> They do disdain us much beyond our thoughts,
> Which makes me sweat with wrath. Come on, my fellows.
> He that retires, I'll take him for a Volsce,
> And he shall feel mine edge.
>
> (1.4.23–29)

This speech and the action of violation that quickly follows it mark the tone of the play and become the pivotal moments for establishing political affect. The key is the amphibolic meanings of "proof." The *OED* cites this very quote as an example of the first adjectival definition of proof, "Of tried or proven strength or quality; (originally *esp.* of armour) of tested power of resistance. *fig.* and in extended use: impenetrable, impervious, invulnerable, resistant (now the usual sense)."[28] This is the clear, expected definition of proof in this instance. Martius wants his soldiers to fight with heart, something that cannot be exactly defined; however, when placed in opposition or comparison to the soldiers' shields, the supposed proof of their hearts becomes a thing more tangible. They become, in this sense, like a wall built against the tide of Volscians, impenetrable, impervious, and resistant. For the audience's ears, this is one of the ways the play makes an emotional connection, by linking the Roman soldiers' hearts to their (hopeful) prowess as fighters. It helps fuel the metaphor that would make the soldiers' shields less necessary because they would be fighting so rigorously that they would have little need of shields to defend themselves. Whether an audience member backs the Romans, the Volscians, or even if he or she is a neutral spectator, there is a conspicuous connection to a feeling action here. By having the heart to complete the undertaking, Martius involves his soldiers in his own emotion and, consequently, so too does the audience feel this involvement. This is the moment of the embodied emotion; as Mullaney reminds us, this is the social nature of how the text transmits emotional affect. Thomas Heywood captured this moment in a similar manner. In *An Apology for Actors*, he writes, "What English blood, seeing the person of any bold English man presented and doth not hugge his fame and hunnye at his valor . . . offers to him in his hart all prosperous performance . . . that it hath power to new mold the harts of the spectators and fashion them to the shape of any noble and notable attempt."[29] Even Heywood believed in the power of the actor to move the feelings of the audience in some manner. Though not as technical as Mullaney, Heywood's terms show that there is a measure of involvement when seeing actors on the stage; I think it is no coincidence that Heywood writes about the heart being the vessel through which the audience apprehends involvement. When Martius demands that his soldiers show their hearts to be "more proof than shields," we can reasonably identify that there is a moment of social exchange of emotion taking place and that the adjectival meaning of proof generates this feeling.

Unsurprisingly, it is more complicated than this. The multivalent signifi-cations of "proof" show that there is a deeper level to the political substance of this moment in the play. Proof is also a noun, of which many of the senses were in use well before Shakespeare wrote the play. Upon examination, there are many different meanings of proof that could take the place of the adjective form as well. There is the first definition, "Something that proves a statement; evidence or argument establishing a fact or the truth of anything, or belief in the certainty of something,"[30] which would seem to fit especially well in this case as Martius is attempting to establish the fact of his soldiers' hearts as capable of meeting the challenge, implying his belief of that thing. Perhaps the second definition fits more aptly, wherein the *OED* defines it as "the action of evidence in convincing the mind."[31] This iteration would make the heart evidence to the mind, of Martius or the spectators, of something more than a shield; it is an index that points to something deeper connecting the soldiers to their duty.[32] We might even point to another definition of proof, which states, "The action or an act of testing or making trial of something; the condition of being tested."[33] This connotation builds upon the emotional involvement of the soldiers as they would make trial of whether their hearts are more tested in battle than their shields. I do not mean to be tedious, but this listing could continue. However, the many different definitions are not necessarily the critical point of this exercise. What matters here is the way in which the word proof functions as an amphiboly that forces the audience to reckon with the meaning of proof and the way in which it causes that audience to form a connection to the walls onstage. This happens because of the many ways that proof draws different connections between Martius and his men, which in turn become part of the fabric of the audience's apprehension of involvement. These actions take place in the spatial vicinity of the city walls, leading inevitably toward the inclusion of the spatial semiotics into the spec-tators' visual reading of the action. The locus of city walls in this key scene

(as well as the ones I discuss below) provides Shakespeare with the opportunity to draw upon the signification of the city walls as contemporary historical markers for an early modern audience. As I mentioned above, the city
walls provide fodder for critical thinking about boundaries and borders for
readers in the following centuries. Through this complex matrix, the amphibole
of proof presses an attentive audience to think further about how Martius and
the play construct affective meaning while allowing the author to build upon
the political valence inherent in the military actions onstage.

   Coriolanus quickens affective involvement through the association of
amphiboly with Martius's character as well. Earlier, I quoted George Puttenham on the rhetorical term and his virulent distaste for such ambiguity. Putting
the amphibolic word in Martius's mouth is a choice that the playwright makes
to facilitate a mode of affective engagement between Martius and the audience.
Not only does the kind of opacity that comes with amphiboly make Martius
a difficult character to understand in terms of his motivations, but he also
becomes concurrently untrustworthy and prescient. This is, as Mullaney
summarizes, because "Puttenham relates amphibology not to sophistry . . .
but to a pre-Socratic past that is oracular as well as pagan."[34] Martius, in his
oracular mode, would be a figure both wondered at and feared. In the play,
he is already both, so the title of oracle seems to fit, though in this instance,
he seems not to be prognosticating. This will change in the fiery speech in
the Forum upon his banishment in 3.3 and then, a scene later, when he says,
"I shall be loved when I am lacked" (4.1.15). Martius's shiftiness drives much
of the distaste a reader may feel for him. We might respect his military record
and his devotion to the idea of the state of Rome, but he is altogether difficult
to determine when he would exhort his fellow soldiers while simultaneously
threatening to cut them should they retreat.

   For the early modern audience, Martius's amphiboly would be more recog-
nizably troubling in that it was associated with treasonous remarks. We may
recall the witches' prophecy in *Macbeth* and how the characters reacted to
the indeterminacy. I would even invite us to recall Cordelia's amphibolic
"nothing" in response to her father's query of what she might say to outstrip
her sisters' offers and protestations of love. In this case, Lear reads Cordelia's
answer as a treasonous dictate of filial rejection, whatever the actual truth of
the statement may be. This is a particularly troubling quality of amphiboly,
especially in a country experiencing the growth and development of a national
language. Mullaney extrapolates, "Nor are they simply relics of bygone days,
for amphibologies return willfully to trouble both the still developing national
language and the security of the state itself."[35] No stranger to this rhetorical
device, Shakespeare gives us a character that troubles through his very words,
even before we consider his actions. With hindsight, we know that Martius
will be called a traitor; even through his vehement denial, we will still question
just how true this accusation is. Yet, the difficulty of the "proof" remains even

after Martius leaves Rome. Perhaps he goes seeking some other test or trial; maybe, a heart more proof than a shield needs more convincing of his mind rather than testing of his sword. In any case, the uncertainty that Shakespeare develops here pulls a spectator in; it invites the kind of involvement that constitutes the social appropriation of emotion and the transmission of feeling from stage to spectator. That Martius may be treasonous only gives further texture to the political context of these feelings.

Caius Martius's entry to Antium does not carry the same kind of frenetic pace that his incursion of Corioles generates. Indeed, he enters the stage "in mean apparel, disguised and muffled" (4.4.0 sd). For this reason, among others that I will note below, the sense of violation is likewise muffled, subdued, but still simmering below the appearance of things. In the 2011 film version, actor and director Ralph Fiennes makes the dramaturgic choice to have the titular character grow a beard, in stark contrast to the entirely clean-shaven face and head of the Martius of Rome.[36] Caius Martius enters Antium on foot, clothes disheveled, and looks around at the seaside town. The buildings are non-Roman, and his dress clearly marks him as out of place. In this reading of the play, the film production makes it clear that the normal order of things is not as it was. Martius's beard is in full defiance of the militaristic codes that the viewer would expect, based on the hyper-martial setting, war scenes, and fatigues that almost all the men in the play wear. Violation is written plain upon Martius's face.

In the play text, Martius signals his awareness of the spatial violation from the first line of the scene. In a rare moment of solitude on stage, he muses,

> A goodly city is this Antium. City,
> 'Tis I that made thy widows. Many an heir
> Of these fair edifices fore my wars
> Have I heard groan and drop. Then know me not,
> Lest that thy wives with spits and boys with stones
> In puny battle slay me.
>
> (4.4.1–6)

Addressing the city, Martius acknowledges his deeds in war may not be the most kindly looked-upon actions in the heart of the territory of his former enemies. He caps this by willing the city not to recognize him, though there is a measure of situational irony in his invocation against death in "puny battle." When he does meet his end, Martius is called "boy" by Tullus Aufidius, and the conflict is no great war wherein he might perform deeds heroic; but rather, he dies in an ambush, infantilized and alone. This type of battle, one that the character cannot foresee for himself, echoes the subtle undercurrent of violation introduced here by Martius's solitary musing. Additionally, we must consider the fact that Martius really does want to be recognized, perhaps not by the wives and children in the streets, but ultimately by the men, and by Tullus Aufidius, specifically. This would confirm his martial prowess, by being the man who was an "eagle in a dovecote" (5.6.113), and intriguingly, he cannot refrain from trying to give himself away before the proper moment of reveal when he has this brief exchange with one of the servant men,

THRID SERVINGMAN: Where dwell'st thou?
CORIOLANUS: Under the canopy . . .
THIRD SERVINGMAN: Where's that?
CORIOLANUS: I' th' city of kites and crows.

(4.5.40–45)

Further, the trope of the avian metaphor allows Martius one last jab at his bitter rival before joining with him, wherein he replies to the serving man's incredulous response to the above exchange by calling Tullus Aufidius a daw. The language of birds of prey and the behaviors of fowl in general do some work that almost gives away the identity of Martius before the more dramatically appropriate moment. By telling the servant that he dwells in the city of kites and crows, he is aligning himself with those prey birds that hunt and attack (language that he employs in the final scene of the play, as quoted above) while offsetting his conception of self by affirming once more that he thinks Tullus Aufidius to be a silly thing, a daw (now called a jackdaw). In sum, Martius seems aware of the kind of the perception of violation that his presence in Antium invokes in all parties (the fictional Volsces, the early modern audience, and the reader). The tension of the scene builds with the half confessions that hint at Martius's undisguised identity.

In this very specific instance of a violation of space, we are dealing with walls and boundaries that are not physically present on stage.[37] Shakespeare labors to distinguish the type of connections that the surrounding characters have to the space they inhabit through the language of the servers that enter and exit rapidly in the scene following Martius's arrival in Antium. In this way, the play gives voice to Martius's own sense of being an outsider, one who has usurped or incurred upon a space where he is, at least, not welcome, and at most, subject to execution. As I interrogate the language of the scene further, I will show how the cultural significations of walls and boundaries coupled with emotional connections emerge in the spatial semiotics of the stage. Above all, I wish to highlight the linguistic keys that exemplify how the play provides an instance of a violation of space to understand a conception of the cultural significance of what walls and borders represent.

Martius moves from outside of the borders of Antium to the inside, perhaps even to the very heart of the enemy's territory when he enters the house of Tullus Aufidius. Though much of the language I quote above exemplifies how he feels a sense of unwelcome,[38] Martius is at his most straightforward when he says, "A goodly house. The feast smells well, but I/Appear not like a guest" (4.5.5–6). As is so often the importance of the trope for the dramatic medium, how Martius looks determines who he is and how he feels. His awareness of the violation of space that his Antium incursion represents allows the audience to understand the gravity of the emotional force that humans imbue in particular spaces. Nevertheless, it is not only Martius's awareness of place, but the concurrent disavowal of Rome that his journey enfolds that brings the affective politics into relief. As Martius moves closer to his encounter with Tullus Aufidius, the dynamics of the space change as well. The audience sees the serving men working (at least nominally busily), there is talk and preparation for a feast, and at the reveal, Aufidius's language echoes that of a man speaking of his spouse. Throughout, the language of plenty and the behavior of the serving men of Antium provide stark contrasts to the characterization of the Roman citizens and their appeal for food in a time of dearth. In this development especially, the political affect must be understood to illuminate the way the play brings into focus the cultural attitudes towards spaces and the inherent emotion embodiment of them.

The violated space in this scene differs in its substance from the scene that takes place before the walls of Corioles. In this instance, the subtle cues that the drama gives the audience accumulate to form a distinct setting with a violation that stands as a particular affective product. Though Martius does not stand before any physical wall, his awareness of the strangeness of the situation and his sustained disruption of the serving men's labor draw an audience member to deduce a violation or misappropriation of the space. At the core of this is the moment when Martius reveals himself to Aufidius; however, Shakespeare writes a scene that does more than confirm one man's identity. It cements how uncharacteristic Martius's decision is and how greatly it is at odds with the play's previous political current.

Coriolanus presents the conflicts of gender dynamics when Martius and Aufidius meet. Rather than being at odds with the martial nature of the play, the scene serves to set in relief how Martius struggles to play a more domestic and marital (as opposed to martial) role. Here, Martius and Tullus Aufidius play the roles of husband and wife in the struggle for the domus. The interplay begins with Martius saying he was "Whooped out of Rome. Now this extremity/Hath brought me to thy hearth" (4.5.82–83). In submissiveness, he makes his gesture a physical one, "[I] Present/My throat to thee and to thy ancient malice . . . And cannot live but to thy shame unless/It be to do thee service" (4.5.99–100, 104–5). Driven to the hearth of his enemy, Martius goads Aufidius still, daring him to cut his throat or to use him. In a somewhat reduced way, Martius presents his body to Aufidius for him to do as he pleases. To kill Martius with a knife is a kind of penetration (an act one might anticipate on a wedding night); Tullus Aufidius does not disappoint the viewers. His reply is rather stunning,[39]

> O Martius, Martius! . . .
> Let me twine
> Mine arms about thy body, whereagainst
> My grained ash an hundred times hath broke
> And scarred the moon with splinters
>
> (105–13)

> . . .
> Know thou first,
> I loved the maid I married; never man
> Sighed truer breath. But that I see thee here,
> Thou noble thing, more dances my rapt heart
> Than when I first my wedded mistress saw
> Bestride my threshold.
>
> (117–22)

The sexual tension of this passage is palpable, and many critics have done much work to unpack the meanings, overt and subvert, of the erotically charged language.[40] Rather than understanding this relationship to be pathological or problematic, or, as Kuzner does, to see it as liberating to the point of "dissolve[ing] personal boundaries . . . reduc[ing] themselves to surfaces,"[41] I see this as an underutilized strategy of placing both men in domestic roles wherein they will play out (or fight out) the struggle for dominance in a power relationship. In this vein, I believe it is reductive to posit that Martius takes on a feminized role, though Aufidius's language would place him in such a one. Thus, here is the tension and the struggle. As he speaks these lines, the audience must wonder if these two men can fight together if one is meant to be subservient. *Coriolanus* is novel in that it creates, in miniature, a domestic quarrel over a gendered power struggle.[42] Hopkins almost captures this when she writes, "Having returned from combat to the domestic sphere, he then travels back to the place of war, albeit in a quasi-domestic capacity as a guest and dependent of Aufidius, and exposes the vulnerability of his home not on an emotional plane but on a military one."[43] I think that there is very clear domestic setting in place for this encounter between Martius and Aufidius; one of the servants even describes Aufidius's treatment of Martius thus, "Our general himself makes a mistress of him; sanctifies himself with's hand, and turns up the white o' th' eye to his discourse" (4.5.203–5). It is here that the audience gets drawn deeper into the emotional investment that constitutes the politically affective content of the play. No matter the individual viewer's feelings about Martius's decision, he or she is involved and the violation of the domestic space of Aufidius's hearth is the vehicle for attaining such affective involvement. It is another kind of wall that has been breached, but it is the violation of this space that brings to bear the interrogation of the use of boundaries that enemies keep between each other and that domestic partners (of whatever gender) erect as they contrive to maintain a delicate balance of power and affection.

Earlier, I wrote about the guildhalls' responsibility for maintenance and upkeep of the London city wall. It is the sense of community that I would like to invoke here to enhance the picture of the complex matrix of political and emotional connections represented by Martius's breaching of Aufidius's walls. This strange scene presents the initial stages of an unexpected community being built. The complex, obsessive, and often sexual nature of the ties that bind Martius and Tullus Aufidius provide a rough foundation for the kind of community that a wall helps define, whether that is by exclusion or inclusion. Of note, the wall itself acts as a kind of definition or test; the liminal nature of the space of a city wall also becomes a potential site of judgment and assay. As the action of the play progresses, the audience notes the previously violated space of the wall; they must wonder what kind of a wall, and by extension, what kind of city, that an alliance between these two leonine warriors would create. Perhaps we may impute this impulse to the patricians of Rome, who, upon hearing of the alliance, make a desperate attempt to stop the "lonely dragon" (4.1.30) they once turned away.

In this third analysis of a spatial violation, there is a question about the "end" of walls or borders, a useful bit of an amphiboly that encapsulates the disquieting feeling of peace that characterizes the last few scenes of the play. In the argument above, I have focused on the way that Shakespeare's deployment of walls in this play connects to the very real unrest that was a consequence of the grain riots in the years preceding the performance. This text fits into the larger cultural landscape as a mode of reflecting the steady reorganization and redefinition of the use of space, both public and private, in the years beginning the seventeenth century. Specifically, this play creates and invites the apprehension of politically motivated affect, a kind of feeling about the working of governance, through the violation of city wall spaces, which have palpable political import. I script this brief summation to introduce the way in which this study now takes on the last of the violated wall spaces, the incursion of Volumnia, Virgilia, and Young Marcus into the Volscian camp, outside of Rome. This violation pairs with the ambiguity of the notion of an "end" of walls. In the sense of termination or finality, there is no more need for the defensive or militaristic wall because Volumnia and Martius make peace with the Volsces. We may recall the closeness that Hopkins infers about the Romans and Volsces[44] and gather that the amount of shared cultural practices may revoke the need for any walls, thus making the end of the walls and the walls a thing of the past. However, in its less obvious or expected usage, end means the point, purpose, or use of the wall. This article is heavily interested in the notion of boundaries and how humans choose to define these. From the microcosmic domestic spaces to the macrocosmic city walls, there is an intense need to examine how the creation of these boundaries indicate the way in which people determine them. This is especially pointed when we look at the violation of these walls or borders. Though there is little violence to the entrance of Volumnia, Virgilia, and Young Martius's into the Volscian camp, this is an incursion that leads Martius to conclude that his mother has "prevailed" "most dangerously." The difficulty in reading this scene (though it is a pleasant one) is the necessity to draw conclusions that go beyond the scope of Martius's character and specifically his relationship with his mother. In what follows, I will trace through pertinent lines of speech and attempt to extrapolate how this is an invocation for the political affect Shakespeare uses to make sense of this breach of a wall or boundary.

The long speeches of 5.3, made mostly by Volumnia, attempt to give definition to the reason for the familial incursion in such a way that might persuade Martius to break off the impending attack on Rome; he says to Aufidius, "We will before the walls of Rome tomorrow / Set down our host" (5.3.1–2). Walls are on the mind, of Martius, Aufidius, the Volsces, and the audience as well. The offstage physical proximity underscores the less tangible wall that Volumnia, Virgilia, and Young Martius must overcome. As we near the end of the scene, the audience begins to understand that Martius's decision to make peace with the Volsces has more to do with the purpose of walls and their use as things of definition and division. Though I cautioned against making conclusions based solely on Martius's character, the plea that finally wins him over is one that points to the difficulty he has defining himself within the world of the play. This also serves a secondary, but no less important, purpose of illuminating the magnitude of his wife's words and what she represents as one who must make her life within the strict walls and boundaries that define her role as a wife and a woman in Rome's militaristic patriarchal society.

Volumnia begins to frame the request to her son with an affective appeal to the sense of Rome as a place to which she cultivates attachment,

> For how can we,
> Alas, how can we for our country pray,
> Whereto we are bound, together with thy victory,
> Whereto we are bound? Alack, or we must lose
> The country, our dear nurse, or else thy person,
> Our comfort in the country. We must find
> An evident calamity, though we had
> Our wish which side should win. For either thou
> Must as a foreign recreant be led
> With manacles through our streets, or else
> Triumphantly tread on thy country's ruin,
> And bear the palm for having bravely shed
> Thy wife and children's blood.

(5.3.106–18)

This is a deft rhetorical action; Volumnia uses lineal anaphora to cement her connection to both Rome and to Martius. The preposition "whereto" strongly signifies the place related nature of the question. In her conception, the country and Martius's victory are both places to which she is bound, therefore, they are both places that need definition and delimitation. I read this as a moment of apprehension for the audience when their involvement in the emotional valence of the scene creates a blending of affect and politics. Volumnia is especially provocative by implying that this outcome arrives with a loss of at least one kind of space. The theatrical medium makes excellent use of this spatial metaphor in its semiotic representation of London through the Rome of the stage. She ties her suffering to Rome; though an audience may not necessarily empathize, Volumnia's words still force them to reckon with the walled aspect of the London performance. This is, perhaps, a moment of national consciousness for the early modern theatergoer. The destruction of the "country," whereto the audience is bound, surely calls upon the awareness of the changing nature of the social, political, and economic uses of space.

Victory for Caius Martius will be achieved only through the loss of place in some way, Volumnia suggests. In this loss of space comes the re-definition of Martius's person. He would be a "foreign recreant;" tellingly, this expression is less effective. Repeatedly, Martius desires some measure of outsider status; he famously exhorts, "There is a world elsewhere" (3.3.136), or as a strained attempt to live in a post-Rome world, he claims, "I go alone, / Like to a lonely dragon" (4.1.29–30). Martius is solidly foreign to the audience as his time with Aufidius and the Volsces shows. Nevertheless, this is clear evidence of Volumnia's politic feelings, the blend of the affective social ties with her son and his and her political affiliations. There is even a measure of heterodoxy or mistake with her term "foreign recreant." If Martius is a recreant, he must have abdicated his role and his allegiances; he is faithful to Rome no more. How can one fitting this description not be foreign to the Roman state?[45] He is either foreign, and thus has not effectually renounced any fealty to Rome, or he is recreant, and is thereby tied to the breaking of an oath through an indigenous tie to Rome. The richness of this sequence is the character's ability to be both and Volumnia's naming it as such. The characters' and spectators' politic feelings are not bound to be absolute—a truth that complicates the interpretation of the play.

At a break between the two long speeches that she gives, Volumnia risks losing Martius to the disinterest he has shown to Cominius and Menenius. She forces upon him a recognition of the automatic connections to family, which doubles when Young Martius (on stage with his father for the first time) speaks. Volumnia reminds the senior Martius of "thy mother's womb / That brought thee to this world" (5.3.124–25). Young Martius's defiance must also smack of Martius's need to resist this entreaty, "A shall not tread on me! / I'll run away till I am bigger, but then I'll fight" (5.3.127–28), perhaps a sentiment shared by his father in this very moment. Both lines enforce a thing automatic that Martius would rather make for himself. In the way that he seeks to tear down the walls of Rome to make a new name for himself,[46] he would also deny the old definitions and the connections that these deterministic relationships enforce. He claims, "I have sat too long" (5.3.131), which Volumnia reads as a threat that he will abandon their audience and end the conversation. This is a moment where Martius does not yet grasp the way his attachment to walls or his usurpation of those walls and borders has defined him. The invitation to remember his mother and his son is like being called across the border of a permeable boundary that needs no violence or subterfuge to be accessed. This is not an act that will allow him to create. Traditionally, these ties do the work to define the man. Indeed, even in his alliance with Aufidius, he does not join so much as he makes his own way; he is no part of the community of Volsces until he is the pinnacle of such. Aufidius's Lieutenant wonders at his charisma, "I do not know what witch-craft's in him, but/Your soldiers use him as the grace 'fore meat,/Their talk at table, and their thanks at end;/And you are dark'ned in this action, sir" (4.7.2–5). Martius is messianic to Aufidius's men, which is not like saying he joined them, but that his immersion was a revelation wherein he was carried out or beyond, just as in his conquering of Corioles, which made him Cori-olanus, a name beyond Caius Martius. Contrarily, Volumnia's plea is at risk because she invokes a turning inward directionality when urging association with Young Martius. Martius acts as though all walls should be broken through and undone, the boundless solipsism he develops as the narrative progresses is a biconditional definition of the violence done around walls in this play.

Volumnia's two long speeches culminate with the detail that finally breaks Martius's will to holdout. She says, in what must be a tone of exasperation and exhaustion, tinged with resignation,

> Come, let us go.
> This fellow had a Volscian to his mother;
> His wife is in Corioles, and this child
> Like him by chance.

$$(5.3.177–80)$$

According to Alexander Leggatt, this is "the barb that finally sticks."[47] Though he contends that Martius can no longer play the part once he is confronted with the dishonesty of that part, I think the crucial aspect of these lines is not so much in the part, but what Martius has urged through his actions to define his role. Volumnia exposes the exterior or outward associations as being accidental rather than deliberate. It is almost as if she says to Martius that the name he would forge in Rome's fires would come to him anyway or not at all, regardless of what he wills. The three familial connections that Volumnia paints above are not deliberate and Martius takes them for being happenstance; by convening with Aufidius, he would be born of another country, thus another mother. He loves war so much more than his wife that it is fitting for her to point to his victory in Corioles, yet, it could have been any of his many victories that she named. If Young Martius looks like him, it is by chance, which affirms the lack of certitude about any of the connections that Martius has forged in his solipsistic, self-destructive path from potential consul of Rome to the spiritual leader of his former great adversaries. In the presence of his family and amongst the enemy who he has allied with, Martius finally sees that he has lived life outside of boundaries for too long. His desire to rage against and simultaneously define the walls and borders of his life is unsustainable.

As the counterpoint to Martius's failure to understand and erect proper metaphorical walls, Shakespeare gives us Virgilia. Where her husband would tear down and overleap walls to suit his personal desires and political or martial needs, Virgilia expertly maneuvers within the many walls that necessarily define her as the wife of this man and as a woman in the militaristic state of Rome. Her single interjection in the middle of Volumnia's long speeches is the precise answer to Martius's dilemma, the one he cannot see. She says, after Volumnia's invocation of the womb that brought Martius into the world, "Ay, and mine, / That brought you forth this boy, to keep your name / Living to time" (5.3.125–27). Volumnia urges the remembrance of the name Coriolanus and how it would be tainted with the conquering of Rome. Virgilia makes an important distinction, reminding Martius that his son will keep his name "living to time." She presses the notion that the connections we forge and the boundaries we keep live on in vibrancy, rather than in a type of memento mori. Her power in this moment has been remarked upon, with one critic arguing, "Her insistent femininity and protection of the domestic sphere represent Shakespeare's particular critique against Rome's hypermasculine ideology."[48] She will not go out of doors until Martius returns from Corioles, early in the play. Against Valeria and Volumnia's imprecations, she sets her boundary and establishes her character as the picture of consistency. One scholar reminds us that her fortitude is not initially clear, "The first impression of weakness fades as we sense an inner strength of will. Utterly at odds with Coriolanus' life as a warrior, she presents an image of that private integrity he has tried, and failed, to live by."[49] Even Martius would seem to confound the audience, to wit, "Though Coriolanus calls Virgilia 'my gracious silence' (2.1.172), it is less to signify wifely subjection than the feminine complement to his marital austerity."[50] This same critic makes a further point, "The understated personal and civic tragedy of *Coriolanus* lies in that despite Coriolanus's expressions of love, Virgilia, like her epic forbear, Dido, is ultimately powerless against the imperatives of his hypervirtue."[51] There is much to connect Virgilia and Dido, but I think that fate plays a bigger role in the heroine of Virgil's epic. Though Aeneas and Martius may be driven by the same "hypervirtue," Martius has more choice, more agency to align with his wife. In accordance with Leggatt's premise, the tragedy is more in keeping with Martius's inability to maintain private integrity. Though he shuns public recognition of such, he must make it for himself and seemingly report it for himself as well. None can express the virtue of Martius unless it is himself. He is at war with himself from without and from within. The play materializes walls and boundaries to allow Martius to act on a macrocosmic scale this internal strife. He is unwilling, or unable, to learn anything from Virgilia's example.

Martius's death is the brief coda to this article. He predicts correctly that his mother has "most dangerously . . . with him prevailed." Following textual clues, Martius rejoins Tullus Aufidius in Corioles (AUF: "Dost thou think/I'll grace thee with that robbery, thy stol'n name/'Coriolanus' in Corioles?" [5.6.87–89]). Aufidius unmans him entirely. He calls him "boy" and "traitor," words anathematic to Martius's ears and sense of self. The irony is fitting; Martius dies in Corioles, the place where he won his name in the play's first act. Unlike Virgilia, he has not managed to tread the borders and boundaries with skill. His death is remarkable in terms of the walls in the play because he entered the city freely. The violation of the space of city walls becomes a lesson, for the London of 1609 and for the reader now. According to Leah Marcus, the play "enacts a civic victory like the expansion of London author- ity; it does so by casting out a symbolic representative of the artificial con- straints imposed on the city from above."[52] This is, I think, a bit idealistic. Martius is more unique than simply a "representative" of the artifice of civic and royal power structures. He may eventually represent those things, but as I have attempted to show earlier in this article, the ever-shifting attitude toward the use of space and the popular relationship to that does not need a Martius- like figure to demonize or to scapegoat. Rather, the play dwells upon the universality of the issue by investing time and stage space to a character that is at war with both sides of the question. Martius cannot live within Rome's walls and he cannot live without them. The play cultivates political affect by allowing the struggle to be personal while still carrying political and civic consequences. Marcus's historicizing of the political gains London achieved against the stricter authority of the Crown is useful, but city centric. We know that many people came to the theater from outside of the London walls. Even if the more affluent theatergoers of Blackfriars did not necessarily pass among the city walls, they were aware of the unrest ranging far across the country. The success of the play, then and now, is how it calls us to consider what walls we must negotiate and how inextricable our personal feelings are from the explication of those walls.

Coriolanus celebrates the victory of a more modern conception of the civic landscape. Rome is London and London is London, and in this sense, the city is victorious. However, this point seems hollow to me if we discount the injection of the personal. Shakespeare's play makes the spectator wrestle with a figure that inspires many conflicting emotional reactions. Simultaneously, it brings to bear the bodies of the spectators as active agents in the thematic concerns of the violation of space and the changing nature of the sociality of space as both a concrete thing and an idea. The play cannot claim to be the very moment of the shift in English culture that marked a definitive beginning to the decline of royal authority and the rise of civic-based government. But it persists in the imagination for all the reasons that theater still lives and vibrates within our culture now. It is incumbent upon us not to stop thinking about walls, civic, national, or neighborly, and borders, and the things that they represent as signifiers of the ways we understand social space. It should make us emotional; it means we are involved.

Notes

I want to thank Adam Zucker, Jane Degenhardt, Liz Fox, Catherine Elliott Tisdale, Sean Ash Gordon, and Kate Perillo for their generous feedback on previous versions of this paper.

1. For more on the early attempts to enwall London, see John Stow, *The Survey of London* (London: J.M. Dent & Sons, Ltd.; E.P. Dutton & Co., Inc, 1960), 7–12.

2. One visual example of the mayoral processions and their role in fixing borders as sites of civic authority is Jonathan Norden's *Civitas Londini*. The map can be viewed here: https://dl.wdl.org/14397.png. For more on this map, see Andrew Gordon, "Performing London: the map and the city in ceremony," in *Literature, Mapping, and the Politics of Space in Early Modern Britain*, eds. Andrew Gordon and Bernhard Klein (Cambridge: Cambridge University Press, 2001), 69–88.

3. For more on the political unrest and food riots specifically, see Elyssa Y Cheng, "Moral Economy and the Politics of Food Riots in Coriolanus," *Concentric: Literary and Cultural Studies* 36, no. 2 (September 2010): 17–31; Alex Garganigo, "*Coriolanus*, the Union Controversy, and Access to the Royal Person," *Studies in English Literature, 1500–1900* 42, no. 2 (2002): 335–59; L.A. Parker, "The Agrarian Revolution at Cotesbach 1501–1612," *Transactions of the Leicestershire Archaeological Society* 24 (1948): 41–77; E.C. Pettet, "*Coriolanus* and the Midlands Insurrection of 1607," *Shakespeare Survey* 3 (1950): 34–42.

4. For a brief introduction of the changing nature of social space in early seventeenth-century London, see Garrett A. Sullivan, *The Drama of Landscape: Land, Property, and Social Relations on the Early Modern Stage* (Stanford: Stanford University Press, 1998), 31–56; Julie Sanders, *The Cultural Geography of Early Modern Drama, 1620–1650* (Cambridge: Cambridge University Press, 2011), 1–15; and Denis E. Cosgrove, *Social Formation and Symbolic Landscape* (Madison: University of Wisconsin Press, 1998).

5. On theatrical semiotics, see Erika T. Lin, *Shakespeare and the Materiality of Performance* (Palgrave Macmillan, 2012), 41–69. Her method of understanding the way the stage space can signify depends on how the viewer sees the space. It is a process "where the signifier does not resemble the signified but rather gestures toward it" (47). I think many of the characters' actions in this play do not necessarily resemble feelings but do gesture toward them. For more on politic feelings and affective affinity, see my discussion of Steven Mullaney's work below.

6. Henri Lefebvre, *The Production of Space*, trans. Donald Nicholson-Smith (Malden: Blackwell, 1991), 85.

7. Jean E. Howard, *Theater of a City: The Places of London Comedy, 1598–1642* (Philadelphia: University of Pennsylvania Press, 2007), 14.

8. Steven Mullaney, *The Reformation of Emotions in the Age of Shakespeare* (Chicago: The University of Chicago Press, 2015), 21 and 190n.

9. Ibid., 22.

10. Ronda Arab, Michelle M. Dowd, and Adam Zucker, eds. *Historical Affects and the Early Modern Theater* (London: Routledge, 2015), 5.

11. Drew Daniel, *The Melancholy Assemblage: Affect and Epistemology in the English Renaissance* (New York: Fordham University Press, 2013), 9–10. Daniel uses another metaphor to describe emotional transmission, writing, "An affective bond-which-is-also-a-gap emerges," and, "The more witnesses, the greater number of bonds and exterior relations joined together to consolidate the assemblage" (3, 26). This coheres nicely with the way that Arab, Dowd, and Zucker and Mullaney emphasize the cultural aspect of the proliferation and construction of emotion as it applies to a theatrical experience. Arab, Dowd, and Zucker define affect "as created within economies of or circulations between human bodies, non-human bodies, and material things, mediated by social, cultural, and economic systems and practices" (4). Bailey and DiGangi further reify this idea when they write, "Questions of affect might be productively articulated with early modern understandings of bodies, passions, and social relations" (5). See Amanda Bailey and Mario DiGangi, eds., *Affect Theory and Early Modern Texts: Politics, Ecologies, and Form* (New York: Palgrave Macmillan, 2017), 1–23. An explanation of Mullaney's affective technologies can be found in his essay, "Affective Technologies: Toward an Emotional Logic of the Elizabethan Stage," in *Environment and Embodiment in Early Modern England*, eds. Mary Floyd-Wilson and Garrett A. Sullivan (New York: Palgrave Macmillan, 2007), 71–89.

12. Pettet, 36; see David Underdown, *Revel, Riot, and Rebellion: Popular Politics and Culture in England, 1603–1660* (Oxford: Clarendon Press, 1985) and Robert Wilkinson. *A Sermon Preached at North-Hampton the 21. of Iune Last Past, before the Lord Lieutenant of the County, and the Rest of the Commissioners There Assembled Vpon Occasion of the Late Rebellion and Riots in Those Parts Committed.* (London: Printed . . . by George Eld for Iohn Flasket, 1607).

13. William Shakespeare, *Coriolanus*. ed. Jonathan V. Crewe (New York: Penguin Books, 1999). Further references in the text will appear parenthetically by act, scene, and line number.

14. On *Coriolanus* and politics, Annabel Patterson alleges, "Political theory is its *raison d'etre*, and if we try to set it aside nothing of interest, of plot or character, remains." I find that this contention understates the play's potential as a cultural work of art. James Kuzner, writing on republicanism and the play, remarks, "Advancing a prorepublican reading of *Coriolanus* is thus quite difficult to do." See Annabel Patterson, *Shakespeare and the Popular Voice* (Cambridge, MA: Blackwell, 1989), 120, and James Kuzner. "Unbuilding the City: *Coriolanus* and the Birth of Republican Rome," *Shakespeare Quarterly* 58, no. 2 (Summer 2007): 174–99. For more on Shakespeare's political language, see Cathy Shrank, "Civility and the City in *Coriolanus*," *Shakespeare Quarterly* 54, no. 4 (Winter 2003): 406–423.

15. Shannon Miller, "Topicality and Subversion in William Shakespeare's *Coriolanus*," *Studies in English Literature, 1500–1900* 32, no. 2 (1992): 288, 291.

16. Garganigo, 336.

17. Patrick Ashby, "The Changing Faces of Virtue: Plutarch, Machiavelli and Shakespeare's *Coriolanus*," *Early Modern Literary Studies* (2016): 2–3.

18. For more on political contexts, see Ann C. Christensen, "The Return of the Domestic in *Coriolanus*," *Studies in English Literature, 1500–1900* 37, no. 2 (1997): 295–316; A. Crunelle, "*Coriolanus*: The Smiling Belly and the Parliament Fart," *ANQ: A Quarterly Journal of Short Articles, Notes, and Reviews* 22, no. 3 (Summer 2009): 11–16; John M. Wallace, "The Senecan Context of *Coriolanus*," *Modern Philology* 90, no. 4 (May 1993): 465–78.

19. Leah S. Marcus, *Puzzling Shakespeare: Local Reading and Its Discontents* (Berkeley: University of California Press, 1988), 202–3.

20. Ibid., 211.

21. Mullaney, 2015, 53.

22. Roger Ascham, *The Schoolmaster (1570)*, ed. Lawrence V. Ryan (Ithaca, N.Y: Cornell University Press, 1967), 60.

23. Shrank, 410–11.

24. Shrank's concern here is with what she calls the "indecorous speech" of Caius Martius. By not speaking well, he cannot participate in the civic affairs of Rome, hence the inevitable banishment from the city. I think this tells only part of the story, especially since Martius's speech is not always indecorous. The emotional valence of his banishment relies upon how the play materializes Martius's and other characters' attachment to the spaces of the play, how it sets up that exchange of feelings that are embodied in the thoughts and emotions of the characters and audience. See Shrank, 2003, 411.

25. As I quoted from Mullaney previously, "The apprehension of involvement, the social element of an emotion, is also the moment of embodiment" (2015, 22).

26. Lisa Hopkins, *Renaissance Drama on the Edge* (Burlington, VT: Ashgate, 2014), 12. Hopkins is illustrative of the way in which walls confound critics; I do not quite agree that it has no obvious political agenda, in which walls play a crucial role. Kuzner would argue that the play's political agenda, or utility, is in the way Martius seeks not autonomy, but undoing (179–80), in opposition to Hopkins. I think the agenda is in the affective relations the play materializes. However, Hopkins writes a delightfully succinct account of one possible source for the play's action, especially as it concerns Martius's mother, Volumnia. For her sustained work on borders and the spaces separating nations, see *Shakespeare on the Edge: Border-Crossing in the Tragedies and the Henriad* (Burlington, VT: Ashgate, 2005).

27. Qtd. in Mullaney, 1980, 36.

28 *Oxford English Dictionary*, 3rd ed (2007), s.v. "Proof." This definition also recalls a line from *2Henry VI*, where King Henry exclaims, "What stronger breastplate than a heart untainted!" (3.2.232). Though Martius may seem to lack the moral aspect of Henry's metaphor of the heart as armor, his love for Rome is akin to a demonstration of devotion.

29. Thomas Heywood, *An Apology for Actors Containing Three Briefe Treatises. 1 Their Antiquity. 2 Their Ancient Dignity. 3 The True vse of Their Quality. Written by Thomas Heywood.* (London: Nicholas Okes, 1612), B4r.

30. *Oxford English Dictionary*, 3rd ed (2007), s.v. "Proof."

31. Ibid.

32. There is an implication of a type of Cartesian duality here, with the heart being the thing that convinces the mind of strength or validity. Though Martius does not appear to be making an ontological argument here, there is a weird twist to this definition that lends itself to this kind of reading.

33. *Oxford English Dictionary*, 3rd ed (2007), s.v. "Proof."

34. Mullaney, 1980, 36

35. Ibid.

36. *Coriolanus*, directed by Ralph Fiennes (Anchor Bay Entertainment, 2011), Blu-ray.

37. I suppose that one might stage the city walls of Antium as well as Tullus Aufidius's house, however, I do not assume that the early modern stage would have been large enough, nor would there have been need. The actor playing Martius might have been able to encounter the various serving men as they entered and exited through the tiring house door in the rear of the stage to make it appear that he was in the rear of a large house.

38. One might also consider how Martius is here an alien, outsider, or other, though these are all weighted terms that have their own subsets of significations. In a way, Martius is like an immigrant in Antium, though not really an alien one. As Hopkins reminds us, "The Romans and the Volsces already talk the same language, worship the same gods and eat the same food, and both have a political structure involving senators; total assimilation can then hardly be far away" (2014, 15). For contextual-ization of Martius's alien status, see Lloyd Edward Kermode, *Aliens and Englishness in Elizabethan Drama* (Cambridge: Cambridge University Press, 2009), Emma Smith, "'So Much English by the Mother': Gender, Foreigners, and the Mother Tongue in William Haughton's *Englishman for My Money*," *Medieval & Renaissance Drama in England* 13 (2001): 165–81, and Alan Stewart, "'Euery Soyle to Mee Is Naturall': Figuring Denization in William Haughton's *English-Men for My Money*," *Renaissance Drama* 35 (2006): 55–81. My sincere thanks to Catherine Elliott Tisdale for pointing these out to me.

39. I saw a filmed stage performance of the play in which the actor playing Martius was seated in a chair at Aufidius's hearth and the actor playing Aufidius was very literally crawling all over the other man, his hands gratuitously roaming the other's body. I thought it a smart choice; it was evocative and discomfiting simultaneously. Perhaps for these very reasons, a different production that I saw live cut these lines entirely. Without the language to form the homo-social and homo-sexual bond between these two characters, the play lost some of its luster.

40. See Kuzner, especially 193–99. Other works that explore this issue are Daniel Juan Gil, "Before Intimacy: Modernity and Emotion in the Early Modern Discourse of Sexuality," *ELH* 69 (2002): 861–67; and Bruce R. Smith, *Homosexual Desire in Shake-speare's England: A Cultural Poetics* (Chicago: University of Chicago Press, 1991).

41. Kuzner, 197.

42. See Christensen, 301–2

43. Hopkins, 2014, 15.

44. Ibid.

45. In this moment, Volumnia would have Martius be both things, foreign and not-foreign, recreant and not-recreant. This recalls the theme of anthropological resent-ment; see Richard Van Oort, *Shakespeare's Big Men: Tragedy and the Problem of Resentment* (Toronto: University of Toronto Press, 2016), 162–65. In the Big Man's quest for centrality, the protagonist must become all things and risks becoming none of the things, hence the concurrent resentment from those who are not "big men."

46. Recall Cominius's report of his meeting with Martius, "'Coriolanus'/He would not answer to, forbade all names./He was a kind of nothing, titleless,/Till he had forged himself a name o' the fire/Of burning Rome" (5.1.11–15).

47. Alexander Leggatt, *Shakespeare's Political Drama: The History Plays and the Roman Plays* (London: Routledge, 1989), 208.

48. Unhae Langis, "*Coriolanus*: Inordinate Passions and Powers in Personal and Political Governance," *Comparative Drama* 44, no. 1 (2010): 19.

49. Leggatt, 208.

50. Langis, 19.
51. Ibid., 20.
52. Marcus, 209–10.

Bibliography

Arab, Ronda, Michelle M. Dowd, and Adam Zucker, eds. *Historical Affects and the Early Modern Theater*. New York: Routledge, 2015.

Ascham, Roger. *The Schoolmaster (1570)*. Edited by Lawrence V. Ryan. Ithaca: Cornell University Press, 1967.

Ashby, Patrick. "The Changing Faces of Virtue: Plutarch, Machiavelli and Shakespeare's *Coriolanus*." *Early Modern Literary Studies* (2016): 1–21.

Bailey, Amanda, and Mario DiGangi, eds. *Affect Theory and Early Modern Texts: Politics, Ecologies, and Form*. New York: Palgrave Macmillan, 2017.

Cheng, Elyssa Y. "Moral Economy and the Politics of Food Riots in *Coriolanus*." *Concentric: Literary and Cultural Studies* 36, no. 2 (September 2010): 17–31.

Christensen, Ann C. "The Return of the Domestic in *Coriolanus*." *Studies in English Literature, 1500–1900* 37, no. 2 (1997): 295–316.

Cosgrove, Denis E. *Social Formation and Symbolic Landscape*. Madison: University of Wisconsin Press, 1998.

Crunelle, A. "*Coriolanus*: The Smiling Belly and the Parliament Fart." *ANQ: A Quarterly Journal of Short Articles, Notes, and Reviews* 22, no. 3 (Summer 2009): 11–16.

Daniel, Drew. *The Melancholy Assemblage: Affect and Epistemology in the English Renaissance*. New York: Fordham University Press, 2013.

Fiennes, Ralph, dir. *Coriolanus*. Anchor Bay Entertainment, 2011. Blu-ray.

Garganigo, Alex. "*Coriolanus*, the Union Controversy, and Access to the Royal Person." *Studies in English Literature, 1500–1900* 42, no. 2 (2002): 335–59.

Gil, Daniel Juan. "Before Intimacy: Modernity and Emotion in the Early Modern Discourse of Sexuality." *ELH* 69, no. 4 (Winter 2002): 861–87.

Gordon, Andrew. "Performing London: the map and the city in ceremony." In *Literature, Mapping, and the Politics of Space in Early Modern Britain*, eds. Andrew Gordon and Bernhard Klein, 69–88. Cambridge: Cambridge University Press, 2001.

Heywood, Thomas. *An Apology for Actors Containing Three Briefe Treatises. 1 Their Antiquity. 2 Their Ancient Dignity. 3 The True vse of Their Quality. Written by Thomas Heywood.* London: Nicholas Okes, 1612.

Hopkins, Lisa. *Renaissance Drama on the Edge*. Burlington, VT: Ashgate, 2014.

———. *Shakespeare on the Edge: Border-Crossing in the Tragedies and the Henriad*. Burlington, VT: Ashgate, 2005.

Howard, Jean E. *Theater of a City: The Places of London Comedy, 1598–1642*. Philadelphia: University of Pennsylvania Press, 2007.

Kermode, Lloyd Edward. *Aliens and Englishness in Elizabethan Drama*. Cambridge: Cambridge University Press, 2009.

Kuzner, James. "Unbuilding the City: 'Coriolanus' and the Birth of Republican Rome." *Shakespeare Quarterly* 58, no. 2 (2007): 174–99.

Langis, Unhae. "*Coriolanus*: Inordinate Passions and Powers in Personal and Political Governance." *Comparative Drama* 44, no. 1 (2010): 1–27.

Lefebvre, Henri. *The Production of Space*. Translated by Donald Nicholson-Smith. Malden: Blackwell, 1991.

Leggatt, Alexander. *Shakespeare's Political Drama: The History Plays and the Roman Plays*. London: Routledge, 1989.

Lin, Erika T. *Shakespeare and the Materiality of Performance*. New York: Palgrave Macmillan, 2012.

Marcus, Leah S. *Puzzling Shakespeare: Local Reading and Its Discontents*. Berkeley: University of California Press, 1988.

Miller, Shannon. "Topicality and Subversion in William Shakespeare's *Coriolanus*." *Studies in English Literature, 1500–1900* 32, no. 2 (1992): 287–310.

Mullaney, Steven. "Lying Like Truth: Riddle, Representation and Treason in Renaissance England." *ELH* 47, no. 1 (1980): 32–47.

————. "Affective Technologies: Toward an Emotional Logic of the Elizabethan Stage." In *Environment and Embodiment in Early Modern England*, edited by Mary Floyd-Wilson and Garrett A. Sullivan, 71–89. New York: Palgrave Macmillan, 2007.

————. *The Reformation of Emotions in the Age of Shakespeare*. Chicago: The University of Chicago Press, 2015.

Norden, John. "Civitas Londini." World Digital Library. Accessed February 6, 2017. https://dl.wdl.org/14397.png.

Parker, L.A. "The Agrarian Revolution at Cotesbach 1501–1612." *Transactions of the Leicestershire Archaeological Society* 24 (1948): 41–77.

Patterson, Annabel M. *Shakespeare and the Popular Voice*. Cambridge, MA: B. Blackwell, 1990.

Pettet, E.C. "*Coriolanus* and the Midlands Insurrection of 1607." *Shakespeare Survey* 3 (1950): 34–42.

Puttenham, George. *The Art of English Poesy*. Edited by Frank Whigham and Wayne A. Rebhorn. Ithaca: Cornell University Press, 2007.

Russell, John. "Treatise of the Happie and Blissed Union Betuixt the Tua Ancienne Realmes of Scotland and Ingland (1604)." In *The Jacobean Union: Six Tracts of 1604*, edited by Bruce Galloway and Brian P. Levack, 1–46. Edinburgh: Printed for the Scottish History Society by C. Constable, 1985.

Sanders, Julie. *The Cultural Geography of Early Modern Drama, 1620–1650*. Cambridge: Cambridge University Press, 2011.

Shakespeare, William. *Coriolanus*. Edited by Jonathan V Crewe. New York: Penguin Books, 1999.

Shrank, Cathy. "Civility and the City in *Coriolanus*." *Shakespeare Quarterly* 54, no. 4 (2003): 406–23.

Smith, Bruce R. *Homosexual Desire in Shakespeare's England: A Cultural Poetics*. Chicago: University of Chicago Press, 1991.

Smith, Emma. "'So Much English by the Mother': Gender, Foreigners, and the Mother Tongue in William Haughton's *Englishman for My Money*." *Medieval & Renaissance Drama in England* 13 (2001): 165–81.

Stewart, Alan. "'Euery Soyle to Mee Is Naturall': Figuring Denization in William Haughton's *English-Men for My Money*." *Renaissance Drama*, New Series 35 (2006): 55–81.

Stow, John. *The Survey of London*. London: J.M. Dent & Sons, Ltd; E.P. Dutton & Co., Inc, 1960.

Sullivan, Garrett A. *The Drama of Landscape: Land, Property, and Social Relations on the Early Modern Stage*. Stanford: Stanford University Press, 1998.

Underdown, David. *Revel, Riot, and Rebellion: Popular Politics and Culture in England, 1603–1660*. Oxford: Clarendon Press, 1985.

Van Oort, Richard. *Shakespeare's Big Men: Tragedy and the Problem of Resentment.* Toronto: University of Toronto Press, 2016.
Wallace, John M. "The Senecan Context of *Coriolanus.*" *Modern Philology* 90, no. 4 (May 1993): 465–78.
Wilkinson, Robert. *A Sermon Preached at North-Hampton the 21. of Iune Last Past, before the Lord Lieutenant of the County, and the Rest of the Commissioners There Assembled Vpon Occasion of the Late Rebellion and Riots in Those Parts Committed.* London: Printed . . . by George Eld for Iohn Flasket, 1607.

Reviews

Ben Jonson and Posterity: Reception, Reputation, Legacy, edited by Martin Butler and Jane Rickard. Cambridge: Cambridge University Press, 2020. pp. xv + 255. Hardcover. $99.99.

Reviewer: MARK BAYER

"That Bard, that glorious Bard . . . So great his Art, that much which he did write / Gave the wise wonder and, and the Crowd delight" (25). We've encountered so many similar encomiums to Shakespeare that discussions of the playwright's rise to cultural prominence have become sufficiently commonplace in our critical discourse. This quotation by Lucius Cary, however, eulogizes not William Shakespeare but Ben Jonson—forcing us to reconsider the reputation of not just Jonson but of other dramatists from the entire early modern period. Martin Butler and Jane Rickard's collection of essays, *Ben Jonson and Posterity*, traces the fascinating afterlife of that playwright and poet from the seventeenth century to the present. Jonson's legacy does not follow the meteoric rise of Shakespeare's. As the contributors to this volume demonstrate, Jonson's reputation is, by turns, elusive, ambiguous, obscure, and even contradictory—in short, it's a lot messier, and deserves our attention precisely because of its fascinating complications and nuances.

The volume is divided into three sections that dissect discrete aspects of Jonson's reputation. The first three chapters attempt to conceptualize Jonson's constantly shifting place in the canon of non-Shakespearean early modern drama. James Loxeley first assesses Jonson's extremely calculated efforts to create and manipulate his posthumous reputation during his lifetime. He interrogates Jonson's journey, on foot, in 1618 to Edinburgh, where by all accounts Jonson was greeted as a celebrity, as a telling example of the almost obsessive ways that Jonson curated his own popularity from a very early age—a project perhaps best exemplified in the 1616 *Works*.

Why is Jonson always considered pedantic, and why is pedantic considered such a negative and even insulting label? In the following chapter, Adam Zucker attempts to change our mind not just about Jonson's alleged pedantry, but also about the adverse connotations of that term. He suggests that many of the aspects of his work that readers have often found pedantic actually point towards new and remarkably modern ways of constructing and classifying specific audiences with the necessary cultural vocabulary to understand and appreciate Jonson's more idiosyncratic and complex dramatic works. And what about Jonson's reputation for corporality, a man grown fleshy due to his overindulgence in food and drink? Jean Howard traces the construction of the "corporeal Jonson," suggesting that this particular impression of Jonson is a product of the "the various forms of urban literature he composed" (64–65). The characters that populate Jonson's city comedies, Sir Epicure Mammon, Ursula, and the equally rapacious Volpone and Mosca, are driven and even defined by their excessive appetites—connotations that later commentators easily reconciled with Jonson's own 285-pound frame.

The remainder of the collection turns towards more familiar avenues of reception on stage, in print, and in popular culture from the seventeenth century to the twenty-first. In the fourth chapter Jane Rickard builds on Jonson's own instruction to those "that taks't my book in hand,/To read it well: that is to understand." Her fascinating study of the extensive marginalia in 30 copies of Jonson's *Works* held by the Henry E. Huntington Library assesses how readers really did understand Jonson—an important question given Jonson's obsessive desire to control his reputation. The evidence Rickard compiles suggests that at least the readers who annotated these copies during the seventeenth century were willing to take up Jonson's challenge, that they were tracing his abundant classical allusions, and engaging the plays in ways Jonson would have approved.

An equally important element of Jonson's legacy lies in the performance history of his plays. As Jennie Challinor argues in chapter 5, Jonson had a head start during the Restoration. When theaters reopened in 1660, they were in desperate need of plays to perform while a new generation of playwrights slowly emerged. In the absence of new material, the King's Company (one of two active troupes) turned to plays by Jonson, who could serve as a bridge to a violently ruptured dramatic past and whose heavily satirical plays could also be retooled for an era that had undergone enormous cultural and political change. With Jonson's dramatic authority assured during the early years of the Restoration, the new breed of dramatists readily adapted his plays to capitalize on his popularity and navigate a much different theatrical milieu—to varying degrees of success.

The following three chapters grapple with the forces that helped shape Jonson's complicated legacy through the seventeenth, eighteenth, and nineteenth centuries. Tom Lockwood looks at Jonson's politics as understood during the Romantic period, using John Thelwall and Charles Lamb as examples of political interpreters of Jonson. As in other facets of Jonson's reception, Lockwood concludes by wondering why these figures failed to draw the same kinds of political engagement that they so readily found in Shakespeare. In the next two chapters, Paul Menzer and Steven Orgel trace two other cultural forms that helped solidify Jonson's reputation over against that of Shakespeare. Menzer traces the set of anecdotes that consistently praise Jonson's learning, but subtly twist this erudition into a demerit compared to Shakespeare's allegedly more 'natural' brilliance. He argues that these same anecdotes that denigrate Jonson's learning helped to elevate the comedies to an enduring position of prominence in the Jonsonian canon as opposed to the allusive and Latinate tragedies. Orgel considers the mechanism of the edition. He suggests that eighteenth-century editions of Jonson lagged behind the more innovative editions of Shakespeare produced by the firm of Jacob Tonson. Because the

House of Tonson was so influential in constructing the canon of English literature as we now know it, their heavy investment in an extensive editorial apparatus and intricate illustrations to accompany their Shakespeare editions, ultimately left Jonson "in the shadows"—something underscored by the rather unflattering visual images of Jonson that accompanied editions of his works.

The book's concluding chapters move us into the present. Richard O'Brien examines three twentieth-century adaptations of *Volpone*, one of the few plays that found a regular place onstage in a Shakespeare-centric dramatic marketplace. O'Brien posits that *Volpone* is uniquely suited to modern sensibilities because of its focus on financial power and its tendency towards corruption. Finally, Martin Butler takes us through a fascinating assortment of images, films, TV shows, songs, advertisements, novels, and comic books to point out the "disconnections that exist between Jonson as he is known to scholars and the image of him that circulates in the broader consciousness" (216). Despite Jonson scholarship's laudable efforts to offer an authentic portrayal of Jonson and his work, the general public's view of him is probably forever distorted by these other, and significantly more popular, cultural forms—a situation where dubious stories of hijinks at the Mermaid Tavern are far more well-known than any of his plays. A brief afterword by Julie Sanders reassesses the volume's contributions and brings Jonson into our digital present, reimagining Jonson's popularity in the age of Twitter (where, she argues, Jonson's wit would be a distinct advantage).

Ben Jonson and Posterity is an important book on an understudied topic. I learned much from these essays, and I imagine that all but the most specialized scholar in Jonson would say the same. Despite the rich variety of topics traversed in these essays, all of them in some way struggle with the same question: how can we address Jonson's posterity without immediately invoking Shakespeare? Must Jonson always remain an irascible foil to Shakespeare's genius, a subplot in the master narrative? Perhaps the book's greatest contribution, then, is its implicit entreaty to scholars to move beyond Shakespeare in considering the long-term cultural authority of early modern drama.

Religious Conversion in Early Modern English Drama, by Lieke Stelling. Cambridge: Cambridge University Press, 2019. Pp. xi + 226. Hardback, $99.99.

Reviewer: Catherine Winiarski

This fine new study offers an impressive, comprehensive analysis of the theme of conversion in early modern English drama. It provides apt religious contextualization and a masterful typology of more than 40 conversion dramas of various genres across the transformative period of 1558–1642, proceeding from late morality plays through the rise of the commercial theater. Stelling distinguishes her study with "a broad, cross-confessional and pan-religious approach" that examines patterns in the portrayal of conversion both within Christianity and between Christianity and Judaism, Islam, and various forms of paganism (11). In addition to extensive readings of canonical conversion plays like *The Jew of Malta* and *Othello*, the book provides comparative analysis of lesser-known works like Richard Zouche's *The Sophister* and James Shirley's *St. Patrick for Ireland*. It divides its large body of evidence into those (mostly earlier) plays concerned with "spiritual conversion," understood as an act of repentance and deepening of devotion within the same religious identity, and those (mostly later) ones concerned with "interfaith conversion," involving the replacement of one religious identity by another. It accounts for this historical shift by thoroughly immersing the plays in their contemporary religious contexts, especially sermons, pamphlets, and spiritual autobiographies concerned with England's state-enforced adoption of a singular Protestant theology (including the Calvinist doctrine of double predestination) in the midst of a "diversification" of confessional positions within Protestantism and increasingly frequent encounters with non-Christian others. Stelling's central argument expresses the paradox that early modern conversion drama both glorifies conversion as evidence for the righteousness and power of Christian faith while expressing profound anxiety about its ability to destabilize group identity; ultimately, she argues, this drama asserts religious identity to be an inherent and immutable basis for group identity.

The first half of the book examines how the staging of spiritual conversion in late medieval morality plays comes to be inflected by the doctrinal innovations of Protestantism. Typical medieval morality plays stage conversion events as *exempla* for their Christian audience and encourage a renunciation of sin, renewal of piety, and even embrace of the monastic life that define the "spiritual" form of conversion in the book's analysis. This form of conversion takes place not between distinct faiths but within Christianity itself. As the Protestant Reformation takes hold in England, dramatists have to reckon with the doctrine of predestination, which takes the agency of spiritual conversion and salvation away from the believer and puts it entirely in the hands of God. Stelling expertly shows how this doctrinal turn affects dramatic plotting, for example, and the use of allegorical characters like Faith, Law, and Repentance in a play like Lewis Wager's *The Life and Repentaunce of Marie Magdalene* (c. 1550–66). One chapter focuses on Protestant sermons of the early Elizabethan period, which underline this new Protestant theory of spiritual conversion and rail against the theater as a vehicle of conversion. Even as the representation of spiritual conversion declines due to these efforts and to government censorship, dramatists continue to respond to the challenge posed by Calvinist predestination by staging tragic, failed attempts at conversion by inveterate sinners (as in *Doctor Faustus*). Later, the book claims, spiritual conversion re-enters the drama as a comic device to facilitate a happy ending (devoid of its prior moral gravity), as a nostalgic turn to the medieval past, or as relief from the intense politicization of faith in early modern Europe.

The second half of the book concerns dramatizations of interfaith conversion, which become the dominant form of conversion drama after 1590. Stelling sees these as an effort on the part of dramatists to address the problem of sectarian diversification within Protestantism, as well as the perceived dangers and opportunities of contact with non-Christians, in imperial circumstances. She again refers to English Protestant sermons, in this case Foxe's *The Sermon Preached at the Christening of a Certain Jew* and Hanmer's *The Baptizing of a Turke*, for religious context. Contrary to many readings of interfaith conversion plays that see them as enacting social transgression and demonstrating cultural flexibility, this reading perceives a fundamental suspicion of interfaith conversion and of the integration of interfaith converts into Christian communities, in line with the conversion ideology of the sermons. This reading aligns Stelling with Jane Hwang Degenhardt and Dennis Austin Britton, who have traced the limits of the potential for Christian conversion in this historical and cultural context.

The later chapters present a stunning catalog of the ways in which the possibility of full interfaith conversion is undercut or foreclosed in this drama. Interfaith conversions are treated as comically futile (*The City Madam*); opportunistic and expedient—and satirized as such (*The Three Ladies of London*); pre-conditioned by the convert's already Christian-like character or empathy for Christians, as well as the physical beauty and fairness that were thought to manifest Christian virtues visually (*Selimus*); stabilized by a female convert's incorporation into her Christian husband's identity (*The Merchant of Venice*); or doomed by the convert's internalization of Christian doubts about conversion (*Othello*). Stelling convincingly argues that the plays impose racial, national, and gender markers onto religious group identities which serve to create impenetrable boundaries around them.

The many dramatic examples the book presents in the interfaith conversion chapters support the ultimate claim that "the early moderns could not conceive of the concept of conversion as a radical transformation of religious identity" (154). The book's brief references to Paul's conceptualization of the "new man" do prompt the question of what a truly "radical" interfaith conversion would consist of and why this is inconceivable in early modern culture. If Paul is an authoritative source for understanding conversion in early modern culture, how did religious thinkers and dramatists interpret (or misinterpret) the epistles on this point?

Stelling qualifies her useful division between spiritual and interfaith conversion by noting that interfaith conversion was sometimes defined according to the model of spiritual conversion. This raises the question of whether spiritual conversion might have been understood on the model of interfaith conversion. In the medieval and early modern context, to what extent was sin regarded as apostasy or idolatry (of self, money, fame, or the material world) and spiritual repentance as (re)conversion from these forms of idolatry?

This book offers especially valuable insights into how the affordances of drama itself (and of tragedy and comedy specifically) influence the conceptualization of conversion in early modern English culture. As mentioned, it discusses how tragic genre conventions are used to depict failed attempts to enact spiritual conversion through personal agency, thus asserting the Protestant doctrines of grace and predestination. Comic plots and devices are used to ridicule conversions to Christianity as inconstant, expedient, and ultimately absurd. However, the book insists that early modern conversion drama carefully avoids an analogy between dramatic transformation (actors transformed into characters, men into women, Christians into "infidels") and religious conversion, which would be too threatening to the group identities it seeks to consolidate.

Religious Conversion in Early Modern English Drama fulfills its ambitious goal of giving an account of the whole corpus of early modern English conversion plays, perceiving salient patterns and crucial nuances across a vast array of genres, historical settings, and confessional contexts. The book provides a valuable counterpoint to a subfield of religious and literary studies that has perhaps given disproportionate attention to the "greatest hits" of conversion drama, from Marlowe and Shakespeare. It will certainly interest those looking to broaden and diversify the canon of early modern literature and those seeking to understand the complex interdependencies of religious and dramatic expression in early modern England.

Conceiving Desire in Lyly and Shakespeare, by Gillian Knoll. Edinburgh University Press, 2020. Pp. 288. Hardcover, $110.

Reviewer: LINDSAY ANN REID

Taking its opening cue from a speech delivered by Nick Bottom in act 4, scene 1 of *A Midsummer Night's Dream*, Gillian Knoll's *Conceiving Desire in Lyly and Shakespeare* begins with the assertion that it "is a book about tongues that conceive" (1). Just what Knoll means by this requires considerable unpacking. *Conceiving Desire in Lyly and Shakespeare* is broadly aligned with the field of cognitive literary studies, and it tackles interrelationships between thought, language, and metaphor. More specifically, Knoll sets out to probe "the capacity of language to create, to transform and to dramatise the *erotic experiences* of [theatrical] characters" (241; emphasis my own). The cognitive lens Knoll applies to early modern drama's linguistic engagements leads her analysis in multiple directions: this approach not only highlights "the potential of words to create eros and conjure the beloved," but also allows Knoll to explore how dramatic "characters experience eros by analysing how they conceptualise it" (13).

Conceiving Desire in Lyly and Shakespeare makes a welcome addition to the modest body of existing scholarship on Lyly's dramatic works. "To date," as Knoll observes in her introduction, "no full-length study has paired Shakespeare's and Lyly's plays" (16). Her rhetoric here may sell the study's novelty somewhat short, for—Shakespeare pairing aside—only a handful of prior monographs have given extended consideration to Lyly's dramatic oeuvre: G.K. Hunter's *John Lyly: The Humanist as Courtier* (1962); Peter Saccio's *The Court Comedies of John Lyly* (1969); Michael Pincombe's *The Plays of John Lyly: Eros and Eliza* (1996); Andy Kesson's *John Lyly and Early Modern Authorship* (2014); Theodora A. Jankowski's *Elizabeth I, the Subversion of Flattery, and John Lyly's Court Plays and Entertainments* (2018). It comes as little surprise that Kesson's relatively recent work on Lyly is a recurring point of reference for Knoll; slightly more surprising, given the small size of the field, is the absence of both Saccio and Jankowski from *Conceiving Desire in Lyly and Shakespeare*'s bibliography.

It is not only the relative paucity of Lyly criticism that has drawn Knoll to the early modern author's plays. Rather, she also validates her emphasis on his dramatic works by arguing that "the language of desire is spoken more exhaustively by Lyly's characters than by any other playwright's in the sixteenth century" (14). The broader question of why Lyly *and* Shakespeare have been specifically paired is treated less thoroughly. Indeed, Shakespeare's inclusion receives little justification at the study's outset: it is taken as a something of a given—though perhaps reasonably so?—that he, too, "created characters who speak erotic language at considerable length and in extraordinary depth" (2).

The six body chapters in *Conceiving Desire in Lyly and Shakespeare* are organized according to a tripartite scheme: two chapters each are grouped under the headings of "Motion," "Space," and "Creativity." These sections are meant, as Knoll explains, to function as expansive categories that "constitute significant building blocks for erotic experiences such as sensation and arousal (motion), intimacy and connection (spatiality), and lovemaking (creativity)" (19). Each of these three sections is prefaced, in turn, by a local introduction that seeks to elucidate "the underpinnings of its metaphor, drawing from a range of ancient, early modern and modern philosophical models" (19).

Knoll's first section on "Motion" is equally concerned with stasis. Chapter 1, which looks at Lyly's plays, centers on metaphors of erotic motion—and, more significantly, stillness—that appear across a selection of plays in Lyly's dramatic oeuvre. The reading presented here runs through some briefly sketched examples of erotic idleness in *Endymion* and *Sappho and Phao* before delving much more deeply into a rich analysis of the "idle and circuitous language that prolongs desire" in *Galatea* (39). Chapter 2 shifts attention (back) to Shakespeare, whose *Measure for Measure* was also a significant focal point in the section introduction. Here, Knoll returns to *Measure for Measure* and considers the play alongside *A Midsummer Night's Dream* and *Othello* in a broader discussion of eros and movement.

In the monograph's primary introduction, Knoll is rightly critical of what she describes as the "teleological" slant often taken when critics engage with Lylian drama (which can reduce the value of Lyly's work to the light that it can shed on Shakespeare's career), and she indicates that she has been careful to avoid replicating the fallacies of this approach in her own study. The act of "reading Lyly alongside Shakespeare, Shakespeare alongside Lyly," Knoll avers, need not be "teleological nor strictly comparative" (17). While the position that she stakes is well-articulated, in practice, it also means that the majority of monograph's body chapters present readings of Lyly *or* Shakespeare rather than Lyly *and* Shakespeare. This authorial segregation is particularly pronounced in sections 2 and 3.

Section 2 on "Space" considers spatial metaphors for love and desire. This expands to include considerations of place and displacement, and Knoll underscores how these issues intersect with conceptions of selfhood. Following a section introduction that primarily draws its examples from *The Two Gentlemen of Verona*, we find two chapters respectively dedicated to Lyly's *Endymion* and Shakespeare's *Antony and Cleopatra*. As these chapters attest, Knoll excels at presenting detailed and sensitive close readings of individual plays.

Knoll's final section on "Creativity" seeks to "explore the role of the erotic instrument as a medium of mutual creation and lovemaking" (179). *Twelfth Night* serves as the main textual referent in the section's introduction as Knoll discusses the collaborative dynamics of constructing a "mutual erotic fantasy" (175). Following the pattern established in earlier sections of the study, "Creativity" features discrete and largely self-contained chapters on Lyly and Shakespeare. The Lyly chapter provides a lively and thought-provoking analysis of *Campaspe*: Knoll examines this seldom-discussed play's metaphors of erotic creation in light of the visual artistry of Apelles. The Shakespeare chapter looks instead at verbal artistry, noting how "the process of storytelling (making fiction, twisting language, telling lies) instrumentalises Petruchio's erotic interactions with Kate" in *The Taming of the Shrew* (180). A common argumentative thread woven through both of these chapters involves the complicity or collaboration of female characters who are simultaneously shaped by men's artistry and "become co-creators as well" (180).

Despite some quirks and limitations in its framing, *Conceiving Desire in Lyly and Shakespeare* deserves to be commended as a study of great inventiveness. Its skilful and engaging readings of individual plays model how early modernists interrogating the facets of eros might productively turn to cognitive literary studies for inspiration.

Prodigality in Early Modern Drama, by Ezra Horbury. Cambridge: D. S. Brewer, 2019. Pp. x + 284. Hardback, $130.

Reviewer: DAVID LANDRETH

Prodigality in Early Modern Drama is an impressive and valuable contribution to our field. The last book-length study of this central thematic in the literary history of early modern drama was Alan Young's *The English Prodigal Son Plays*, more than 40 years ago. Ezra Horbury brings his own compendious mastery of these dramatic texts into conversation with the most vital contemporary scholarship on education, debt and usury, sexuality, and urban form in the period.

Horbury begins with a puzzle from the early sixteenth century: a series of English school plays plainly based on the parable of the prodigal son in Luke 15, which discard the redemptive climax of the Gospel story and leave their protagonists to hang. What, he asks, could motivate so savage an attitude toward prodigals in early Tudor culture? And how then did the English drama come over the next hundred years to forgive the wastefulness and disobedience of scapegrace youths, and even to celebrate them?

Through a nimble and deeply read analysis of the exegetical tradition, Horbury demonstrates that the parable was a central nexus for the coordination of Christian soteriology with Aristotle's ethics. The Aristotelian matrix, which defines virtuous living as the mean between contrary vices and gives such prominent place to the instance of proper and improper spending, encouraged the literal reading of the prodigal's story as an ethical exemplum, and marginalized its parabolic formulation of the saving power of forgiveness and grace. This dismal interpretation generated these punitively didactic and patronizing, scared-straight interludes for schoolboys, which Horbury delineates with rueful wit. He situates them very effectively in the environment of doctrinaire cruelty that was the Tudor schoolroom.

The relationship of these earlier school plays to the texts of the post-1576 commercial theater is left undefined in a chapter break—I infer it's that some of the boys subjected to the prodigal interludes at school grew up to engage these themes from a very different perspective and institutional position than that of their old teachers. Horbury is concerned in his second chapter to demonstrate the continuity of Aristotelian categories across that gap, and I'm certainly persuaded that that's the case. But it would also have been helpful to define at this point the most salient differences that overtake the prodigal motif in its move to the public stage. Horbury's chapters on the commercial drama are instead arranged topically rather than chronologically, and the sequence presents some challenges to the reader. One is that of frequent, confusing references in early chapters to ideas and explanations that only emerge in later chapters: Horbury alludes familiarly to the matters that interest him in Heywood's (less than familiar) *The English Traveller* nine times before he presents the play to the reader in the last chapter. More important is that Horbury asserts throughout the book that the ideologeme of prodigality goes through a metamorphosis over the course of early modern dramatic history—from pernicious caterpillar to delightful butterfly—but the non-sequential structure of the book occludes the inflection points of that narrative and slackens the momentum of the argument.

The chapter that best anchors this larger narrative is the fourth, which shrewdly presents the dyadic relation between stage prodigal and usurer as a revision of the generational conflict between the parable's liberal father and wasteful son. The usurer arrives as a typical foil to the prodigal as soon as the prodigal appears on the commercial stage: his advent pleasurably reorients the singular ethical burden borne by the prodigal in the interludes into an *agon* between more and less sympathetic vices, and vastly complicates the conceptualizations of value and of excess upon which the reproach of prodigality depends. Situating the emergence of this dynamic in the 1570s, amid the prodigal's transition to the commercial theater—i.e., as the point of departure of the second chapter—might have made it easier to orient changes and continuities among the other aspects of the motif that Horbury is tracing (which include the relation of prodigality to urbanization, and the symmetry between sex work for daughters and prodigality for sons), as the joint progress of prodigal and usurer through this dramatic history seems to me best to represent the transformation of value that he points to.

Prodigality in Early Modern Drama is remarkably comprehensive, and Horbury guides the reader with fluency through the breadth of his expertise. More than two dozen plays are presented in thoughtful detail, with as much care and attention given to little-known texts like *Greene's Tu Quoque* as to benchmarks of youthful deviance like *Henry IV*. Those readings are in turn grounded in a much larger awareness of the dramatic field, and of the ways in which different aspects of the prodigal motif are woven into it. (For example, Horbury remarks suggestively that *Measure for Measure* showcases almost every aspect of the prodigal motif in its difficult salvation ethics, except for the prodigal son himself.) I wish Horbury had taken some space to make explicit a distant reading of his field as a whole, to complement the close readings of representative instances—that is, to enumerate how many plays engaged the different aspects of prodigality that concern him, and to track the prevalence of new developments in statistical terms (if the sample is large enough) or at least in a timeline. I gather from his citations that Horbury avoids this because Alan Young and Ervin Beck already did such work in the 1970s, but he mentions that he disagrees with their taxonomies, so it would be helpful to see his own; and it's not like his reader has those studies to hand. Horbury is often deferentially evasive of his predecessors in this way, and can impose arbitrary boundaries on his own discussions for fear of reinventing their wheels, when it would be more productive to engage them as interlocutors.

Such local frustrations don't diminish my appreciation of the large ambition and varied contributions of the book as a whole. By attending to the intertextual forms and tropes of prodigal drama, Horbury develops valuable insights into a range of topics that engage scholars of today as much as they did the staged prodigals of the sixteenth and seventeenth centuries: commercialization and consumption; the pressured affordances of urban living; inheritance and usury; forgiveness and punishment; luxurious idleness and sexual labor; and the self-destructive glamour of "riotous living."

Fictions of Credit in the Age of Shakespeare, by Laura Kolb. Oxford: Oxford University Press, 2021. Pp. ix + 223. Hardback, $80.00.

Reviewer: BRIAN SHEERIN

With *Fictions of Credit*, Laura Kolb contributes to an increasingly crowded body of recent scholarship studying the intersection of economic life and literary imagination in early modern England. Kolb's interest here has to do with the complex—and usually contradictory—representation of "credit culture" by Elizabethan and Jacobean writers. Her study prioritizes attention to correspondence, advice treatises, and other "practical literature" (33) from the period that speak to the interpersonal delicacy of borrowing and lending. These artifacts then provide a rhetorical vantage point for examining a handful of noteworthy Renaissance dramas in a manner that is consistently engaging.

Kolb's work builds on an interdisciplinary foundation that is sometimes referred to as "the New Economic Criticism." In recent years, perhaps no scholar has been more influential to this field than Craig Muldrew, whose landmark historical work *The Economy of Obligation* (1998) inspired a rich vein of literary studies focused on how systems and relations of monetary credit are reflected—and interrogated—by imaginative fiction. Muldrew persuasively demonstrated just how ubiquitously the English populace relied on complex debt relations long before paper money or banking became systematized. But what, we might wonder, was the psychological effect of such economic interdependence? Did it generate pervasive cultural anxiety amidst the ever-immanent threats of defaulting on one's obligations? Or did it normalize debt relations and solidify communal bonds in ways that would eventually be threatened by emergent capitalism? Literary scholarship in the wake of Muldrew has generally found itself favoring one or the other of these alternatives, with plenty of primary source evidence to argue just about any point on the spectrum between them.

Kolb's intervention within this debate involves refusing to take a side—or rather, taking both sides at once. She argues persuasively that early modern culture was not merely conflicted on its attitudes toward borrowing and lending, but deeply contradictory. Noting some of the Elizabethan financial advice as it was expressed in the form of proverbs, for instance, Kolb finds that injunctions such as "don't stand surety, even for a friend" were no less prevalent than the insistence that "among friends, all things should be common" (86). And while these attitudes might seem at first to be mutually exclusive, they were often found grouped together or even uttered side-by-side. Such incongruity is thus not something we should be trying to iron out, but a constructive starting place for rhetorically nuanced analysis. Indeed, with this approach, Kolb is able to shift the emphasis of her study away from *economy* per se—i.e., the figures and facts of actual lending practices—to focus principally on the *rhetoric* of economic life, the realm of language by which subjects attempted to make sense of their experiences. After all, navigating a world of finances grounded primarily in interpersonal trust fundamentally involved skills of "reading others," of interpreting reliability, of constructing appearances of solvency. Credit, in short, worked as a kind of *fiction*, one requiring a hermeneutics that "both augmented and unsettled credit's grounding" (11); establishing this hypothesis with an engaging rhetorical flair of her own, Kolb is able to navigate several instances of Renaissance drama as "emplotted analyses" of such a hermeneutics.

After the Introduction, *Fictions of Credit* contains four chapters, each of which elaborates a different aspect of the irreducible interpretive ambivalence intrinsic to early modern credit relations. The focus here is more-or-less equally divided between a survey of instructional and advice texts (on the one hand) and economically themed dramas (on the other). The first instance of this pairing is particularly effective, as Shakespeare's *Othello* is read alongside sixteenth-century arithmetic treatises that demonstrate the ambiguities of "reckoning" in mercantile contexts. Calculations that seem straightforward on paper have a way of getting blurred when human bonds, ethnic tensions, and the risk of disaster enter the picture. In the case of *Othello*, the "opposition between two models of self-evaluation and reckoning" (59)—one grounded in social trust and the other in the calculation of intrinsic value—demonstrates the tragic potential of such rhetorical confusion.

And yet, such tragedy is not inevitable amidst ambivalence: the "social and verbal slipperiness necessitated by credit relations" (99) take a comic turn in *The Merchant of Venice*, where the protean Bassanio shows himself much more adept at navigating the theatricality of credit relations than the all-too-consistent Antonio. Although Kolb's reading of *Merchant*—cogent though it is—mostly travels well-worn territory amidst a plethora of other financially themed scholarship, her juxtaposed treatment of Heywood's *A Woman Killed with Kindness* offers one of the most interesting analyses of the book. In the case of this latter play, irreconcilable economic impulses overlap with homo-social dilemmas that place marital relationships in tension with (male) friend-ship. In this instance, boundaries between tragedy and comedy become provocatively blurred.

Kolb returns to Shakespeare (and Middleton) in her next chapter with *Timon of Athens*, cleverly initiating the discussion by taking note of how the play-wrights supplemented their source material: most significantly, they added *debt* and *poetry* to the existing narratives. As we might expect, what these two things have in common is not only their correspondence to fiction making, but their tendency to generate contradictory rhetorical descriptions. Are the imaginative falsehoods involved in social narratives (both financial and liter-ary) deceptive and blameworthy, or are they constructive and unavoidable? Once again, the answer is both, depending on one's rhetorical perspective. Timon expresses each extreme in the same play; but in doing so, he also embodies merely an exaggeration of *everyday* economic tensions at the turn of the seventeenth century.

The impressive consistency of *Fictions of Credit* only threatens to be diverted by the final chapter, which seems to take the argument in a new direction. As her focus shifts forward into the Jacobean era, the opposition at hand becomes not so much a rhetorical as a temporal one. Here Kolb traces a tension between an earlier paradigm of credit grounded in objects and material wealth, and a later paradigm in which debt is conceptualized more abstractly, in the realm of numbers and calculating tables. The opposition is reinforced by a reading of two plays by Ben Jonson, the early *Volpone*—in which wealth is overwhelmingly comprised of gold and the "stuff" it can buy—and the late *The Magnetic Lady*, where the usurer figure is more of a theoretical mathematician or investment banker than a coin counter. It is a line of argument that ventures somewhat murkily into the quagmire of capi-talist teleology, and its dubious quest to pin down cultural "shift." While the tension between the material and abstract wealth is certainly important and compelling, it is one that could more convincingly be represented as something *rhetorical* rather than *historical*, applicable to both earlier and later writers than Jonson. (In a Coda, Kolb acknowledges precisely the durability of this tension, continuing as it has into the world of modern finance.) Fortunately, Kolb's relentless focus on ambivalent economic rhetorics in the previous chapters makes this leap an easy one for the reader.

Overall, Kolb's study is focused and insightful, especially in the rhetorical domain in which it specializes. Beyond this domain, however, the workings of actual economic practices in early modern England can sometimes feel a little hazy. Topics as significant as currency circulation, debasement, usury, banking, and promissory notes all receive brief explanation, but no sustained investigation or analysis. And while Kolb's research clearly has great breadth, sometimes she neglects studies that are closer to home. Several recent scholarly studies clearly relevant to her discussion—including Martha Wood-mansee and Mark Osteen's *The New Economic Criticism: Studies at the Intersection of Literature and Economics* (1999); Jill Phillips Ingram's *Idioms of Self-Interest: Credit, Identity, and Property in English Renaissance Literature* (2006); Bradley D. Ryner's *Performing Economic Thought: English Drama and Mercantile Writing, 1600–1642* (2014); and my own *Desires of Credit in Early Modern Theory and Drama: Commerce, Poesy, and the Profitable Imagination* (2016)—do not ever seem to be acknowledged, and do not appear in the Bibliography. And yet, these works are all intensely interested in the very entanglements of monetary credit and imaginative fiction that Kolb is examining.

In the end, however, *Fictions of Credit* stands on its own as a solid contribution to the field—even one of the most readable on the topic. Amidst the bustling arena of economic literary scholarship, Kolb manages infuse fresh energy into this marketplace of ideas, and to craft inspired readings of several Renaissance plays.

Shakespeare's Domestic Tragedies: Violence in the Early Modern Home, by Emma Whipday. Cambridge: Cambridge University Press, 2019. Pp. xi + 270. Hardback, $99.99.

Reviewer: SID RAY

Reading Emma Whipday's *Shakespeare's Domestic Tragedies: Violence in the Early Modern Home* is eerily similar to the progress Whipday traces of murderers and thieves from ballads, pamphlets, and plays who breach the thresholds of domestic spaces and creep room by room to the treasure chamber. The book argues that in *Taming of the Shrew, Hamlet, Othello, Macbeth,* and *King Lear*, Shakespeare redeploys and transforms tropes from plays we now categorize as domestic tragedies—a genre that stages crimes of the home perpetrated by ordinary people as in *Arden of Faversham* (c. 1590), *Two Lamentable Tragedies* (1595), *A Warning for Fair Women* (1598), *A Woman Killed with Kindness* (1603), *A Yorkshire Tragedy* (1605), *The Witch of Edmonton* (1621), *The English Traveller* (1624), and sometimes *Othello* (c. 1605).[1]

The book is organized around domestic spatial concepts: "Home," "Household," "House," and "Neighborhood." Each of these chapters begins with an illustrative piece of "street literature"[2]—a broadside ballad or a crime pamphlet—followed by similar archival material that Whipday connects to a Shakespeare play. As home architecture is literal, figurative, and/or staged in the works Whipday examines, the reading experience dovetails with the themes and the patterns found in the domestic tragedies.

The structure is clever but not entirely cohesive. The vast range of texts calls for a stronger apparatus—a tight framework with appendices that list the plays and the adjacent popular literature, and a more expansive index that includes secondary sources. The analysis of the rich primary materials is more insightful than the effort to read Shakespeare through those materials. Part of the problem is that Whipday is overly reliant on essential scholars such as Frances E. Dolan and, particularly, Lena Cowen Orlin, and less so on more recent work by Catherine Richardson and Viviana Comensoli. She has the tendency, too, to generalize about scholarly trends without adequately citing them.[3]

Whipday departs from Orlin's *Private Matters and Public Culture in Post-Reformation England* (1994) "in focusing not on isolated correspondences between a Shakespearean tragedy and a domestic tragedy, but on the ways in which Shakespeare borrows formal tropes and thematic concerns from domestic tragedy and cheap print, and, in so doing, creates his own hybrid versions of the genre, in conversation with wider theatrical and cultural concerns about patriarchal authority, female agency, privacy, and neighborhood" (19). But Whipday actually does focus on isolated correspondences between Shakespeare's plays and tropes from domestic tragedies. That part of her argument is not particularly innovative—that the plays blend public and private spheres, that Shakespeare revamps popular forms and mixes genres, and that Gertrude, Desdemona, and Lady Macbeth are wives with quotidian wifely duties that they subvert. None of this is new. Much more valuable is Whipday's attention to underexamined broadsides and pamphlets, her investigation of domestic architecture, and her insights on the staging of homes.

The first chapter, "Home: Contesting Domestic Order in *The Taming of the Shrew*," argues that Shakespeare's *Shrew* works with later shrew-taming offshoots to "encapsulate the concerns of domestic tragedy." Whipday dates the play around 1592 (34), meaning *Shrew* exemplifies a genre for which, in 1592, there was only one example—*Arden*. In fact, *Shrew* might have been written before 1592. The engagement with popular beliefs about shrewish women and the reading of Petruchio as "equally unruly" (46) in his marriage to Katherine retreads ground covered 20 to 30 years ago. Whipday has a better purchase on John Fletcher's sequel/revision of *Shrew*, *The Tamer Tamed*.

The book finds its stride in chapter 2, "Household: Performing Domestic Relationships in *Hamlet*," which builds from an exploration of adulterous wives in ballads and plays such as *Arden of Faversham*, *Warning for Fair Women*, and *A Woman Killed with Kindness*, to a fresh reading of Shakespeare's inscrutable Gertrude as a variation on the adulterous wife complicit in spousal murder. Whipday is a deft close reader of texts, and her analysis of Gertrude in light of Alice Arden, Anne Sanders, and Anne Frankford is subtle and illuminating.

The book's most compelling and most troubling section is chapter 3. It considers early modern architectural advances and the blending of public and private spaces in home building that playwrights adopted to stage thresholds, doors, rooms, and windows. In analyzing the complex position of women in these new, more permeable buildings, Whipday finds architectural correspondences in rooms described in *A True Report of the Horrible Murther* (1607), *The Rape of Lucrece*, *Much Ado about Nothing*, and *Cymbeline*. Whipday places the permeability of Brabanzio's Venetian estate in thought-provoking juxtaposition with the locked door and drawn bed curtains of Desdemona's bedchamber in Cyprus. What gets lost in this broad review is any mention of the mixed-race marriage or the colonial setting at the heart of *Othello*, an inexplicable oversight. In Whipday's thesis, an upper-class white woman marrying a formerly enslaved African man would seem to be a clear example of Shakespeare transforming a trope. The lapse becomes more vexing when, referring to the bedchamber, Whipday observes, "here as elsewhere, darkness is associated with misdeeds" (144) and leaves the color bias hanging. That the extraordinarily important recent work done on *Othello* by scholars of color such as Ayanna Thompson, David Sterling Brown, and Matthieu Chapman is neither consulted nor cited is frustrating.[4]

Chapter 4, "Neighborhood: Crossing Domestic Boundaries in *Macbeth*," shifts to exteriors, as Whipday explores treatises such as Reginald Scot's *The Discoveries of Witchcraft*, focusing on the ways in which communities policed wayward female behaviors. Whipday makes an important connection between neighbors shaming and punishing "undomestic" women believed to be witches to "the vulnerable domesticity of the Macbeths' castle" (161). In impressive detail, she suggests that Shakespeare engages and transforms domestic tropes associated with air in and around the uncanny home, gate keeping, and superstitions such as cruentation. But again, an important scholarly step is omitted. A chapter intensely focused on witches should have discussed Thomas Middleton's hand in *Macbeth* especially in light of Middleton's probable authorship of an actual domestic tragedy, *A Yorkshire Tragedy*.[5]

The afterword, "Homeless: Outside Domestic Tragedy in *King Lear*," shifts from houses to homelessness and masterless men in *Lear*. There is useful analysis here of the play's concept of shelter as a disruption of domestic tropes.

Whipday concludes by suggesting that Shakespeare's purpose in adopting and transforming domestic tropes is "to unsettle or even challenge popular ideas about the dangers of domestic insubordination, the agency of adulterous wives, the perils of female privacy, and the consequences of criminality" (214)—ground that has been well and ably trod. But Whipday then argues that early modern domestic narratives continue "to shape our institutions, narrative, and metaphors today." She asserts that the rights to privacy claimed at the 2012 trial of Joseph Naso for rape and murder "were forged through the impact of, and in reaction to, these early modern discourses" (218). She then cites a line from a Woody Allen script replaying the early modern adage that a man's home is his castle. This unexamined, unironic reference to Allen in a book on domestic violence should have been edited out.

This is another missed opportunity to edit this book into a tighter piece of scholarship. The oversights do Whipday a disservice because the book is otherwise full of trenchant local insights on a wide range of texts and attends thoughtfully to many under-studied archival sources.

Notes

1. Whipday's dating of these plays differs from the dates I include here, which come from Martin Wiggins' edited collection, *A Woman Killed with Kindness and Other Domestic Plays* (Oxford: Oxford University Press, 2008). Whipday tends not to follow debates about dating, but she needs a footnote on her reasons for assigning these dates to these plays. Lena Cowen Orlin places *Othello* with other domestic tragedies in *Private Matters and Public Culture in Post-Reformation England* (Ithaca: Cornell University Press, 1994); Sean Benson also considers *Othello* among the domestic tragedies in his book, *Shakespeare, Othello and Domestic Tragedy* (London: Continuum, 2012). Wiggins includes 15 "domestic plays" in his list, including five that are lost.
2. The phrase is from Sandra Clark, *Women and Crime in Street Literature of Early Modern England* (Basingstoke: Palgrave Macmillan, 2003).
3. Here are five examples: "Many critics . . . argue . . ." (47); she cites one. "Many scholars argue . . ." (76); she cites one. "Modern critics have a tendency to read . . ." (89); she cites two. "It has been observed by numerous critics . . ." (171); she cites none. "Many critics have observed . . ." (190); she cites one.
4. See for example, Ayanna Thompson, *Passing Strange: Shakespeare, Race, and Contemporary America* (Oxford: Oxford University Press, 2011), and the introduction to her revised edition of Shakespeare's *Othello* (Arden Third Series, 2016); David Sterling Brown, "(Early) Modern Literature: Crossing the Color-Line," *Radical Teacher*, Vol. 105 (July 2016): 69–77, and Matthieu Chapman, *Anti-Black Racism in Early Modern English Drama: The Other Other* (NY: Routledge Press, 2017).
5. See Stanley Wells, "A Yorkshire Tragedy," in *Thomas Middleton: The Collected Works*, ed. Gary Taylor and John Lavagnino (Oxford: Clarendon Press, 2007), 452–55.

Telltale Women: Chronicling Gender in Early Modern Historiography, by Allison Machlis Meyer. Lincoln: University of Nebraska Press, 2021. Pp. 354. Hardcover, $60.00.

Reviewer: EMMA KATHERINE ATWOOD

In her monograph *Telltale Women: Chronicling Gender in Early Modern Historiography*, Allison Machlis Meyer provides a welcome intervention in a nexus of divergent fields—source studies, feminist criticism, and historiography. By considering the shifting ways in which early modern queens have been represented across genres, Meyer offers a new treatment of the relationship between historical narratives and history plays, making a case for the ways in which history writing—in all of its myriad forms—wrestles productively with larger cultural desires. With critical elegance, Meyer revises a number of assumptions held by even the most astute scholars of early modern history. First, she revises the feminist tradition that has largely deemed chronicles and political histories patriarchal and anti-feminist, instead connecting the rather contradictory treatment of early modern queens in the historical record with a political shift from dynastic rule to emergent nationalism. Second, she rejects the literary tradition that has placed drama on a pedestal without rejecting the importance of the history play; she still delivers careful close readings of dramatic scenes that contextualize this literary genre in a wider conversation about women's political representation. Third, Meyer rejects the hierarchical treatment of fiction endemic to traditional source studies and instead opts for an intertextual and infracontextual methodology that recognizes historiography as an expansive, cumulative, and flexible practice.

In her first chapter, Meyer sets the groundwork for her exploration of "telltale women," arguing that narrative histories of the kind composed by More, Vergil, and Hall located a great deal of dynastic political power in women. This is a significant intervention, reframing a genre that is often considered patriarchal at best and misogynist at worst. While previous feminist critics have argued that narrative historiography "negatively evaluates or excludes women" (49), Meyer rejects this assertion, using depictions of Elizabeth Woodville as a case study to prove the opposite. Though she concedes that early modern narrative historiographers tend to focus on women's emotions, Meyer contends that this demonstrates the way women could use emotion as a vehicle for public political action. The history play, in contrast, eliminates women from political action. Meyer shows how Shakespeare's *Richard III* strips Elizabeth Woodville of her intercessionary power and only affords women sympathy when they are denied political participation (68). This "new model of queenship" (26) that emanates from the history play reduces women's political agency and constitutes what Meyer calls a "significant rewriting of royal women's roles" (61). Meyer connects this generic shift between narrative and dramatization with a larger cultural shift from a dynastic to nationalistic model of government.

Chapter 2 further explores the political role of queenly influence under a dynastic model, and their limited—even eliminated—political role under emergent nationalism. Focusing on the treatment of "illegitimate" women's power, Meyer considers the representation of Jane Shore in Thomas Churchyard, Thomas Heywood, and the anonymous play *True Tragedy of Richard III* to show how dramatic representation reduced otherwise powerful historical women to fictionalized domestic subjects. Significantly, Meyer contends that this shift in approach to queenship promoted a version of English nationalism that located its power within fraternal citizenry rather than dynastic family networks, a move that "implicitly excludes England's sovereign ruler Elizabeth I from its vision of ideal queenship" (120). By connecting the historiographic record to critiques of Elizabeth I, Meyer makes a case for the way popular attitudes towards politics, nation, and women in power were shaped through the discursive practice of history writing.

Chapter 3 continues the treatment of dynastic queens' political interventions through a consideration of competing historiographic accounts of Queen Isabel's power and influence. Meyer argues that two divergent traditions emerge from historiographic sources: one that foregrounds her active, legitimate political agency, and another that emphasizes her illegitimate passion and seeks to punish her transgressions. For instance, in Richard Grafton's generous account *A Chronicle at Large*, Isabel is politically empowered as an agent of order and justice. However, in Marlowe's more critical and punitive *Edward II*, Isabel is driven by private concerns and personal motivations, resulting in her presumed execution in act 5. Once relegated to dramatic representation, Isabel's affective power becomes a liability, or what Meyer deems "an example of the problems of royal women's political participation" (125).

In contrast to Marlowe's unflattering depiction of Isabel in *Edward II*, chapter 4 moves into a consideration of Isabel in Elizabeth Cary's *The History of Edward II* that reveals a gap between the queen's powerful actions and men's unwillingness to take her seriously. While some critics have previously argued that Cary's work is anti-feminist, others have argued the opposite, finding moments of proto-feminism in her treatment of Isabel. Meyer acknowledges that both approaches are defensible and that the text itself is frustratingly ambivalent, but she reframes this ambivalence to argue that indeterminism is a component of historiography more broadly; these incongruities are to be expected when you engage both chronicle history and dramatic sources. While Cary has been treated as an anomaly, Meyer argues that Cary's approach is part of the historiographic tradition of paradoxical depiction, thus revising the assumption that "early modern historiography . . . is unconcerned with women" (180). In refusing to "condemn queenship as a structural position" (205), Cary legitimizes the institution. At the end of Cary's *The History of Edward II*, Isabel laments a future in which she will be relegated to the margins, "quoted in the Margent of such a story" (218). In this way, Cary's Isabel recognizes her own precarious role in the historiographic process, even—especially—when effacement and abnegation is part of the expectation for women's personal behavior.

This tension between the political and the personal is taken in up chapter 5 when Meyer considers the way dramatic adaptations privatize the role of queenly authority in favor of a "fantasy of apolitical queenship" (223). Informed by Queen Anna's and Queen Henrietta Maria's own political influence during the respective reigns of James I and Charles I, Meyer shows the

way historiographic depictions of queenship interrogate—and disagree about—
the appropriate role for a queen consort. While Francis Bacon's *The History
of King Henry VII* makes an argument for the public function of queenship,
John Ford's *Perkin Warbeck* undercuts the legitimacy of women's political
power. Queen consorts who are shown to choose wifely devotion over political
engagement enact the "fantasy of a wholly domestic marriage alliance" (258)
that helped solidify a national identity that located its power in the male head
of state.

Despite juggling dozens of dense primary sources, Meyers's close readings
are consistently engaging and well-supported. The kind of work that Meyer
undertakes in *Telltale Women* necessitates a kind of "in the weeds" methodology that requires nuance, specificity, and attention not just to detail but to
minutia in the "multiplicity of historical perspectives" (268). Sometimes this
has the potential to confuse matters (i.e., whose version of Queen Isabel are
we analyzing now? Marlowe's? Cary's? Grafton's? Holinshed's? Stow's?).
Yet overall, Meyer navigates this dizzying field of alternative histories with
confidence and clarity. As Meyer's argument hinges on a distinction between
narrative and drama, the project may further benefit from an application of
performance theory, dramaturgy, or embodiment that considers extratextual
expressions of queenly authority on stage. Meyers's study leaves me with a
few big-picture questions: how connected were the reigns of Queen Elizabeth
I, Queen Henrietta Maria, or Queen Anna to the historical queens depicted
in the historical record? To what extent did the genre of early modern drama
engender nationalism, and to what extent was this simply a product of late
16th-century sentiment? How might writings and speeches by these historical
queens themselves intersect with the largely male-authored historiographic
record? How connected are critiques of queenship with broader political
critiques of monarchy and absolutism? But perhaps these lingering questions
are part of the project: Meyer ends her study with a coda that provides an
open invitation for more "capacious" (268) approaches to English history. In
doing so, she self-consciously positions her own work in the historiographic
lineage with an acute awareness of the way academic arguments *about* history
also become an integral part *of* history.

Communal Justice in Shakespeare's England: Drama, Law, and Emotion,
by Penelope Geng. Toronto: University of Toronto Press, 2020. Pp. 280.
Hardback, $75.00.

Reviewer: JESSICA APOLLONI

Penelope Geng's *Communal Justice in Shakespeare's England* is an inspiring
addition to the field of law and literature. Geng builds from current scholars in
the field, such as Lorna Hutson and Jessica Winston, to chart new ground within

her focus on communal feeling within justice systems. Through her analysis of popular texts, Geng examines a critical counternarrative of the professionalization of common law in early modern England. This was especially apparent in plays, where authors produced "resistant narratives which depicted justice as the product of collective and communal action" (xii). Geng thoughtfully connects this communal experience of watching legal dramas in the theater to a kind of civic consciousness, weaving in a range of sources from sociology to the study of emotions and affect theory. At the same time, the monograph's clear storytelling makes Geng's narrative accessible and useful for scholars outside of the fields of law and literature or early modern studies.

In each chapter, Geng elucidates the emotional experience of the law as something that would stem from both an individual's "embodied legal experience" when attending a court session, for example, and from one's "imagined legal interactions" in plays and other popular texts (xiii). As a result, Geng effectively demonstrates how this combination could shape popular expectations on issues ranging from individual responsibility in the law to community reactions to crime and judgment. *Communal Justice* consequently adds a new layer to law-literature studies by focusing on the kinds of knowledge and experience that became valued within increasingly competing and often conflicting notions of legal authority.

The introductory sections establish the historical and cultural background of the book's central argument as well as its deep roots in sociolegal issues of the time. Geng's preface on Yarington's *Two Lamentable Tragedies* (1594), a play based on an actual double murder case, effectively draws the reader into her focus on communal action in the law. Geng uses the term "lay magistrates" to signify "those who stake their legal authority on conscience and moral feeling, not on book-based knowledge or professional legal expertise" (xi). Geng then explains how English subjects were under a "double obligation" vis-à-vis the law, according to which they were expected both to adhere to the authority of magistrates and to actively participate in crime detection and the presentation of evidence. The introduction provides a clear overview of the origins of English law as a distinctly "communal" justice system; the key changes occurring in the late sixteenth century such as the professionalization and equation of legal knowledge and authority; and the importance of Protestant theologies, including Calvinism, that could emphasize the forensic capacity of conscience. Consequently, we come to see the competing viewpoints about "the source of legal authority, the nature of knowledge, and the degree to which laypeople could exert legal judgment" (4–5). These various sociocultural threads all nicely lead up to Geng's investigation of the tension between professional and nonprofessional understandings of magistracy and the continued impact of communal action in law.

Chapter 1 turns to assize sermons, an important genre often overlooked in law-literature scholarship, to explore how lay or nonprofessional magistracy centered legal authority in conscience. Geng traces the foundations of communal justice in England when focusing on the "evolution of the assize from a legal process to a metaphor for the lay conscience" (23). This led to a "juridical feeling" for both individuals and the spiritual community (49). By integrating the history of trial by jury with new changes in the assize system, Geng establishes the importance of religious writing within English understandings of law. This first chapter thus acts as a nice setup to expand our view of legal history and explain "how deeply embedded concepts of communal justice and lay magistracy were in everyday legalities" (49). This chapter is also an ideal frame to elucidate the longer history of communal justice in England's legal system and the larger tensions between professional and non-professional authority in the law, allowing her to turn effectively to the late sixteenth-century playhouses.

The next set of chapters focus on theatrical texts, where this tension between professional and lay authority became a perfect source for playwrights. Geng illustrates how authors invited audiences to imagine the power of non-professional legalism and communal action in the law. Chapter 2 delineates tensions between royal and communal justice with a focus on Shakespeare's *Henry IV, Part 2*, particularly the character of the Lord Chief Justice. Geng cleverly blends her reading of Shakespeare with contemporary representations of judges in the popular imagination. This synthesis complicates the view of the Lord Chief Justice as a static symbol of the law and showcases the competing popular and professional legal expectations of such officials, and it leads to a discussion of the significance of his removal from *Henry V*. Chapter 2 addresses the ways in which early modern plays can raise questions about the multiple legalities arising from the relationship of royal and communal justice and the various viewpoints that relationship produces. Chapter 3 moves to the role of neighborliness in criminal inquests. Geng returns to Yarington's *Two Lamentable Tragedies* and pairs this text with the anonymous *A Warning for Fair Women* to show how plays could stage participatory justice in which crimes are resolved by a local community. Geng brings these plays into conversation with the economic instabilities of the 1590s, when this focus on communal ability to detect and investigate crimes was especially welcome. These two chapters further demonstrate how audiences in such legal plays are invited to be a part of judicial power within a sense of communal feeling.

Chapter 4 builds from recent criticism connecting bodily suffering in *King Lear* to martyr narratives such as those in John Foxe's *Acts and Monuments*. This connection speaks to the power of empathetic witnessing and its potential to restore communities—even ones on the edge of destruction—and to create different kinds of social bonds. Geng's close reading of the play does not limit itself to violent scenes like Gloucester's blinding but instead reveals different forms of witnessing that occur throughout the narrative to analyze communal action within the play itself and in the playhouse. Social bonds in the play and surrounding audience "are forged through a highly theatrical mode of witnessing: seeing, imagining, and feeling—seeing with the mind's eye to seeing with actual eyes and feeling with the other bodies in the playhouse" (121). These shared experiences of bodily feeling break through traditional bonds and Geng illuminates how "this blurring of embodiment and imagination foments ethical, political action that cuts across class, status, and gender" (121). Looking at *Henry VI, Part 2* and *Macbeth*, chapter 5 makes an interesting turn to group spectatorship in public penance and the possible communal defiance of legal ceremonies and forms. Geng synthesizes the ordered "open penance" of Eleanor Cobham, the Duchess of Gloucester, and Lady Macbeth's sleepwalking scene to expose our underlying assumptions about remorse. This comparison exhibits both the intimate or private aspect of remorse as well as the law's obsession with making conscience and remorse legible to a community. Geng claims that "remorse, like any enduring fiction, is a product of our ungovernable imagination," and she asks "if this key legal emotion of communal justice is socially, culturally, and theatrically constructed, then does it not suggest that communal justice itself hinges on the communal imagination?" (144). This chapter's focus on the power of legal narratives and customs to shape our collective understanding of remorse illustrates the enduring power of such concepts in courtrooms today.

Geng brings out some of these contemporary connections in the postscript, where she notes that this is a project that "has settled into its present form as popular distrust of legal institutions has grown to epic proportions" (148). By demonstrating the role of plays in shaping a communal sense of legal culture, Geng adds new insights into sociocultural underpinnings of collective knowledge making as well as the communal nature of theater. The postscript also provides larger reflections about how authors in the early modern period worked through clashes in professional and nonprofessional conceptions of authority at a key moment in the development of English law.

The postscript thus provides a strong conclusion to the narrative arc of Geng's manuscript. The overall arrangement of chapters and their focuses on different concerns of communal justice generally follow the pattern of a case—moving from inquest and the collection of evidence to witnessing and confession. Such organization allows the text to have a strong cohesion of ideas but also keep a refreshing flexibility to investigate the complexities of communal justice as a phenomenon that also challenged legal professionalization in early modern law. Geng's wide-ranging interests and methods in each chapter would consequently benefit a variety of scholars. The book is a captivating read with new approaches to law, community, and culture.

Ghosts, Holes, Rips and Scrapes: Shakespeare in 1619, Bibliography in the Longue Durée, by Zachary Lesser. Philadelphia: University of Pennsylvania Press in cooperation with the Folger Shakespeare Library, 2021. Pp. 232. Cloth, $49.95.

Reviewer: MOLLY YARN

In scientific terms, the existence of gravity is a fact. The apple falls from the tree. Our understanding of its mechanics, however, is a theory, and that theory is subject to constant revision based on new evidence. In *Ghosts, Holes, Rips and Scrapes: Shakespeare in 1619, Bibliography in the Longue Durée,* Zachary Lesser argues that the conclusions reached by the New Bibliographers in the early twentieth century about the so-called Pavier Quartos (a group of quarto editions printed in 1619 and sold both singly and as a bound-together set) have been too often treated as settled fact, rather than theory. Lesser sets out to reexamine this bibliographical mystery from the ground up, to contribute new facts and data to the preexisting body of evidence, and to remind the field that, however canonical Pollard's and Greg's theories have become, there's always an Einstein just around the corner, ready to throw Newton and his apple for a (curved) loop.

Due to their emphasis on edition over copy, neither Greg nor Pollard examined a large number of extant Pavier Quartos. As Lesser reminds us, the New Bibliographers were almost myopically focused on textual transmission, ignoring evidence of circulation and reception; however, interest in those very details has increased significantly in the intervening century. Scholars have come to value the "fossil record" (25–26) contained in each copy that reveals clues about its life (as it were) past the printing house doors. Surveying the last century of criticism about the Pavier Quartos, Lesser establishes that recent revisionist work still relies on two problematic assumptions: namely, that Pavier was the driving force behind the quartos' publication, and that the 1619 quartos were an attempt to create a collection of works by Shakespeare. To thoroughly reassess the quartos, Lesser argues, one must abandon those preexisting suppositions and return to the most significant source of evidence—the surviving copies themselves.

As the first bibliographer to study over 340 of the extant 372 copies, Lesser has a lot of ground to cover. The large number of images in this book—52, by my count, most of them in full color—were a wise investment; after all, Lesser's premise rests on the importance of reexamining the surviving copies themselves. The plentiful visual links between Lesser's descriptions and that key material evidence strengthen the book, both practically and conceptually. The images allow the reader to see things as Lesser saw them, and, as a lifelong reader of Sherlock Holmes stories, I found something Holmesian in Lesser's ability to synthesize evidence in new ways and see clues others have missed (an impressive feat not even slightly diminished by the modern imaging techniques that facilitate his viewing). Throughout the book, Lesser acknowledges the pervasive analogies made between bibliographical work and detective stories, returning several times to Sherlock Holmes' famous adage that "when you have eliminated the impossible, whatever remains, *however improbable*, must be the truth" (123). Lesser's aim, however, is to push back against the imposition of detective fiction's neatly tied-up solutions on bibliographical work, urging his readers to "remain wary of the detective genre's march toward a triumphant unmasking" (124). Lesser creates a rhetorically effective tension between himself, the postmodern seeker of truth, open to uncertainty and messy endings, and the traditional literary detective, whose stock in trade is sweeping pronouncements and pat conclusions. In doing so, he navigates a rhetorical tightrope that allows him to lay out evidence and explain his own theories while leaving the door open for other possibilities.

Lesser differs from Holmes in another key way. In Conan Doyle's stories, John Watson, Holmes's associate, rarely comes off well. In marked contrast, Lesser introduces us to a whole cast of impressive collaborators and co-investigators. Librarians, curators, and cataloguers are named and credited for their contributions to Lesser's project and for their own independent discoveries. Thanks to this, there's no sense of the tiresome narrative in which a scholar "discovers" something that has been "lost" in a fully catalogued library or archive. Instead, Lesser cites generously, reminding the reader that these books are not moldering, forgotten, in some dusty box—they are cared for, examined, and catalogued by highly trained professionals, whose knowledge of said items often eclipses the visiting researcher's own. Moreover, their actions and methods, along with those of owners, booksellers, and other agents, alter each copy throughout the longue durée, creating the evidentiary fossil record of circulation that Lesser excavates.

In Chapters 1 and 2, "Ghosts" and "Holes," Lesser examines how acceptance of what an "ideal version" of a bound volume of Pavier Quartos should look like—namely, a set of plays, all ostensibly by Shakespeare, bound in a certain order—has, through its incorporation into cataloguing and collecting practices, influenced both critical understanding of the Pavier Quartos and the material forms of the surviving copies themselves. Collectors and institutions have literally remade bound volumes based on what they "ought" to be, unintentionally destroying evidence and reinforcing the original incorrect premise. In Chapter 1, he begins with bibliographic "ghosts," not just the phenomenon created by the residue of linseed oil from formerly bound facing pages, but the ghosts of bound volumes that no longer exist in their previous state—who have crossed over, as it were. Various types of "ghostly" evidence offer clues as to how often early modern booksellers sold Pavier Quartos as bound volumes. Although most of those volumes have been disbound in the centuries since, Lesser's resulting census of currently or formerly bound volumes of the 1619 quartos indicates that they were originally purchased bound, or as a set to be bound, much more frequently than was previously believed. Chapter 2, "Holes," dives into how the surviving stab-stitch evidence supports this hypothesis; ultimately, Lesser estimates that around half of the extant 1619 quartos were originally sold as part of a bound volume.

The questions that grow from the enigmatic presence of Thomas Heywood's *A Woman Killed With Kindness* among the supposedly Shakespearean quartos bridge the first two chapters.[1] The first major assumption of bibliographers— that the quartos were intended to be a collection of Shakespeare plays—comes under attack here. Lesser identifies two additional instances in which "ghostly evidence" indicates that *Woman Killed* was bound together with the Shakespearean quartos, bringing the total to four. The two previously known instances of *Woman Killed* in bound Pavier volumes have traditionally been explained as sammelbands—owner-designed bound collections. The existence of *four* volumes with *Woman Killed* makes this unlikely. Taken in conjunction with the evidence from his bound-volume census, Lesser concludes that the printers and publishers conceived of the Pavier Quartos, including *Woman Killed*, as a collection of plays that were marketed and sold as a bound volume, as a set to be bound, and as individual quartos.

If that is the case, the presence of *Woman Killed* also weakens the second assumption bibliographers since Greg have been making—that Thomas Pavier was the shady force responsible for the whole volume. In fact, Lesser relegates Pavier to the role of junior partner in the enterprise. Instead, Lesser suggests, we should focus on the agents who were definitely involved in the production of all nine playbooks *and* had a vested interest in including *Woman Killed*—the printers, William and Isaac Jaggard, who had printed and published an edition of *Woman Killed* in 1617 and, Lesser hypothesizes, still had extra copies in stock. Having refigured the forces behind the quartos' publication as a willing consortium of stationers centered around the Jaggards, Lesser rechristens the playbooks, referring to them throughout the remainder of the book as the "Jaggard Quartos."

The questions of who the publishers were trying to deceive with the falsified title pages and why have long been central to studies of the quartos. Lesser offers commentary on various theories and some hypotheses of his own, but much of his new evidence complicates these issues significantly, as exemplified in Chapter 3. "Rips and Scrapes" presents an intriguing body of previously-unexamined evidence—a collection of 12 to 14 Jaggard Quartos, the dates on whose title pages have been deliberated altered in various ways after printing. The complex details and labyrinthine "branching paths" of hypothetical explanations for this evidence make this the chapter which most requires the reader to think critically about method and to accept ambiguity. Lesser summarizes his evidence and thoughts, but withholds any Poirot-esque denouement. The book's finale is, in both content and form, a rebuke to the idea that one can "solve" bibliographical mysteries; while he calls the chapter a conclusion, its title is "Questions," a nice paratextual wink. And Lesser means "questions" quite literally—he begins the chapter by describing a final ghost, one he has few explanations for, and ends with a detailed list, several pages long, of unanswered, and perhaps unanswerable, questions for future bibliographers to address.

While framed as a reexamination of accepted evidence, Lesser's book is ultimately a manifesto about the aims and practices of bibliographical study, including the motivations and methods of weaving narratives to explain evidence. Each bibliographer, Lesser reminds us, is thoroughly situated in their own moment, subject to biases, assumptions, abilities, and circumstances that shape their research and conclusions. We, restless seekers, must constantly reflect upon and challenge ourselves and our field; like the books we study, we are unfinished, always becoming. Elementary.

Note

1. Although *A Yorkshire Tragedy* and *Sir John Oldcastle* are no longer included in the Shakespearean canon, he is named as the author on their title pages in the Pavier Quartos.

Index